THE EARLY MODERN CHILD IN ART AND HISTORY

The Body, Gender and Culture

Series Editor: Marjorie Levine-Clark

Titles in this Series

1 Courtly Indian Women in Late Imperial India
Angma Dey Jhala

2 Paracelsus's Theory of Embodiment: Conception and Gestation in Early Modern Europe
Amy Eisen Cislo

3 The Prostitute's Body: Rewriting Prostitution in Victorian Britain
Nina Attwood

4 Old Age and Disease in Early Modern Medicine
Daniel Schäfer

5 The Life of Madame Necker: Sin, Redemption and the Parisian Salon
Sonja Boon

6 Stays and Body Image in London: The Staymaking Trade, 1680–1810
Lynn Sorge-English

7 Prostitution and Eighteenth-Century Culture: Sex, Commerce and Morality
Ann Lewis and Markman Ellis (eds)

8 The Aboriginal Male in the Enlightenment World
Shino Konishi

9 Anatomy and the Organization of Knowledge, 1500–1850
Matthew Landers and Brian Muñoz (eds)

10 Blake, Gender and Culture
Helen P. Bruder and Tristanne J. Connolly (eds)

11 Age and Identity in Eighteenth-Century England
Helen Yallop

12 The Politics of Reproduction in Ottoman Society, 1838–1900
Gülhan Balsoy

13 The Study of Anatomy in Britain, 1700–1900
Fiona Hutton

14 Interpreting Sexual Violence, 1660–1800
Anne Greenfield (ed.)

15 Women, Agency and the Law, 1300–1700
Bronach Kane and Fiona Williamson (eds)

16 Sex, Identity and Hermaphrodites in Iberia, 1500–1800
Richard Cleminson and Francisco Vázquez García

17 The English Execution Narrative, 1200–1700
Katherine Royer

FORTHCOMING TITLES

British Masculinity and the YMCA, 1844–1914
Geoff Spurr

Infanticide and Abortion in Early Modern Germany
Margaret Brannan Lewis

THE EARLY MODERN CHILD IN ART AND HISTORY

EDITED BY

Matthew Knox Averett

LONDON AND NEW YORK

First published in paperback 2024

First published 2015 by Pickering & Chatto (Publishers) Limited

Published 2016 by Routledge
4 Park Square, Milton Park, Abingdon, Oxon OX14 4RN

and by Routledge
605 Third Avenue, New York, NY 10158

Routledge is an imprint of the Taylor & Francis Group, an informa business

© Taylor & Francis 2015
© 2015, 2016, 2024 selection and editorial matter, Matthew Knox Averett; individual chapters, the contributors

The right of Matthew Knox Averett to be identified as the author of the editorial material, and of the authors for their individual chapters, has been asserted in accordance with sections 77 and 78 of the Copyright, Designs and Patents Act 1988.

All rights reserved, including those of translation into foreign languages. No part of this book may be reprinted or reproduced or utilised in any form or by any electronic, mechanical, or other means, now known or hereafter invented, including photocopying and recording, or in any information storage or retrieval system, without permission in writing from the publishers.

Trademark notice:
Product or corporate names may be trademarks or registered trademarks, and are used only for identification and explanation without intent to infringe.

Publisher's Note
The publisher has gone to great lengths to ensure the quality of this reprint but points out that some imperfections in the original copies may be apparent.

To the best of the Publisher's knowledge every effort has been made to contact relevant copyright holders and to clear any relevant copyright issues. Any omissions that come to their attention will be remedied in future editions.

BRITISH LIBRARY CATALOGUING IN PUBLICATION DATA

The early modern child in art and history. – (The body, gender and culture)
1. Children in art. 2. Art, European. 3. Children – Europe – History.
I. Series II. Averett, Matthew Knox, editor.
704.9'425-dc23

Typeset by Pickering & Chatto (Publishers) Limited

ISBN: 978-1-84893-579-2 (hbk)
ISBN: 978-1-03-292497-7 (pbk)
ISBN: 978-1-315-65361-7 (ebk)

DOI: 10.4324/9781315653617

CONTENTS

Acknowledgements ix
List of Contributors xi
List of Figures xv

Introduction: The Early Modern Child in Art and History
 – *Matthew Knox Averett* 1

Part I: Infants
 1 Cradle and Grave: Commemorating Individual Victims of
  Infant Mortality – *Margaret Elizabeth Hadley* 21
 2 'Little Idols': Royal Children and the Infant Jesus in the Devotional
  Practice of Sor Margarita de la Cruz (1567–1633) – *Tanya J. Tiffany* 35

Part II: Children and Violence
 3 *E Riluttante Ragazzotti*: Youths as Hesitant Participants in the
  Crucifixion – *Margaret Flansburg* 49
 4 'These Stories Are Not for Children': Misbehaving Children in
  'World Upside Down' Prints and the Origins of Folk Tales
  – *Rachel L. Chantos* 67

Part III: Picturing Children and Childhood
 5 Dynastic Identity in Renaissance Court Life: Dynastic Privilege in
  Portraits of Children – *Jasmin W. Cyril* 83
 6 'You Will Be a Man, my Son': Signs of Masculinity and Virility in
  Italian Renaissance Paintings of Boys – *Fabian Lacouture* 99
 7 Dressing the Part: Picturing and Promoting the Early Modern
  Child – *Parme Giuntini* 117

Part IV: Great Expectations
 8 Princely Portraits of Adolescence in the Habsburg Court of Philip II
  in the Mid-Sixteenth Century – *Lisa Tom* 133
 9 Titian's *Clarissa Strozzi*: The Infant as Ideal Bride – *Brian D. Steele* 153
 10 Uncle Urban Raises the Barberini Nephews: The Education and
  Expectations of Papal *Nipote* – *Matthew Knox Averett* 171

Notes 185
Index 227

Love childhood, indulge its sports, its pleasures, its delightful instincts.
—Jean-Jacques Rousseau, *Émile*, Book II.

ACKNOWLEDGEMENTS

This book was born out of papers delivered for sessions at two academic conferences that I organized in 2013 and 2014. The first session, 'Children in the Renaissance', was organized for the Renaissance Society of America meeting held in San Diego, in April 2013, and was sponsored by the South-Central Renaissance Conference and the Society for Renaissance Art History. The second session, 'The Early Modern Child in Art and History', convened for the College Art Association meetings in Chicago, in February 2014. Additional contributions to this book were solicited from other authors. The goal of these conference sessions was to present art-historical investigations of earlier conceptions of childhood and to help reconstruct various aspects of the lives of early modern children. While individual contributors have made acknowledgements in their chapters, I would like to thank a number of people who helped make this project possible. First, of course, are the other contributors: each of your papers was interesting and educational, affording a new look at some exceptional art. Thanks to the organizers of the RSA meetings in 2013 and the CAA meetings in 2014. At Creighton University, my thanks to Bridget Keegan, Fred Hanna and Rose Hill, all of whom gave continuous support to this project from its inception several years ago, and to the College of Arts and Sciences and the Department of Fine and Performing Arts who helped fund this book. My thanks also to Keith Eggener at the University of Oregon, who helped me get this project organized and off the ground. A profound thanks to Janka Romero at Pickering & Chatto for her enthusiasm for the project and for shepherding it through to completion, and to Sarah Thomas who led the team at P&C that put the book together. My deep gratitude to my wife, Erin Walcek Averett, who encouraged me to begin this project and who helped me think about children, be they ancient, early modern, or modern. Above all, though, I wish to thank my daughters, Annabel, Chloe and Lily, who were the inspiration for this project.

LIST OF CONTRIBUTORS

Matthew Knox Averett is Associate Professor of Art History at Creighton University. He took his PhD in Art History and Archaeology at the University of Missouri where he specialized in Italian Renaissance and Baroque Art and Architecture. His recent publications include 'Becoming Giorgio Cornaro: Titian's *Portrait of a Man with a Falcon*' in the *Zeitschrift für Kunstgeschichte* (2011), 'The Annual Medals of Pope Urban VIII Barberini' in the *American Journal of Numismatics* (2013) and "*Redditus Orbis Erat*': The Political Rhetoric of Bernini's Fountains in Piazza Barberini' in the *Sixteenth Century Journal* (2014). He is currently completing work on a book on Bernini's *Triton Fountain*.

Jasmin W. Cyril has a PhD in the History of Art from the University of Michigan, Ann Arbor. Her Masters, also in Art History, is from the University of Oregon, Eugene. Dr. Cyril's research interests include the Medieval and Renaissance Italy and the Mediterranean basin. She has publications in the art of Ancient Rome, Medieval Italy and the Renaissance in Tuscany, primarily in Florence and Siena. Most of her research has lately focused on women and identity. Dr. Cyril has participated in four NEH Summer Seminars, three in Italy.

Margaret Flansburg is Professor Emerita in the Department of Humanities and Philosophy at the University of Central Oklahoma. She took her PhD in Interdisciplinary Fourteenth-century Italian Studies at the University of Oklahoma. Primary research interests are fourteenth-century altarpieces and frescoes of Tuscany and Umbria and patronage of the Augustinian Order. A current interest is the detached fresco from Fabriano, Italy, that is in the Boston Museum of Fine Arts. Her publications include 'Simone Martini's Beato Agostino Novello Altarpiece and Reliquary Altar: Sienese Program and Augustinian Agenda' in *Imagery, Relic and Devotion in Medieval and Renaissance Italy*, edited by Sally Cornelison and Scott Montgomery (Tempe, 2005); 'Painted Memorials: Four Augustinian Coffins', *Explorations in Renaissance Culture* 26, n. 1 (Summer 2000); 'The South Chapel Fresco Cycle of Sant' Agostino, Fabriano', pp. 687–706 and 'The Sacristy Frescoes of Sant' Agostino, Montefalco', pp. 707–26 in Augustine, in *Iconography: History and Legend* edited by Joseph C. Schnaubelt, Frederick Van

Fleteren, and George Radan (New York, 1999); 'Publications reçues: The Miraculous Heart of St. Claire of Montefalco', *Analecta Bollandiana* (Summer 1998); and 'The Mystical Heart of Clare of Montefalco', *Collectanae Augustiniana, Vol. 2: Mysticism* (Villanova, PA, 1991). No longer engaged in classroom teaching, Margaret is currently working with some 1940s WPA murals in an Oklahoma City elementary school, and with her three grandchildren.

Rachel L. Chantos, a native of Kansas City, MO, is an art historian specializing in early modern Italian art history, with a particular focus in social history and gender studies. Dr. Chantos' doctoral thesis focused on Saint Mary Magdalene in early modern Venice and Rome and the saint's relationship to prostitution reform, providing an evocative intersection between social, political and religious contexts. Dr. Chantos' research interests include the history of printmaking, costume studies, religious studies and American photography. Also an active artist, Dr. Chantos has received formal training in painting, photography, printmaking, clothing construction, ceramics and furniture restoration. Currently her research is focused on the study of early modern popular prints and their relationship to the development of folk tales and marriage reform across Protestant and Catholic regions.

Parme Giuntini joined the faculty of Otis College of Art and Design after completing her doctorate at UCLA with a scholarly focus on eighteenth-century English portraiture, gender and domestic representation. As the Assistant Chair of Liberal Arts and Sciences and Director of Art History, she has been instrumental in teaching, designing and supervising courses that address both fine art and visual culture. Her involvement with studio faculty nurtured an interest in fashion and culture and led to a collaboration with Kathryn Hagen, the former head of Fashion Illustration at Otis and current Chair of Fashion at Woodbury University. This resulted in the 2007 publication of *GARB: A Fashion and Culture Reader*. For the past five years her scholarly focus has been curriculum design, educational technology and pedagogy. She is currently involved in designing and teaching art History MOOCS and in developing ways that MOOC material can be critically implemented in both online and traditional learning environments.

Margaret Elizabeth Hadley specializes in the study of late Medieval and Early Modern manuscripts. Expanding the discourse on missals in French translation before 1500, she earned a PhD from Yale University for a dissertation on fifteenth-century manuscript illumination in Tours, France. She has taught courses on philosophy, literature, architectural history and art at Lawrence Technological University in Southfield, Michigan. Her most recent essay considers hybridity in macaronic illuminated manuscripts, and she is preparing a new book on problems in heraldry of the Middle Ages and Early Modern Period.

Fabien Lacouture is based at the Paris I Panthéon-Sorbonne University, where he works as a teaching assistant and is preparing a PhD dissertation on Children history and representation, from the fourteenth to the sixteenth century, in Northern and Central Italy. Lacouture has a particular interest in the Italian Renaissance and in the representation of children and family in art history. He organized a one-day conference about the current researches on the representations of children in art history at Paris I University in November 2013. His research on children, family and women is interdisciplinary in nature, incorporating studies from art history as well as modern history and anthropology.

Brian D. Steele (PhD University of Iowa) is Associate Dean for graduate, faculty and research issues in the College of Visual & Performing Arts at Texas Tech University, Director of its Fine Arts Doctoral Program and associate professor of art history in its School of Art, where he teaches courses in Renaissance art history. His research interests focus upon painting in Venice during the sixteenth century. Previous papers have explored issues of sexuality, pictorial intelligence and imaginative vision in later works by Titian; current work on sacred imagery engages issues of iconography, site, function and viewer reception. Presentations for the Renaissance Society of America and the Sixteenth Century Studies and Conference include 'Veronese and the Art of Contemplation: On the Role of Splendor in the *Marriage at Cana*' and 'Giovanni Bellini's *Frari Triptych* (1488) Reframed: Wisdom and Redemption'. Steele has published in the *Sixteenth Century Journal, Source: Notes in the History of Art* and *Studies in Iconography*.

Tanya J. Tiffany is an associate professor of Art History at the University of Wisconsin-Milwaukee. Her research focuses on the visual culture of early modern Spain and its empire, with a particular emphasis on the intersection between religious imagery and gender. Her first book, *Diego Velázquez's Early Paintings and the Culture of Seventeenth-Century Seville* (Penn State Press, 2012), examines Velázquez's visual interpretations of cultural debates, ranging from the role of women in religion to the place of African slaves in Spanish society. Her current book project, 'Visual Culture and Feminine Devotion in the Early Modern Spanish Empire', explores how images and objects constituted the foundation of the rituals, prayers and visions of late sixteenth- and seventeenth-century nuns. In addition, her articles have appeared in publications such as *Art History* and *Sixteenth Century Journal*.

Lisa Tom's research on portraiture in early Modern Europe looks at how portraits contributed to definitions of princely identity and authority, representations of gender and normalized perceptions of warfare. Her research engages with the interaction of images across a broad spectrum of mediums, examining the patterns of their dissemination and varied receptions. She received her

PhD in 2014, from the History of Art and Architecture Department, at Brown University under the guidance of Evelyn Lincoln. She earned her Masters at the University of California, Los Angeles, and BA in Art History and Computing, in the Arts at the University of California, San Diego. She currently teaches at the University of Rhode Island.

LIST OF FIGURES

Figure I.1: Anonymous, *Three Young Girls* (1627) — 2
Figure I.2: Luca della Robbia, *Boys Singing from a Book* (early 1430s) — 11
Figure I.3: Peter Paul Rubens. *The Education of the Princess Maria de' Medici* (1622–5) — 13
Figure I.4: Jean-Honoré Fragonard, *A Young Girl Reading* — 16
Figure I.5: The author's children with a *Cantoria* relief panel by Luca della Robbia at the High Museum of Art in Atlanta, Georgia — 20
Figure 1.1: *Pietà* and *Macé Prestesaille's Family with St. Michael* — 22
Figure 2.1: Juan Pantoja de la Cruz, *The Infanta María in Her Coffin* (probably 1603) — 39
Figure 2.2: Juan Pantoja de la Cruz, *The Infanta Ana as a Baby* (1602) — 43
Figure 2.3: Anonymous, *The Christ Child with a Bird* (early seventeenth century) — 44
Figure 2.4: Anonymous, *Prince Ferdinand as the Christ Child* (c.1635) — 45
Figure 2.5: Anonymous, *María Ana, Queen of Hungary, with her Son Ferdinand* (1634) — 46
Figure 3.1: *Via Crucis*. Miniature in the *Supplicationes variae* — 52
Figure 3.2: Simone Martini. Piercing with the lance (Crucifixion from the Orsini Polyptych) — 54
Figure 3.3: Barnaba da Modena, *Crucifixion* (c.1374) — 56
Figure 3.4: Master of the Urbino Coronation, *Crucifixion* — 58
Figure 3.5: Pietro da Rimini, *Crucifixion* — 61
Figure 3.6: Giuliano da Rimini, *Crucifixion* pinnacle. Polittico dell'Incoronazione della Vergine, Santi e scene della Passione, 1315–c.20, tempera e oro su tavola, Rimini, Fondazione Cassa di Risparmio, on deposit in the Museo delle Commune. — 63
Figure 3.7: Baronzio, Giovanni (d.1362), *Crucifixion* pinnacle Polyptych, Madonna, Saints, and Scenes from the Life of Christ (1345) — 64
Figure 4.1: Nicolò Nelli, *Il Mondo alla Riversa* (c.1575–90), etching — 68
Figure 4.2: Ewout Cornelisz Muller, publisher, *De verkeerde wereld* (c.1595), broadside — 69

Figure 4.3: Detail from Nelli, *Il Mondo alla Riversa* — 70
Figure 4.4: Detail from Muller, *De verkeerde wereld* — 70
Figure 4.5: Detail from Muller, *De verkeerde wereld* — 72
Figure 4.6: Detail from Muller, *De verkeerde wereld* — 73
Figure 4.7: Detail from Nelli, *Il Mondo alla Riversa* — 77
Figure 4.8: Detail from Muller, *De verkeerde wereld* — 78
Figure 5.1: *Ara Pacis Augustae* (13–9 BCE) — 85
Figure 5.2: Niccoló Gerini and Ambrogio Baldese, *The Brotherhood of the Mercy Receiving the Orphans* (1386) — 87
Figure 5.3: Desiderio da Settignano, *Laughing Boy*, marble (*c.*1430) — 89
Figure 5.4: Benozzo Gozzoli, *Procession of the Magi*, Medici Chapel, Medici-Riccardi Chapel, Florence (1459) — 91
Figure 5.5: Domenico Ghirlandaio, *Confirmation of the Rule of St. Francis*, Sassetti Chapel, Santa Trinitá, Florence (*c.*1480–5) — 93
Figure 5.6: Andrea Mantegna, *Court scene, Camera Picta*, Ducal Palace, Mantua (*c.*1465–74) — 94
Figure 5.7: Andrea Mantegna, *The Meeting, Camera Picta*, Ducal Palace, Mantua (*c.*1465–74) — 95
Figure 5.8: Justus von Ghent or Pietro da Spagna, *Federigo da Montefeltro and Guidobaldo Montefelto*, Galleria nationale delle Marche, Urbino (*c.*1475) — 97
Figure 6.1: Bartolomeo da Fruosino. Desco da parto (1428) — 102
Figure 6.2: Giovanni di Ser Giovanni, called Lo Scheggia, *Desco da Parto with the Game of Civettino* (1455) — 103–4
Figure 6.3: Paolo Veronese. *Portrait of Iseppo Da Porto and His Son* (1551) — 106
Figure 6.4: Paolo Veronese, *Portrait of Livia Da Porto Thiene and Her Daughter* (1551) — 107
Figure 6.5: Titian, Portrait of Ranuccio Farnese (1542) — 109
Figure 6.6: Paolo Veronese, *Boy with a Greyhound* (1570s) — 112
Figure 6.7: Bronzino, *Portrait of a Young Man* (1530s) — 114
Figure 7.1: Anonymous. *A Family Group in a Landscape* (*c.*1750) — 121
Figure 7.2: William Hogarth. *The Graham Children* (1742) — 122
Figure 7.3: Thomas Gainsborough. *The Painter's Daughters* (1756) — 124
Figure 7.4: Sir Joshua Reynolds. *Lady Elizabeth Delmé and her Children.* — 126
Figure 7.5: Sir Joshua Reynolds. *The Age of Innocence* (*c.*1788) — 127
Figure 7.6: Francis Bartolozzi after Sir Joshua Reynolds, *Miss Theophilia as Simplicity* (1989) — 128
Figure 7.7: Girls' dress designed by Joan Calabrese, (*c.*2015) — 131
Figure 8.1: Anthonis Mor, *Portrait of Alessandro Farnese* (1557) — 135
Figure 8.2: Anthonis Mor, *Portrait of Alessandro Farnese* (1561) — 136

Figure 8.3: Alonso Sánchez Coello, *Don John* (1560)   143
Figure 8.4: Alonso Sánchez Coello, *Don Carlos* (1564)   144
Figure 8.5: Alonso Sánchez Coello, *Emperor Rudolf II* (1567)   148
Figure 8.6: Copy after Alonso Sánchez Coello, *Archduke Albert with a Hound* (1574)   151
Figure 9.1: Titian, *Portrait of Clarissa Strozzi at the Age of Two Years* (1542)   154
Figure 9.2: Titian, *Eleonora Gonzaga della Rovere, Duchess of Urbino* (c.1536–8)   154
Figure 9.3: Titian, *Portrait of Pietro Aretino* (c.1545)   156
Figure 9.4: Paolo Veronese, *Giustiniana Barbaro and the Wetnurse with the Dog Standing at a Balcony*, Villa Barbaro, Maser (c.1560)   160
Figure 9.5: Titian, *Presentation of the Virgin in the Temple* (1534–8)   164
Figure 9.6: Titian, *Presentation of the Virgin in the Temple*, det. (1534–8)   165
Figure 9.7: Titian, *Offering to Venus* (1518–19)   166
Figure 9.8: Titian and Workshop, *Venus and the Lute Player* (c.1565–70)   168
Figure 10.1: *Pope Urban VIII Barberini* after Peter Paul Rubens (1630s)   172
Figure 10.2: *Portraits of the Barberini Nephews* by Johann Friedrich Greuter after Andrea Camassei, in the *Aedes Barberinae* (1642)   172
Figure 10.3: *Urban VIII Receiving from His Great-Nephews a Copy of the* Aedes Barberinae *by Girolamo Teti*, by Johann Friedrich Greuter after Andrea Camassei, in the *Aedes Barberinae* (1642)   180
Figure 10.4: *Apollo in Parnassus* by Johann Friedrich Greuter after Andrea Camassei, in the *Aedes Barberinae* (1642)   182

INTRODUCTION: THE EARLY MODERN CHILD IN ART AND HISTORY

Matthew Knox Averett

This book uses art historical evidence to illuminate early modern children: their births, lives and early deaths. The topics range chronologically from the fifteenth century to the eighteenth, and geographically across England, France, Germany, Italy and Spain; the essays cover a variety of media, including painting, sculpture and the graphic arts. The book is comprised of ten essays organized in four parts. The two essays in *Part I: Infants* consider different and unusual ways in which adults deal with the absence of infants. Taken together, the essays underscore the importance and centrality of children in early modern European society. *Part II: Children and Violence* consists of two essays that examine separate instances of children as perpetrators of violence. These studies elucidate the social attitudes on a range of issues such as childhood innocence, justice, cruelty and morality. *Part III: Picturing Children and Childhood* features three essays that consider paintings of children as means of identity creation. Finally, *Part IV: Great Expectations* presents three essays that consider the education and expectations of children, often in political contexts, shedding light on the demands early modern adults placed on children.

Three Young Girls

Some four hundred years ago, an anonymous follower of William Larkin painted a half-length portrait of three young girls (Fig. I.1). Though ostensibly a simple portrait, the image takes some investigation to gain all the information that the painting gives, affording viewers today a glimpse of the changes in the lives of children that have taken place over the last four centuries. The girls are likely sisters, as they hold hands or link arms familiarly. They are dressed identically and wear identical tiaras, necklaces and earrings. They hold or wear objects given by adults with the intent to teach these children how to be adults. Indeed, the objects which the sitters hold can often convey a wide array of meaning.[1] The artist meticulously depicted fabric, hair, dress, jewelry and other accessories, and the girls' expensive possessions indicate familial wealth. It is hypothesized that the painting was made after the death of the girls' mother; the gold ring on the left hand of the middle child is adult-sized (indicated by the string used to tie the ring to the wrist), suggesting that the ring could have belonged to the girl's mother and is kept now by the child as a memento.[2] The flowers in the children's hair can have a range of meanings in various floral languages. Blue hyacinths, for example, can represent mourning, advancing the idea that the girls' mother has recently died.[3] Meanwhile marigolds can represent obedience, suggesting the need for the young girls to grow up and assume some of the familial responsibilities vacated by the deceased mother. This line of interpretation can perhaps be deduced from the bunch of grapes held in the right hand of the oldest girl and the pears held by middle child: ripening grapes (symbolizing maturation) coupled with pears (traditional symbols of women) could suggest the girl's growth into adulthood, when they will assume the duties of wives and mothers.[4] Indeed, the youngest girl holds a doll, which can be considered a didactic tool to teach young children future social roles. Dolls are well-suited for imitative play, through which young girls learn household responsibilities, and they were frequently employed in this capacity.[5] The girls on either end also wear bracelets made of coral, a material often used in protective talismans.[6]

Figure I.1: Anonymous, *Three Young Girls* (1627). Photo Credit: Denver Art Museum.

This painting, then, reveals a host of concerns associated with pre-modern children. Recent scholarship on the child in history has contributed significantly to our understanding of early modern children and childhood, as this chapter will discuss. Scholars have explored many child-related issues, including the legal rights of children, infanticide and exposure, parental attitudes toward children, kin networks, gender roles, education and expectations, passage into adulthood and children's domestic spaces. Early modern art is full of depictions of children, from princes and princesses to common street urchins, while cities contained children's spaces both in the palace and in the piazza. Yet, art historical inquiry traditionally has focused on studying images of children without deeper investigation into the broader social meanings and functions of these depictions.[7] The frequent and varied representations of children in early modern art demonstrates the central role they played in society. This book examines how images were employed to construct identity, explain conceptions of childhood, elucidate parental expectations and teach children societal norms.

Philippe Ariès's *L'Enfant et la Vie Familiale sous l'Ancien Régime* from 1960 is widely and justifiably considered the foundational work in the study of the child in history.[8] This introductory chapter focuses on Ariès because he is at the foundation of the study of children, but it does not advocate for his positions. His conclusions are irretrievably flawed and, according to some authors, should be 'discarded'.[9] Reference to Ariès creates a common structure for inquiry, however, allowing this volume to more easily integrate with the wider body of literature on the child in history. I have filled in this structure with the strategic selections from the vast scholarship on children; overall, the chapters in this book offer a solid summary of the art historical literature on children and childhood. The book also makes a specific contribution: it focuses attention on childhood education and expectation across Europe, over a few hundred years, and does so by examining a variety of media by which these ideas were communicated. This survey is unified by our investigation into the investment parents made in educating children to assume various social roles.

The Early Modern Child in History

Before Ariès's seminal work, the study of the child in history was *terra incognita*.[10] Ariès established that childhood is not merely a period of biological development, but is also a societal construct. As such, the study of children and childhood can be a tool with which scholars can reconstruct past societies. Children also emerge as subject in and of themselves and, with them, conceptions of childhood. This critical inquiry has added age to categories of critical inquiry, alongside race, gender and sexual orientation.[11] Social studies of the Renaissance must consider children to understand contemporary society: by one estimate in Italian cities, for example, perhaps up to half of population was less than fifteen years old.¹² These numbers seem to hold true generally for Europe: Henry Kamen puts the number of children between one-third and one-half.¹³ Over the last fifty years, scholarship on the child in history has contributed significantly to our understanding of the early modern period, demonstrating the validity and fruitfulness of Ariès's approach, though modern scholarship rejects or at least questions most of Ariès's conclusions. Chief among his conclusions and, fundamentally the most problematic, is the idea that there was no intellectual concept of childhood in the Middle Ages and that this idea emerged only in the Renaissance. Though it is now clear that there were ancient and Medieval unerstandings of childhood, new conceptions of childhood emerged and older ones evolved in the early modern period.

While contemplating questions about contemporary families in Vichy France, Ariès looked at Medieval French painting and contended that these works never really depicted children: there were no depictions of child-specific clothing, food, objects or space. Ariès stated matter-of-factly that, 'Medieval art until about the twelfth century did not know childhood or did not attempt to portray it'.¹⁴ Children appeared in Medieval art but, as with homunculus images of Jesus, children were portrayed as miniature adults because artists and audiences had no conception of childhood and, therefore, would not have been able to understand a childlike Jesus. In short, 'there was not place for childhood in the Medieval world'.¹⁵ Airès argues that ' ... the men of the tenth and eleventh centuries did not dwell on the image of childhood, and that the images had neither interest nor even reality for them. It suggests too that in the realm of real life, not simply in that of aesthetic transposition, childhood was a period of transition which passed quickly and which was just as quickly forgotten'.¹⁶ Instead, Airès claims, before age seven, kids were considered mini-adults and after that, they were simply adults who assumed labor activities or other social roles.¹⁷ This began to change with the dawn of the Renaissance, and the transformation was largely complete by the seventeenth century. Beginning at this time, well-born families became more interested in companionate marriage, family and the well being of children. The child assumed a more central role in the family's concern and, critically, a role that was of the same importance as any other familial concern. Ariès argued that parents had always loved their children, but this was now coupled with concern for how to raise the child which, in turn, resulted in new and better education. Depictions of children begin to change after 1600, reflecting this conceptual change: children were now shown as individuals, with childlike features, holding children's objects, and engaged in children-specific behaviors. As a key example, Airès notes that, '[n]othing in Medieval dress distinguished the child from the adult' but that, in the seventeenth century, middle- and upper-class children 'ceased to be dressed like the grown-up'.¹⁸ As with clothing, Ariès fails to find in the Middle Ages children's toys or games, things that emerge only in the seventeenth century.[19] Ariès also finds evidence of an emerging awareness of the concept of childhood in humor: before the early modern period, children were treated like adults and could be witnesses to crude sexual humor, something that is among the strictest of taboos today.[20] No one at that time, other than prudish moralists, would have thought anything of it. Hence, there was no concern over images, for example, of urinating children or adults fondling genitalia.[21] Later, however, society came to believe that children must be protected from such inappropriate things, and that there is a whole realm of adult knowledge and activity from which children must be protected until they are older. This demonstrates the notion of children as 'innocents', a conception that both contributes to a definition of childhood, as well as marks a change from Medieval attitudes towards young people.

One of Ariès's fundamental arguments, and to many readers the most shocking and contentious, is that because of the ever-present specter of childhood death, Medieval parents invested little emotionally, economically, or otherwise in their children. As Ariès says, 'People could not allow themselves to become too attached to something that was regarded as a probable loss'.[22] Ariès presents anecdotal observations to argue for this lack of parental attachment: for example, Ariès uncritically cites Montaigne's essay 'On the affection of fathers for their children' (Book 2) in which the essayist says, 'I have lost two or three children in their infancy, not without regret, but without great sorrow'.[23] Death did indeed stalk: estimates place childhood mortality rates in the pre-modern period between 20 per cent and 50 per cent.[24] 20–25 per cent mortality was the norm before the first birthday.[25] For comparison, in underdeveloped and developing countries today the rate is about 10 per cent and less than 1 per cent in developed countries. Beyond the birthing process itself, without antibiotics and vaccines, children were subject to infections and viruses and, later, illnesses and accident. There were demographic variables that impacted mortality: death rates were lower among the wealthy and boys survived more than girls in all socio-economic classes.[26] Improvements in childhood mortality and health begin in the early modern period due to improvements in nutrition and various public measures, a change that reflects increasing societal investment in children.[27]

Ariès's impression of childhood before the seventeenth century was that it was not a happy age; parents could be distant or abusive and even abandon or kill their own children. Newborn infants faced infanticide and exposure. In Imperial Rome, exposure rates ran between 20–40 per cent and, while this practice often led to death, it cannot be considered the same thing as infanticide.[28] Indeed, the frequency of exposure made it a recognized social phenomenon with a resulting reciprocal practice– *aliena misericordia*, which saw children taken in by surrogate households. Though the kindness of strangers could not be guaranteed in every exposure event, it still offered the possibility of survival, whereas infanticide simply meant death.[29] Still, upwards of 90 per cent of abandonments resulted in death before the first birthday.[30] The great turning point in combating death by abandonment was likely the emergence of foundling hospitals in twelfth-century Italy, which increased the likelihood of survival over more haphazard abandonments outside public buildings, open urban spaces and churches.[31] The appearance of foundling hospitals and orphanages is a clear indicator that concern for children transcended the parental realm and became an important civic priority.[32] Orphanages and other such institutions perhaps benefitted girls more than boys, as girls were more likely to be abandoned to founding hospitals.[33] Late in the early modern period, illegitimacy was the prime cause of abandonment; in eighteenth-century Paris, upwards of 90 per cent of abandonments were due to illegitimacy.[34] Other causes of abandonment include financial hardship, the death of the mother or both parents, or the presence of a disability.[35] Orphanages and similar institutions also played key roles in protecting children, potentially limiting their roles as perpetrators or victims of crime.[36] Despite the instances of abandonment, for the most part children were raised in families.[37]

Initially, other scholars built on Aries' notion that childhood was a negative time and that it was only recently that parents began to nurture and show affection towards their offspring. Lloyd deMause, for example, asserts that '[t]he history of childhood is a nightmare from which we have only begun to awaken', and argued that childhood was a period of beatings, abandonment, murder and sexual abuse.[38] Edward Shorter declared that, 'mothers viewed the development and happiness of infants younger than two with indifference'.[39] He further argued that this dark childhood ended only around 1750, perhaps with the Romantic movement. The rise of romantic love between parents was seen as a necessary precondition for parental love of children. Such adult love in marriage was not common until the eighteenth century, when the phenomenon of arranged marriages began to wane. Lawrence Stone argued that doting parents can be seen as early as the fifteenth century, but true parental affection for children is not achieved until the industrial period, a phenomenon that coincides with a sharp decrease in childhood mortality rates.[40] Elisabeth Badinter also sees parental affection appearing in the nineteenth century, but argues that industrialism forced fathers out of the home, allowing for the creation of an environment conducive to making women mothers and homemakers.[41]

In the 1980s, however, a more positive view of pre-modern childhood emerged in scholarly literature. Simon Schama sees care for children in the seventeenth century: in the Dutch Republic, medical and pedagogical books for parents taught mothers to give love, engage in play, provide toys, ensure education and provide for financial futures.[42] Linda Pollock argued that parental investment in children can be seen in diaries and letters as early as the late Middle Ages.⁴³ John Boswell argued that abandonment was not necessarily a cruel practice, as de Mause had, but potentially a positive custom; poor parents gave up children they could not support, hoping that they would live, be adopted and perhaps even prosper.⁴⁴ Shulamith Shahar found that parents in fact were quite concerned about the health of their children, from pregnancy on.⁴⁵ Finally, the most recent scholarship offers a nuanced view of parental attitudes towards children. Steven Ozment documents increased concern among middle class parents in the early modern period, revealing a fear that they might lose children during childbirth, or later through accident and disease.⁴⁶ Moreover, should the child survive, there were efforts to prepare the child for later life: by the teens, people entered professional roles as artisans, merchants, clerics, etc. Elsewhere, Ozment argues that, by the Renaissance, fathers and mothers were recognized as forces who could impact their children's futures and, thus, for the sake of social order and eternal salvation, an emphasis was placed on parental involvement in ensuring the physical and moral health of their children.⁴⁷ Ultimately, Ariès's most shocking claim, that there was little concern among parents for children even in death, was debunked by Robert Woods, who thoroughly documented the pain of losing a child among parents prior to the nineteenth century.⁴⁸ While accepting the fact that death could be in the offing was perhaps a coping mechanism, it appears unlikely that parents were unmoved by the death of a child. For example, there are accounts of devastated mothers that had to be counseled by priests and indeed some mothers were said to have gone mad with grief.⁴⁹ Close study has determined that there was always a good bit of parental concern for children.⁵⁰ At a minimum, those who argue that children were not valued by parents overlook a fundamental economic reality: in peasant families, children contributed as potential labour and, among elite families, as inheritors ensuring the continuation of the family line.⁵¹ Eventually historians began to shy away from making large, overarching comments on childhood in history.

Art historical studies have refuted Ariès's claims about Medieval childhood as well and corrected his observations about children in early modern art. The most critical problem with Ariès's thesis is his sample of evidence: it is neither large enough nor properly interpreted. Contrary to Ariès's claim, the artistic and archaeological records in fact produce all sorts of child-specific images and objects, including children's clothes, objects and furniture, and demonstrate both an awareness of childhood and concern for children.⁵² Klaus Arnold notes that toys appear in child burials in sixth-century Gaul and tenth-century Iceland.⁵³ Meanwhile, Dorota Żołądź-Strzelczyk has noted, in archaeological findings and paintings of pre-Modern Poland, parental concern about 'pregnancy and delivery, baptism, the life of the toddler, children's diets, toys, the education of children, [and] dangers for children ... '⁵⁴ Children's possessions demonstrably existed and they indicate the presence of children and conceptualizations of childhood. Children's furniture, for example, existed prior to the modern period and what makes a piece of furniture child-specific is not just a matter scale. Rather, furniture such as cribs and high chairs reflect concerns with safety, discipline, hygiene and play.[55] Moreover, the possession of this age-specific furniture in a household indicates and displays familial social status. Even in seventeenth-century Rome, where a child-centric material culture did not develop, there are surviving inventories that give an idea of the range of furniture elite families bought for children.[56] Like furniture, toys indicate the presence of children and parental response to children. Dolls, for example, are the oldest and most ubiquitous toy. They are found in almost all cultures and date back amongst the earliest artifacts. Dolls are for imitative play and the way children play with them often mirrors what they see in the home. Similarly, dolls could be used to teach expectations, as we have seen in the *Portrait of Three Young Girls*. In some cases, dolls could even be used for religious instruction.[57] Children have certainly always played, but play does require two things: space and opportunity, both of which are more abundant for elite families. Play can also involve objects (either specially purposed or spontaneously used), but they are not required. Play with specifically crafted objects can, therefore, also reflect economic standing. It is also subject to moral discourse; some thinkers, such as Augustine, have defined it as frivolous and sinful, and found no value in it. On the other hand, in Book III of *The Republic*, Plato saw play (especially imitative play) as an anticipatory form of socialization and therefore quite important.[58] Following Plato's lead, Locke and Rousseau ultimately argued that one can teach through play.

The lack of children's objects in Ariès's sample might reflect the lack of worldly goods generally in the Medieval world, goods which, according to some authors, proliferate beginning only in the Renaissance.[59] By the seventeenth century, in the Dutch Republic, consumers had relatively easy access to newspapers, books, wool cloth, beer, herrings, cheese, salt, tobacco, coffee, cauliflower and even exotic flowers, like chrysanthemums. Earlier in the fifteenth century, the Spanish traveler Pero Tafur visited Bruges and described finding there:

> oranges and lemons from Castile, which seemed only just to have been gathered from the trees, fruits and wine from Greece, as abundant as in that country. I saw also confections and spices from Alexandria and the Levant, just as if one were there; furs from the Black Sea, as if they had been produced in the district. Here was all Italy with its brocades, silks, and armour and everything which is made there; and indeed there is no part of the world whose products are not found here at their best.[60]

Works of art themselves emerge as luxury goods in the Renaissance; Wilfried Brulez calculated that some 17 million paints were executed in Europe between 1400 and 1800.[61] Some estimates put the production of paintings at 2.5 million in the Dutch Republic alone by 1650, while others radically increase this number to 5–10 million paintings.⁶² This booming new market in painting supplied the demands of middle and upper class consumers, and even some from the working class. Throughout Europe in the seventeenth century, and particularly in the north, subjects like portraits, landscapes, genre scenes and domestic interiors appear with great popularity alongside religious, history and morality paintings. Portraits of children emerge as good subjects for mercantile families in the seventeenth century, and the genre evolved.⁶³ As children appeared more and more in art, so too did their possessions and the wealthier the family, the more they could afford non-essential, child-specific items, such as toys, clothes and furniture.

While art related to children is overt and abundant in the seventeenth century, even a cursory (though more substantial than Ariès's) survey finds child-centric art much earlier. Stephanie R. Miller demonstrates that in the wake of the 'children's plague' of 1363–4 a much deeper appreciation for children emerged in Florence and this can be seen in 'treatise and records, and in images related to childhood that ornament the city and appear within the home in increasing numbers over the course of the century'.⁶⁴ There was a veritable 'proliferation' of birth objects, such as *deschi da parto* (birth trays).⁶⁵ There was also a wide range of child-specific artifacts in fifteenth-century Florentine homes, including cradles, teethers, rattles, dishes, chests and educational toys.⁶⁶ Protective talismans and amulets appear in abundance and some are even exclusively for children.⁶⁷

Most importantly, a more nuanced interpretation of objects and images than Ariès offers, demonstrates an earlier concern for children even in the kinds of objects Ariès discusses. For example, Ariès identifies at least three 'types' of children that appear in Medieval art and argues that, rather than being true children, they are stand-ins for other things. These images, he argues, do not seek to portray real children and are thus evidence that there was no theoretical conception of childhood in the Middle Ages.⁶⁸ It is true that well into the early modern period, children continue to be used as indicators of other concepts, like the child beggars as symbols of charity in the painting of Le Nain, Ribera and Murillo.⁶⁹ These images, however, were multivalent; the audience of these works of art likely understood more than one message. One type of child that Ariès identifies is the 'adolescent angel'. We see such figures in the relief panels of Luca della Robbia's *Cantoria*, an organ well in the Cathedral of Florence. In the reliefs, adolescent boys and girls sing, dance, and play musical instruments. However, the children stand on clouds and so, by one reading, they are to be considered angels (fig. I.2). Another reading is also likely, however: Luca incorporated real-life human elements, such as the childish interaction among the players, or a foot lifted to keep time, underscoring the childlike character of the figure.⁷⁰ Moreover, we know that Luca used Florentine youths as models.⁷¹ Finally, while the carved figures may have been angels, children (boys, in particular) would still have sung in the cathedral.[72] All of this makes it impossible to think that contemporary audiences, as well as the artist, necessarily divorced the images of children in the *Cantoria* from actual children. Another example concerns the iconography of the biblical figure of David in Florence. The biblical figure of David certainly communicated Florentine civic values, but these images also communicated parental and familial concerns.[73] Meanwhile, paintings may appear in Renaissance homes that do not specifically display 'real' children, but were in fact made for children. Parents in Renaissance Italy were encouraged to have images of saintly children and virgins because they set positive examples for children.[74] Later images of children seemed to be more for parents than for children.[75] Finally, a child-centric image might have been clear to a contemporary audience but utterly lost to us today. Chiara Franceschini, for example, argues that Michelangelo's famed *Doni Tondo* is, in part, a meditation on the souls of infants in Limbo.[76] Indeed, *tondi* in general (often given at marriage or at the birth of a child and nearly ubiquitous in the Renaissance palazzo and casa) attest to the centrality of children in the hopes and aspirations of the Florentine family. Though outside the chronological scope of this volume, Nancy Rose Marshall's excellent discussion in *City of Gold and Mud* of depictions of Victorian-era children demonstrates that earlier images demand sustained analysis as they often convey far more information than meets the modern eye.[77]

Figure I.2: Luca della Robbia, *Boys Singing from a Book* (early 1430s). Photo Credit: Matthew Knox Averett, author.

Over half of Ariès's book discusses education. Early modern art frequently addressed the education of chikdren, and this volume pays particular attention to this subject. Education represents a significant investment in children, by both parents and societies. The study of both formal and informal education helps reveal what people wanted for their children, as well as what they expected their children to do as adults. A key point in Ariès substantial look at the development of education from the Middle Ages to the nineteenth century is that, in the Middle Ages, there was complete 'indifference' toward the age of the student.[78] Students, regardless of age were mingled and, moreover, once they entered school they entered a world of adults, not an institution designed to shepherd the young into adulthood as we often view it today. Ariès concludes that in the Renaissance, however, education became something for children, suggesting a new conceptualization of childhood among early modern adults: all post-Medieval pedagogies are based on a recognition of 'the special nature of childhood, and the moral and social importance of the systematic education of children in special institutions devised for that purpose'.[79] Beginning in the fifteenth century, education changes dramatically: new curricula are introduced, children stay in school longer and education is entrusted to specialists.

A panel from Peter Paul Rubens' *Medici Cycle* illustrates the education of Maria de' Medici and demonstrates both what should be taught and why (Fig. I.3). Maria commissioned Rubens to make a series of twenty-four paintings that would put forth her case for why she should be monarch of France rather than her son, Louis XIII. Some of the panels promote the idea of a divine will that favours Maria over Louis, while others assert her legal rights. Still others tout her diplomatic successes as queen regent. Only one panel directly argues for her qualifications, *The Education of the Princess*, the third panel in the cycle. In it, we see Maria attentively reading from a book placed in the lap of Athena, who teaches the young student wisdom. Above Maria is Hermes, messenger of the gods, who here symbolizes Maria's mastery of languages, an essential skill in international politics. To the left of the painting is Apollo playing a cello and teaching Maria music and mathematics, while to the right Aglaea, Euphrosyne and Thalia, offer a floral headdress to ensure the future queen will grow in grace. The various objects surrounding the young girl demonstrate the multiple fields of inquiry to which an educated person should be exposed: a bust of Homer indicating literature and philosophy, a palette, paint, and brushes for the visual arts. All of this is required for a solid (elite male) education and a solid education is required to be a ruler.

Introduction: *The Early Modern Child in Art and History* 13

Figure I.3: Peter Paul Rubens, *The Education of the Princess Maria de' Medici* (1622–5). Photo Credit: Wikimedia Commons.

Such an image of education seems at odds with the received impression of Medieval education. In the Middle Ages, a good bit of elite male education focused on chivalric and martial arts, and this survived into the Renaissance.[80] Yet it survived largely as ceremony, as a literary education became essential. To that end, formal institutions of learning evolved or emerged in response to the dramatic changes of the Renaissance. At the outset of the early modern period, there were several competing kinds of schools: for example, in most Italian cities between 1300 and 1600, there was a mixture of independent, church and communal schools.[81] Schools could be in competition, particularly over curricula. A spate of new humanists issued writing on education that emphasized knowledge of Greek and Roman history, drawing and painting, reading, literature, and music. Languages were deemed essential and Latin was given the most attention, though some students also learned Greek. Through the fifteenth century, the *studia humanitatis* was established, with the goal to educate the perfect orator, which combined impeccable speaking skills with an excellence of character. Vernacular schools persisted, providing basic instruction generally to both boys and girls in reading, writing and arithmetic. With the emergence of schools run by religious orders in the sixteenth century, these traditions continued (with the Jesuits, for example, continuing the *studia humanitatis* and the Priarists maintaining the vernacular). Similarly, exposure to the visual arts was considered essential to elite education. As early as the sixteenth century, Baldassare Castiglione, in *Il Cortegiano*, matter-of-factly emphasizes the importance of knowledge of art for both men and women.[82]

These dramatic developments indicate that children's social roles were changing. They also illustrate varying conceptualizations of childhood and the character of children. While the notion of the child as innocent did appear, as Ariès notes, so did a competing image: that of the evil child.[83] This was particularly true for girls. Some early modern educators viewed the relationship between children and parents as 'war' in which the will of the child had to be broken.[84] Only then would a child behave in appropriate ways, thus fulfilling social expectations. Physical and psychological coercion were the norm in efforts to control children's behavior. In the early sixteenth century, Erasmus of Rotterdam argued in his treatise 'Declamation on the Subject of Early Liberal Education for Children' (*De pueris statim ac liberaliter instituendis declamatio*, 1529) that parents should invest time and money into ensuring children (or more specifically boys) received a good humanistic education.[85] Like Augustine, Erasmus believed that children are marked with original sin and thus are not born innocent. Education, however, was a path to moral cleanliness and was critical in establishing a desirable society. Erasmus prescribed not just a curriculum based in the study of languages, arts and mathematics, but also called for teachers who would act as fathers towards their students. Teachers would thus be firm, but gentle; Erasmus was 'obsessed' with stories of severe physical abuse and, following the lead of Quintilian, argued against corporal punishment.[86] In 1693, John Locke published *Some Thoughts Concerning Education*, a treatise on the education of gentlemen. Expanding on his notion of a *tabula rasa*, first put forth in *Essay Concerning Human Understanding* (1690), Locke argued that, contra Augustine and Erasmus, people were not born sinful, but were rather blank slates. Children thus could grow into rational beings but only through a proper education that would drive away prejudice and superstition. Wisdom and virtue were the most important goal of an education, even above raw knowledge. Locke argued for spartan conditions, but condemned corporal punishment. Though others in England had similarly argued for curricular reform, it was Locke's treatise that reached a wide audience and would dominate English educational thought for the next century. Eighteenth-century France, meanwhile, embraced Jean-Jacques Rousseau's treatise on education *Émile, ou De l'éducation* (1762). Rousseau presented a new conceptualization of the childhood, defining it as an inherently good and pure state and the child as physically, morally and intellectually vulnerable. This vulnerability required nurturing and education available only from a loving family. Like Locke, Rousseau found children to be valuable people, indeed the future of society. He rejected authoritarian education and sought an educational system that incorporated children's points of view. In theory, the goal of education was to teach boys to lead virtuous lives in a society that was otherwise corrupting.[87] Short of all these moral goals, there was a fundamental utility to a humanistic education: it prepared elite boys for the social political life and business worlds into which their wealth and social position had placed them.[88] For the wealthy, there was also education in the homes, with parents often taking the lead or instruction left to private tutors. Wherever education took place, formal education typically began at age seven and was divided according to gender.[89]

Though girls learned to read and write, their education was a slightly different matter, as schools were more for boys than girls.[90] Still, essentially all noble and wealthy girls were educated, with the number diminishing down the economic latter.[91] At least as early as the sixteenth century, education was viewed an essential means of imparting social norms and expectations to young girls and this was accomplished with a wide array of strategies.[92] Girls' education focused on religious texts as well as handful of approved classical authors, all normally taught under the supervision of men.[93] It was widely considered that, with few exceptions, girls were intellectually inferior and could not achieve as boys did, which justified or lead to the belief that girls should not be taught too much.[94] Instead, the goal of girls' education was to maintain their virtue and virginity, which was perceived to be an extreme challenge for girls.[95] As a result, girls were normally instructed for only an hour or two per day, and only for a few years, with education focused on catechism.[96] Girls were also largely excluded from grammar schools and universities.[97] Eventually the literary education of girls expanded: as early as the sixteenth century, writers following Plato's lead began promoting historical women famous for intellectual achievement as models for girls' education, including Queen Zenobia of Palmyra, Hypatia, Diotima, and Aspasia.[98] Parents were urged to let their daughters study Latin and Greek as well as literature, and elite girls began to read more after eighteenth-century educational reforms. Rousseau's call for a new family was embraced by the elite of eighteenth-century France, and given visual expression by French artists. Whole new depictions of children emerged, including formal and informal portraits of maternal breast-feeding, newly sentimentalized *maternités* and family portraits, and portraits of fathers and daughters. The new conception of childhood, presented in *Émile*, required a new education, which produced dramatic changes when adopted by French society. As an example, the sitter, in Jean-Honoré Fragonard's *A Young Girl Reading* (Fig I.4), reads a small book, possibly a portable novel such as Voltaire's *Candide*, Rousseau's sentimental *Julie*, or a similar such book. A painting such as this documents that reading emerged as a cultural norm for girls among elite society in pre-Revolutionary France. It would remain so long after.

Figure I.4: Jean-Honoré Fragonard, *A Young Girl Reading*. Photo Credit: National Gallery of Art, Washington, DC.

Even for the poor, education was deemed vitally important, though it was different from elite educations. Schools were still mostly for the wealthy as they were expensive and, consequently, only about 10 per cent of the population attended.[99] Still, that parents would pay is further evidence of investment in children. Most Jesuit schools, such as the Collegio Romano, did not charge fees, but male youths who wished to attend these schools (normally beginning at age ten) had to have had some education in Latin before matriculation, thus effectively barring poorer boys.[100] Overall, education for the poor was largely limited to religious instruction.[101] Most everyone, however, was taught basic literacy, as reading and writing were considered essential for potentially securing good jobs in emerging bureaucracies, as well as preparing children to deal with the rules of life that were increasing printed.[102] In Germany, from at least Luther on, society increasingly saw rearing and educating children as an adult's binding duty, as children were future citizens.[103] Thus, despite the costs of education, Protestant cities in the north led the charge for compulsory education.[104] Weimar in 1619, for example, began requiring education for all children between the ages of six and twelve.[105] Later, education was made compulsory everyone across Enlightenment Prussia by Frederick the Great.[106] Frederick's *Generallandschulreglement* from 1763 is a model of modern compulsory education, calling for education at least until the age of 14 and prescribing a common curriculum and textbooks.[107] There were also various kinds of informal education: education could also be found in apprenticeships, which could take place in workshop or in royal courts.[108] For poorer families, children might help on the farm, around the house or in a workshop by age seven, but begin actual training around ten.[109] For non-elite girls, education often focused on sewing, cooking and other household chores, with reading limited to spiritual books, like the lives of the saints.[110]

The Early Modern Child in Art

This volume contributes art historical examinations of the early modern child. Most of the essays this volume contains originated as papers delivered at academic conferences, while a few were solicited to round-out the book. For various reasons, not all the conference participants could contribute and the very nature of an enterprise like this can be idiosyncratic, leaving out an array of important topics, including children's objects and spaces. The study of the early modern child, thus, will continue to be rich for future study. Still, the ten essays in this volume cover a vast collection of art and a broad body of topics. Altogether, the book examines the construction of identity, explores childhood educations, expands on children's participation in government and religious activities, and helps define childhood and parental roles. The accumulation of evidence presented in the book argues that early modern adults (including parents, clergy, princes and philosophers) consciously developed notions of childhood and actively constructed childhood identity. Our survey begins with Margaret Elizabeth Hadley's essay, which examines a fifteenth-century illustrated prayer book that demonstrates that early modern parents deeply mourned the passing of their children. The book was commissioned by Macé Prestesaille, a recent widower, and depictions of his deceased children in the book visually assert their continued growth after death. Prestesaille wished to envision the entire family reunited as though neither his wife, Jehanne, nor any of their children had died. Although the teachings of the church are relevant and the specific texts included in Macé's book help provide immediate interpretive context, one parent's creative and personal work of mourning is paramount for analyzing this case. Further demonstrating adult affection for children, Tanya Tiffany describes the unusual case of Sor Margarita de la Cruz, daughter of Holy Roman Emperor Maximilian II, who, though childless, placed children at the centre of her life and religious rituals. Sor Margarita's love of children was a direct function of her reverence for Christ's humanity. When describing her religious practice, the nun herself contended that the sight of real babies and the sounds of their cries helped her to 'remember' Christ in the manger.

Our next section focuses on children and violence. Children were victims of violence, but could also be perpetrators. As Margaret Flansburg observes, small children and young boys began to appear with frequency in late Trecento and early Quattrocento Calvary scenes as observers of Jesus's humiliation and suffering. Their poses are drawn from the 1293 *Supplicationes varie*, which was an important reference for several centuries. In the *Supplicationes*, some of the children collect rocks in their tunic skirts or carry pails of stones with which to attack Jesus. In the Riminese School, however, similar children appear to be hesitant and watchful rather than aggressive, perhaps demonstrating empathy towards Jesus's suffering. Rachel Chantos, meanwhile, looks at the humor, moral lessons and social instruction of violent children in *World Upside Down* prints. These prints typically feature scenes of peasant life and inversions displaying animals and men, men and women, and children and their parents, with the subjects often deriving from folk tales. In particular, Chantos notes scenes in which boys beat their fathers, revealing an alternate and undesirable reality – a reality often featured in early folk tales – and both were used to teach a moral, cope with hierarchic anxieties and relate to the civilizing process.

The third section looks at paintings of children as means of expressing conceptions of childhood. Jasmin Cyril notes that late Quattrocento and early Cinquecento portraits of Renaissance court family life underscored the significance of the dynastic legacy of the family, implicit in the heraldry and placement of images of privileged children, and introduced an element of familial association that determined the future of the court itself. She traces the tradition from ancient sources and documents its full flowering in the Italian courts of the Renaissance. Their presence emphasizes the importance of children in establishing aristocratic dynasties. Fabien Lacouture analyzes depictions of young boys, identifying three kinds of works of art that correspond to three traditional Italian divisions of childhood. *Deschi da parto*, with their prominent displays of infantile penises, correspond to *infanzia*. Later in life, double portraits of fathers and sons depicts *puerizia*. And finally, individual portraits of older boys suggests *adolescenza*. The inclusion in these images of various attributes, from weapons to books, asserts the masculinity of male children of noble extraction, emphasizing the perpetuation of the family. Leaving Italy, Parme Giuntini demonstrates that the visual culture of early modern childhood in eighteenth-century England was orchestrated in portraits and fancy pictures painted by Sir Joshua Reynolds and exhibited at the newly founded Royal Academy. Many of these images gained even greater visibility and thus influence when they were reproduced as widely-distributed prints. At the precise moment that physicians and philosophers were exhorting the British aristocracy to revise dramatically their parenting practices, Reynolds was capitalizing on his position as President of the Royal Academy, and his reputation as a portrait painter, to re-envision the landscape of childhood. In all of these paintings, one of the distinguishing characteristics was dress. Fashion was a key factor in early modern representation; in particular the new styles that rapidly and simultaneously identified and characterized both childhood and good parenting. From the perspective of the eighteenth century, the emergence of age appropriate clothing for children demonstrated an acknowledgement and commitment to a new notion of childhood as a unique time, with its own set of needs and conditions.

Finally, we conclude with three essays that consider adult expectations of children. Lisa Tom investigates princely portraits completed in the court of Philip II of Spain. The paintings emphasize the connections between the Farnese and Hapsburg families, while projecting ideas of the model character for young princes. The portraits also establish a close connection between all the young princes in Phillip's court, indicating the anticipated alliance between these families within the context of Italian-Spanish politics. Brian Steele analyzes Titian's painting of Clarice Strozzi to reveal references to her anticipated role as wife, focusing on sixteenth-century Italian expectations of female behavior, including controlled movement, beauty inspiring love, chastity, familial responsibility and piety. The essay provides a detailed reading of iconographic features of setting and implications of dress, jewels, comportment and formal design. These factors intimate a transitive process of becoming: that of schooling the infant of childlike demeanor into the desirable Petrarchan beauty and, potentially, ideal wife. Matthew Averett's paper, through an examination of art and literature, discusses the education and expectations placed on papal nephews in Baroque Rome, using the case of Pope Urban VIII Barberini andhis trio of nephews. The result sheds light on the politics of papal nepotism, surrogate parenting, and the role of children in dynastic aspirations of families in early modern Italy.

All of these essays together contribute to the ongoing assessment of childhood as a social construct by arguing that conceptions of childhood existed well before the modern period and that they varied according to time and place, individuals and societies, and by construction and expression. While the study of children and childhood can tell us much about the past, it can also tell us much about ourselves. The roots of modern attitudes towards children and conceptualizations of childhood reach deep into the early modern period. Today we view childhood as a unique period of development and growth, a period we steadfastly guard. We educate children with an eye towards their future lives as adults, exposing them to history, science, literature and the arts (Fig. I.5). In meaningful ways, today's children are not so very different than those three young girls whose portrait was made four centuries ago.

Figure I.5: The author's children with a *Cantoria* relief panel by Luca della Robbia at the High Museum of Art in Atlanta, Georgia. Photo Credit: Matthew Knox Averett, author.

1 CRADLE AND GRAVE: COMMEMORATING INDIVIDUAL VICTIMS OF INFANT MORTALITY

Margaret Elizabeth Hadley

Macé Prestesaille commissioned an idealized pictorial frontispiece to remember and help visualize what family records indicate to have been impossible on earth (Fig. 1.1).[1] An illuminator, who is known as the Master of Prestesaille[2] and who collaborated with the Master of the Yale Missal, represented Macé's family of eight in the style associated with Jean Fouquet of Tours (c. 1420–80).[3] Accompanying the depiction of the Prestesaille family is a green landscape background and a light blue sky. The middle ground contains a round arched portico, leading from the tiled and coffered interior, that recalls Roman architecture. St Michael the Archangel, the warrior who battled the devil, appears in a full suit of fifteenth-century plate armour. Camille Couderc recognized this idealized portrait as an inaccurate representation of the family unit.[4] Rather than providing a straightforward illustration of the text or a traditional portrait, Prestesaille's frontispiece exhibits dissonance between the manuscript's fifteenth-century historical texts and programme of images in order to serve its memorial, spiritual and didactic purposes.

Figure 1.1: *Pietà* and *Macé Prestesaille's Family with St. Michael*, Lat. 1179, MS Paris, Bibliothèque nationale de France, fols 1v–2r.

Reading to the end of the first fourteen folios demonstrates that all of the sitters in this family group would not have been available at the same time for any artist to render likenesses. Macé Prestesaille and Jehanne Prince married in 1468, lived in Tours and had six children in close succession before the end of 1474. Virginia Reinburg recently published a useful translation of the manuscript's dedicatory text during her discussion of family histories in books of hours:

> In honor and reverence of our savior and redeemer Jesus, and of his blessed dear mother, and of all the saints in paradise, this book was created and compiled as a memorial and remembrance of Jehanne, daughter of the late Colin Prince and Jaquete his wife, in her lifetime the wife of Macé Prestesaille, and also as the memorial and remembrance of the children Jehanne bore and conceived while married [to Macé] ... May God by his holy grace and mercy have pity and mercy on their souls. To all lords and ladies, priests, secular clerics, and others who read and hear this tribute read aloud, pray God for the soul of the deceased Jehanne and all the other dead, and say each one Pater Noster and one Ave Maria. This book belongs to Macé Prestesaille and was completed on the penultimate day of May 1475.[5]

This introduction is followed by suffrages with integrated notices of family births and deaths that were transcribed by Couderc.[6] Its plain accounts of a woman and children lost in a short period of time probably demonstrate the narrator's restraint. Jacqueline Marie Musacchio has argued: 'for every stoic, terse statement noting a child's death, a great deal of sorrow was kept at bay'.[7] The manuscript's family history underscored the Prestesailles' fruitful marriage, social ties and spiritual community. Their six children's godparents show links to influential people. They include Master Pierre Huet, who was a canon of Evreux; Guion Moreau, King Louis XI's apothecary; Master Pierre Bechebien, lieutenant of the Tours magistrate; and the extended household of Jean V de Bueil, Count of Sancerre (1406–77).[8] Jehanne Prince's lineage is notably emphasized more than Macé Prestesaille's in the family history; her sister, Andrée Ogière, was a godmother to their eldest daughter.[9] The Carmelite friars of St Saturnin, Tours, received her family's dead, including both of Jehanne's parents, Jehanne herself and at least three of her children.[10] Documentation suggests a favoured placement 'in the church'.[11] According to the manuscript's introductory texts, therefore, a complete family portrait would have been composed of the couple, with girls aged one and two, a four-year-old boy and three deceased children in swaddling clothes.[12]

Prestesaille's manuscript has been imprecisely classified for well over one hundred years as a book of hours. It does not contain the Little Office, or Hours, of the Blessed Virgin Mary, which is the foundational text for works in that genre. Nor does the manuscript include any other abbreviated prayer cycles for the canonical hours that were widely used by fifteenth-century laity for private devotions, such as the Hours of the Cross or of the Holy Spirit. The typical book of hours, in this period, featured the following components: Calendar, Gospel lessons, Hours of the Virgin, Hours of the Cross, Hours of the Holy Spirit, *Obsecro te* and *O intemerata* prayers, Penitential Psalms, Suffrages, Accessory Texts and the Office of the Dead.[13] Books of hours from Fouquet circle workshops include almost every one of these components;[14] for instance, other *horae* that have been associated with the Master of the Yale Missal conform to general expectations for the genre.[15] Prestesaille's manuscript does not contain a Calendar, Hours, Penitential Psalms or the *O intemerata*; instead, it includes the history of Prestesaille's nuclear family,[16] the Office of the Dead,[17] bible excerpts,[18] the Mass of the Holy Spirit,[19] the Mass of the Virgin with variants for the vigil of Advent and feast of the Virgin's birth,[20] the Mass for the Dead,[21] the Preface and Canon of the Mass,[22] didactic texts[23] and additional prayers.[24] Since the Office of the Dead follows a monastic form of prayer, rather than an abbreviated version adapted for lay usage like the Hours of the Virgin, liturgical emphases in Prestesaille's book are on the official and public rituals for mourning and the Eucharist. The more personalized sections in this collection of texts relate to family history, private prayer and Christian education. Because Prestesaille's volume is closer to a book of hours than to other fifteenth-century genres, previous scholarly classifications of this manuscript are readily understandable. Calling the work Macé Prestesaille's *Book of Remembrance* more appropriately reflects this unique compilation's stated purpose as being, literally, 'for memory and remembrance'.[25]

Past discussions of Prestesaille's book generally focus on the frontispiece and specific biographical notices, but a limited approach does not do justice to the material in this customized prayer book. Although it had been published earlier, Prestesaille's *Book of Remembrance* became widely recognized as a dated example of Turonian illumination, deserving a place in the canon at the *Primitifs Français* exhibition of 1904.[26] Its so-called family portrait,[27] accompanied by contemporary biographical information, makes this source precious to scholars. This entirely digitized manuscript is available online for worldwide access, offering researchers unprecedented opportunities for the detailed study of this atypical source.[28] Almost every scholarly treatment of the manuscript has effectively highlighted the same few folios: the frontispiece and historical data. Couderc, logically following suit, focuses on the family in his album of portraits (Fig. 1.1),[29] but the *Arma Christi* and *Macé Prestesaille with St Matthew* (fols 7v–8r) could have facilitated a clearer emphasis on the work's original patron. Nicole Reynaud, by contrast, illustrated the *Martyrdom of St Sebastian* (fol. 164v) because this scene exhibits more refined stylistic quality and closer ties to Fouquet than images depicting the Prestesaille family.[30] The *St Christopher carrying the Christ Child* miniature (fol. 166v), however, could have served the same curatorial purpose of showing the book's most gifted illuminator's hand, the Master of the Yale Missal,[31] and emphasizing its childhood-related content. Digitization now allows a broader audience to study this rich source as a historical model for commemorating children.

The dedication specifically characterized the intended purpose of Macé's unique prayer book as memorial,[32] so the texts and images in this atypical volume help interpret the representation of the Prestesaille family and their stories. This study aims to place the biographical portions of the manuscript, which have been the focus of previous publications, alongside more sustained and substantive references to their immediate context: this customized anthology's own variety of other texts and images. The complex and unusual collection encompasses texts for mourning a spouse under thirty and several children, who died before reaching the age of two years,[33] as well as providing material for practical and spiritual education. The living and dead are united, thus, in an illustrated programme of Catholic literature that evokes significant functions of memory in fifteenth-century Western European society. Prestesaille's book mirrors the contemporary religious practice of rigorously structured and purposefully crafted memorials for departed members of every community, manifesting a sacred obligation and a perpetual occupation for monastics and laity alike. The didactic portions of Prestesaille's *Book of Remembrance*, although appropriate for any Catholic layperson, support the manuscript's commemorative function. The goal of the book is memory; remembering is central to the processes of mourning and learning. Educational texts facilitated the cultural tradition of basic religious instruction at home, whose aims in medieval and early modern educational programmes included long term memory of the material learned. The manuscript's intended emphasis on memory, therefore, provides the key to understanding the relevance of every text and image commissioned and utilized by Macé, as well as his surviving children, to remember their beloved family members, while meditating upon and retaining the anthology's content.

Prestesaille's Memory and Abstracted Family Images

In the opening diptych Macé and his wife kneel near their six children as St Michael directs their attention to the *Pietà* on the opposite folio (Fig. 1.1). Idealized rendering of their faces, relying primarily on outlines with minimal shading to differentiate features, suggests that they do not bear genuinely personalized likenesses. The young women are carbon copies of their deceased mother in visage, pose and dress.[34] Philippe Ariès has noted the importance that funerary monuments played in the contemporary iconographic development of children's portraiture and that, once swaddling stopped, a child 'was dressed just like the other men and women of his class'.[35] The similarity between Jehanne and her daughters could also be linked to the conception of the child as a 'live image' of her mother, who provides a form of immortality for her parent.[36] The idea that Macé's remaining girls were destined to grow up to be replicas of their mother could have been a comforting thought. These depictions of the girls function as signs that Jehanne's best qualities are conserved in youthful versions.

Prestesaille's son Guillaume, on the other hand, appears to resemble the archangel, especially given his neatly curled golden locks that contrast with Macé's straight, dark hair. The angelic image of Guillaume may correspond to a fifteenth-century cultural idealization of the young. One humanist parallel, appropriate for this Fouquet-circle manuscript that distantly echoes Italian art, comes from a description of Jacopo Antonio Marcello mourning his son Valerio in 1461. 'The father clothed in black bore his child clad in white to the funeral of an angel ... The innocence of children dead before the age of ten, contemporaries believed, won them that special place in heaven'.[37] Asserting Guillaume's visual similarity to the archangel, perhaps, also manifests Macé's wish that his son would be protected by powerful intercessors.

Abstracted figural rendering of the Prestesaille family encourages semiotic readings. The frontispiece miniature's idealized style correlates perfectly with its memorial function. These depicted individuals can be read as a series of iconic signs representing a model family. Showing every vivid detail of Macé's deceased loved ones' visages could have hindered his transition from the raw forms of initial grief to the ongoing mourner's work of honouring and remembering those who departed before him. Iconic forms offering an ideal version of his family, therefore, may have helped Macé make psychological progress with these customized visual aids. Although modern connoisseurs certainly would have preferred Macé to commission the finest possible family portraits, such an expenditure could ultimately have hindered the widower's grieving. The Prestesaille family is presented in relative abstraction to support the book's purpose by assisting a man mourn and constructively survive loss.

Abstracted iconic representation manifests the actual limitations of Prestesaille's memory. After losing several children at early ages, his experience with fatherhood was reduced in part to reconstruction or imaginative remembrance. Although he could not know precisely how his children would have looked upon maturity, he envisioned relative height and anticipated some level of family uniformity, if not resemblance. He may have constructed the mental images of his lost children by using familiar models. Perhaps he thought of himself at an earlier age or, in the cases of his girls, envisioned the way his wife, relatives or family friends looked throughout their life cycles. However, he could never have been sure how one or another child would appear when grown up, which demonstrates the superiority of the artist's abstracted representation for his purposes. Prestesaille's choice to commission work from a practitioner, who–although influenced by the famous Turonian master Fouquet–was potentially unable to produce detailed likenesses, served the patron's means as well as his needs in this case.[38]

Representing the living and dead together as though all the children in his nuclear family have grown according to their respective dates of birth must have been requested by Prestesaille. There is biblical precedent for including dead and living children in the exhaustive reckoning of a man's family. The patriarch Job lost ten children during a series of attacks that decimated his household.[39] Job then doubled all that he had lost by the end of the narrative. Since he only begat ten more children after being tested, the deceased ten children are included in the total.[40] Macé and the author of Job were looking forward to the future resurrection prophesied by the patriarch: 'For I know that my Redeemer liveth, and in the last day I shall rise out of the earth. And I shall be clothed again with my skin and in my flesh I shall see God'.[41] Prestesaille may have commissioned this representation of his family as a constant reminder of the immortality of the soul and the hope of future resurrection that would reunite his whole family. The youngest son, unnamed, raises questions because his Christian status is not as securely established by a documented baptism ritual like all their other children.[42] Whether he was officially named or not, midwives in this period were trained and empowered to baptize in utero or immediately after birth when a child was in peril.[43] Although it would be best to find explicit examples of baptized foetuses and neonates in Turonian accounts,[44] Prestesaille documents suggest he benefitted from this creative measure. The family history clearly states that both Jehanne and her youngest son were buried in St Saturnin, which indicates that a baptism probably happened during his half-hour life.[45]

Prestesaille Indexes of Living with Loss

Looking at the individual suffrage images for each family member helps decode the frontispiece with all the Prestesailles (Fig. 1.1; fols 8r, 8v, 9r, 9v, 10v, 11v and 12v). After the opening diptych's collective portrait, the repetition of seven family members' images, before his or her name saint's suffrage, underscores the imprecisely representational nature of every Prestesaille depicted. Whether the individual is Macé (fol. 8r), his wife (fol. 8v) or their youngest daughter Perrine (fol. 12v), the suffrage miniatures show each kneeling family member with the top of his or her head reaching the height of a patron saint's shoulder. This suggests that the soul of each departed child has reached a state of perfected, youthful maturity in the afterlife. It also asserts that the living Prestesaille children will one day pass the milestone of adulthood, despite their current ages under five years. The suffrage miniatures, then, reveal how the Prestesaille children are represented as miniaturized adults. They are pictorially granted the full majority status that Macé hopes and believes they will achieve, either on earth or in heaven.

Due to the courtly context for Prestesaille's Fouquet-circle manuscript and his social connections to noble households, it is reasonable to compare the painted images of his deceased children with the illustrious, monumental funerary portraiture of other minors. King Louis XI (1423–83) and Queen Charlotte of Savoy (1445–83) lost over half of their children within the first two years of life. A funerary sculpture they commissioned differs markedly in character from the Prestesaille frontispiece's vision of infants who grow after death. Joachim of France (d. 1460), Dauphin and son of Louis XI, was buried in St Martin's Basilica of Hal (or Halle), Belgium, where a famous image is housed that facilitated the king's devotion to Mary.[46] This tomb does not show a young adult awaiting Judgment Day, as Prestesaille envisioned his eldest daughter Jehanne (fol. 9r); instead, Joachim is represented as a child.[47] Since *gisant* sculpture on a tomb is designed to relate more closely to the actual scale of the person interred than manuscript illumination does, the medium may have, in part, dictated the royal couple's iconographic choice. The tomb's small size may, additionally, have been politically and economically desirable because Louis XI had not yet become king; his family was living in exile with the support of his uncle Philip the Good, Duke of Burgundy (1396–1467). The differences between minor and monumental arts appear particularly impactful in this case study because Macé aimed to emulate the court in other respects.

In contrast to the equal, mature stature accorded to Prestesaille children in the suffrages, the frontispiece (Fig. 1.1) differentiates between them using height and costume. The tallest child in the miniature, Macé's deceased daughter Jehanne (b. 16 March 1468 [1469 n.s.]), can be read as iconic, which was suggested above, and as indexical. The height of each child in the frontispiece is an index of the amount of time Macé had been her or his father. Rather than necessarily indicating the duration of time she lived under Macé's care, this figure represents more clearly how long Macé lived separated from little Jehanne, who died in the summer of 1470.[48] Prestesaille's experience of being her father rested on the projection of how tall, beautiful and reverent she would have become if she had survived until 1475. Height, therefore, in the frontispiece is like the rising water line during a flood, that indicates either the ongoing work of mourning undertaken by Macé for each lost child or the time spent raising every surviving one.

Fashion signals the gender of the five older children, who mimic their parents while exhibiting some variety in the colour scheme. Costume, however, takes on greater significance in the swaddle of the unnamed infant son, who rests at his mother's knees in the collective family portrait (Fig. 1.1), because it indicates both educational and spiritual themes. Swaddling connotes a labour-intensive wrapping process that announces the beginning of a child's civilizing programme of education.[49] Margaret Mead argued that swaddling be included in discussion of the 'great importance of the very earliest learnings'.[50] The costume of the infant, thus, manifests the care and concern of his parents – living and dead – to oversee his upbringing in all domains from his first minutes of life; it clearly underscores the comprehensive and structured nature of the civilizing process that Macé and Jehanne intended for each of their children.

The swaddled infant looks intently toward the draped body of Christ in the facing *Pietà* miniature (Fig. 1.1) and he functions as a diminutive mirror image of Christ in the two-folio composition. The public nature of how the biblical figures display grief[51] could have validated Macé's endeavours to make the memory of his family publicly known. The dedication of the manuscript, quoted above, requested that those who hear about his family remember to pray for them.[52] Recent experience with death may have reminded Macé how the swaddle itself resembles the process of clothing bodies for burial, which is implied in the scene after Christ was removed from the cross. The swaddle material also serves as an index of age, because a much shorter length of fabric is needed to secure a baby's limbs than to wrap an adult. The idea that a child could emulate Christ dates back to apostolic times when 'Jesus's own statements ... making the child the model of the life of faith ... exactly reversed the expectations of his hearers'.[53] Both the neonate and Jesus exclusively wear white clothing and overlap with the bodies of their mothers, symbolically communicating purity and the close bonds between parent and child, respectively. Prestesaille's youngest, thus, embodies the type of a 'beloved son'[54] who died.

The juxtaposition of the entire family group and the extra-biblical lamentation over Christ's body beneath the cross reveals Prestesaille's acknowledgment of both the Virgin Mary and God the Father as bereaved parents. Macé, in and through the frontispiece miniatures, is literally looking to ancient models of how a parent survives loss. The Virgin dominates the central axis and exemplifies a suffering mother in the *Pietà*. The composition also evokes divine presence within and beyond the earthly realm, just as the contents of Macé's book underscores the role of the Father in creation and the unity of the Trinity. The manuscript's French version of the Creed begins: 'I believe in God the Father omnipotent, who created both earth and firmament'.[55] The presence of God the Father is asserted in the *Pietà* miniature via its landscape background with the hill of Calvary, distant horizon and blue sky that all manifest signs of the Creator's workmanship. By recognizing God as a parent who dealt with loss, albeit temporary and with perfect knowledge of the outcome, the illuminator offers Prestesaille yet another form of consolation. The short term nature of Christ's death could have provided Macé with additional hope for eternity, because the risen Christ foreshadows the future resurrection of all souls. Macé would have read in the vernacular Creed that Jesus was: 'Resurrected and raised above the heavens, where he sits gloriously at the right hand of God. He will come to judge the living and the dead justly'.[56] The alert Prestesaille baby focuses on Christ in the facing miniature, who emblemizes suffering before victory over death. The image of Macé's youngest son, therefore, can be interpreted to signify hope for a rich, eternal life beyond death.

Religious Education and Memory

The swaddled infant and perfectly staged older siblings, in the frontispiece, pictorially manifest the character-based instruction in Prestesaille's *Book of Remembrance* that relies on orderly memorization of basic Catholic texts.[57] When past sources characterized Prestesaille's manuscript as a book of hours, they minimized the importance of its accessory texts that offer a private educational programme for the children's earliest years at home.[58] Parents and godparents were encouraged to make sure that children learn about and memorize the Lord's Prayer, Hail Mary and Creed as they progress through the essential sacraments.[59] Each one of these three key texts are featured in Prestesaille's book at least once. The *Credo* and *Pater Noster* appear in both Latin and French.[60] The *Ave Maria* and the *Alphabetus Christianorum* are in the vernacular.[61] Such essentials were typically taught from a book by the mother,[62] but Macé's situation may have prompted him to integrate these, and additional didactic texts, into his memorial manuscript. The process of teaching his children, even if for a short time due to necessary role reversal, could have been another way Prestesaille was continually aware of his loss.

The primary goal of elementary instruction, in this period, was not to master a marketable skill but to practice reading and memorizing, while solidifying one's Christian identity.[63] Since Macé claimed ties to the Turonian household of King Louis XI, it is relevant to cite the educational philosophy of the king's eldest surviving child, Anne of France, Duchess of Bourbon (1461–1522). She instructed her daughter, Suzanne (1491–1521): 'therefore, it is good to learn how to live well so that, when the time comes, they will know how to die well – but avoid lengthy explanations because it is not the custom of such people [unwise 'masters and mistresses'] to willingly hear about or to speak of death'.[64] Character formation, stressed via liturgy and didactic texts, was thought instrumental in preparing for an optimal life. Prestesaille, weathered by harsh realities, may have considered these religious texts essential to prepare his three surviving children for possible impending mortality because a number of texts resonate with the themes of death and judgment.[65]

Jean Gerson (1363–1429), the influential University of Paris Chancellor, recommended a reading list to help structure princely education. Although his curriculum is far more substantive than one would expect Macé to replicate in teaching his preschool children, there are noteworthy similarities.[66] The bible comes first.[67] Prestesaille's book includes more biblical readings than a typical personal prayer volume. Without counting biblical excerpts in the Office of the Dead and mass texts or scriptural adaptations in prayers, over a quarter of the manuscript contains sections from the bible.[68] Gerson then stipulated treatises on the virtues and vices, works by St Bernard and stories of the martyrs that parallel content in the Prestesaille volume.⁶⁹ Macé's book covers the seven virtues along with the seven mortal sins, includes St Bernard's verses and depicts stories about the saints in the context of suffrages and prayers.⁷⁰ These elements exemplify texts with the broadest appeal and utility for all Catholic children, regardless of social rank or gender. Another text by St Bernard, included in Prestesaille's collection, is beyond the elementary level: the letter Bernard sent to Raymond, Knight of Ambroise Castle.⁷¹ It treats the theme of the vices in the context of household management, proving that Macé was concerned with his own learning as well.

Anne of France prescribed aspects of Christian education for Suzanne to learn and teach future generations; these directly compare to the practical religious texts available to Prestesaille's children. The Duchess suggested: 'if God gives you children, ask Him for nothing ... except goodness and virtue ... teach them as well as you can, and make sure they learn as much as they can, given their limits'.⁷² She recommended: 'articles of faith, the Ten Commandments, the nature of sin, and the Seven Deadly Sins; teach them how to confess ... and how they must welcome their Creator'.⁷³ Macé's text, as mentioned above, included the Creed and a list of vices as well as the *Confiteor*, *Ave Salus* and a version of the Ten Commandments in French.⁷⁴ One can imagine Prestesaille's children listening to and memorizing these texts before they learned to read them, following the accepted pedagogical technique of repetition. These approaches would prepare the Prestesaille children for the way Sharon Strocchia aptly summarized the methods used in older pupils' convent schooling: 'Virtually all learning in the fifteenth-century was based on sight-sound drills'.⁷⁵ Perhaps Anne of France and her contemporaries would also have included, within the potentially broad category of 'articles of faith',⁷⁶ the brief texts on the sacraments, gifts of the Spirit, beatitudes, works of mercy and obligatory fasts discussed in Macé's book.⁷⁷

Beyond content related to these contemporary programmes of education, Prestesaille's manuscript adds a text on the five senses which brings together the importance and impact of both the visual and verbal materials in the *Book of Remembrance*. 'Guard your eye ... Look with pity how he hung on the cross for you. Put his language and his voice in your heart. And embrace him with great love, seeking him with all affection'.⁷⁸ This text encourages mastering the senses as well as channelling their powers toward devotional ends. Vespasiano da Bisticci, a noted fifteenth-century bookseller in Florence, characterized the aim of educating girls to be controlling their senses.⁷⁹ Such advice, however, would be equally applicable for Prestesaille's son, Guillaume, because it relates to the overarching theme of living well that guided early character education at this time.

Godparents were actively co-opted to take part in children's education. Surveying the different posts held by the Prestesailles' godparents suggests that Macé wanted a wide variety of options for his children's advanced learning through traditional job training placements in the future.⁸⁰ The Prestesailles were able to connect their children with godparents representing several distinct sectors: government, military, ministry, construction, leather craft and health care.[81] The network that Macé and his wife built up is analogous to the level of investment in his family that the *Book of Remembrance* exemplifies. David Herlihy encourages historians 'to evaluate, and on occasion even to measure, the psychological and economic investment which families and societies in the past were willing to make in their children'.[82] The unusual contents of Macé's own book,[83] despite the discouragement of repeated losses, suggest that his commitment to dedicate as many resources as possible to his family was undeterred. This conscientious care for all who had been entrusted to him demonstrates how Prestesaille embodied the first principle St Bernard wrote about to the knight: 'The rule of living, however, is to forget nothing'.[84] Macé chose not to abandon the living or dead members of his young family. His diligence logically resulted from the notion that children represent a form of wealth but his book suggests much more than such a calculating attitude.[85] Prestesaille's collection implicitly asserts that forgetting one's wife and children is as unacceptable as not knowing the *Pater Noster*, *Ave Maria* and Creed.

Time and the *Book of Remembrance*

Macé's idealized commission aided in visualizing his children as educated and pious young adults who are accepted into the fold of the Church through sacraments, prayer and the attention of patron saints. The Prestesailles are visually and textually covered by association with the sacraments, because aspects of this complex work corresponded to the stages in their religious lives. Baptism, anointing the sick and extreme unction relate to recurring themes in the family history.[86] Communion is demystified by including the Latin Preface and Canon of the Mass.[87] Confirmation is associated with the texts for religious education that were discussed above. Marriage is celebrated as an enduring bond in the dedication.[88] Holy orders are referenced via the family connection to the Carmelites at St Saturnin in Tours and writings attributed to St Bernard.[89] The collection of texts responds to the full range of life experiences, from birth to commemoration of the dead, and the manuscript shows tangible evidence of extensive, regular use. Macé's book may have, therefore, facilitated devotions carrying him to his own grave and might then have been willed to mourning survivors, or the family parish church, to preserve his legacy.

The *Book of Remembrance*'s personalized images evoke a place beyond time in heaven or at the final resurrection. Although Prestesaille's vision of eternity may seem materially focused because of its pictorial version of his family history, closer attention to the mixed character of signs in the programme of illumination suggests subtler additional readings. Its family pictures, in this unusual case, assert both growth over time and youthful adulthood. Its iconic and indexical signs illustrate flexible modes of picturing family members that are adapted for mourning and long term commemoration. Macé's experience using the book over the years also invites multiple interpretations. Perhaps he may have first read the images as signifying reunited heavenly perfection for his entire household. Meditating on the *Joys of Paradise*, he could have imagined how: 'The just will have very clear vision of the God of love ... agility, impassivity, subtlety ... immortality, joy without end, beauty, wealth, power, honour, health, virtue, youth, lucidity, rest, assuredness, peace, pleasure, glory, sweetness and every other desire'.[90] As time passed, he may have delighted in envisioning how each person he lost might have changed through the years. This range of interpretations corresponds well to models that attribute improvement while grieving to time necessary for healing.[91] Prestesaille gradually could absorb and apply the lessons in his book, using the memory of loved ones and the work of mourning to improve himself and help others. Although only the children are depicted growing in the frontispiece, Macé also changed as his book helped him deal constructively with loss and grief through multiple forms of commemoration.

2 'LITTLE IDOLS': ROYAL CHILDREN AND THE INFANT JESUS IN THE DEVOTIONAL PRACTICE OF SOR MARGARITA DE LA CRUZ (1567–1633)

Tanya J. Tiffany[1]

When Margarita, a daughter of the Holy Roman Emperor Maximilian II, chose to enter a convent, she resisted intense pressure to bear children and extend her royal line. Margarita (1567–1633) was the second youngest of the sixteen children born to Maximilian and his Spanish wife, the Empress María, a sister of King Philip II. At age fourteen, she accompanied her widowed mother from the Viennese court to the Descalzas Reales in Madrid: a convent of Poor Clares (female Franciscans) founded by the empress' sister, Princess Juana of Portugal, and a foundation whose nuns hailed from the royal family and upper nobility. Soon after Margarita's arrival in Spain, her uncle, the aging Philip II (1527–98), sought to marry her in hopes of securing his succession. Philip had recently lost his fourth wife – Ana, the eldest of Margarita's own sisters – and he feared for the notoriously fragile health of Prince Philip, the couple's only surviving son and the king's sole male heir. According to early sources, Margarita outraged court officials by rejecting the marriage proposal in order to pursue religious vows. Her decision to foreswear a life of childbearing was deemed selfish by courtiers, who considered it her duty to ensure the king's succession. Echoing the sentiments of various diplomats, the Empress María's closest advisor cautioned Margarita that 'your Highness was not born for herself alone, but rather for the good of many', and argued that her marriage was crucial 'to the house [of Habsburg] ... and ... your kingdoms'.[2] Margarita nevertheless withstood such rebukes and began her novitiate at the Descalzas in 1584. Her choice was embraced by her mother, who also lived in the convent, although without taking vows. Perhaps surprisingly, Margarita also received the blessing of Philip II and the monarch demonstrated his support by serving as godfather in the ceremony celebrating her profession.

With this conciliatory gesture, he became the first in a long line of Spanish Habsburgs to incorporate Sor Margarita's vow of chastity and, by extension, her refusal to bare children, into the pious self-definition of the royal dynasty.[3]

Yet despite Sor Margarita's celibacy and confinement to the cloister, children became central to her life and religious practice at the Descalzas. Indeed, she developed close bonds with Philip III (Philip II's son, who surprised contemporaries by living well into adulthood) and his children, whom she referred to regularly in her personal correspondence. The king's children often resided for long stretches in the Descalzas's royal apartments, a space just outside the enclosure and one accessible to the monarch and his family. Sor Margarita's royal charges are also mentioned throughout her *Vida* (first published in 1636), in which her confessor, the Franciscan Juan de Palma, characterizes her attachment to children as a function of her love for the Christ Child. According to Palma, Sor Margarita likewise expressed her consummate devotion to Christ's infancy by cradling, feeding and conversing with polychrome sculptures of the baby Jesus.[4]

Palma wrote the *Vida* at the behest of Philip IV, although he may have received significant help in crafting the text from the eminent cleric and man of letters, Juan de Palafox y Mendoza.[5] Philip IV doubtless commissioned the *Vida* with an eye toward the beatification of his aunt (an official beatification cause was opened in 1689), and the text has a clear hagiographical structure.[6] Nevertheless, Palma conformed closely to the portrait that Sor Margarita herself constructed of her devotional practice. Like Palma, Sor Margarita treated her love of children as sacred in her *Exercicios de devoción, y oración para todo el discvrso del año* of 1622, in which she dictated (or perhaps wrote, despite her failing eyesight) a detailed account of her religious practice throughout the liturgical year. In his prologue to the *Exercicios*, the Carmelite royal preacher, Fray Francisco de Jesús y Jodar, praised her religious practice as full of 'such lively, such devout, and such tender sentiment': a fitting description of a piety focused on Christ's infancy.[7]

In examining Sor Margarita's devotion, I expand upon recent discussions of the roles played by the royal nun and by the Descalzas as a whole in the sacred rituals of the Madrid court. Magdalena Sánchez has shown that the Descalzas was an especially 'permeable cloister' because of its ties to the royal family, and she has highlighted Sor Margarita's regular contact with Habsburg family members and court officials.[8] In a study of the children of Philip III, Martha Hoffman has shed new light on the activities of Sor Margarita's nieces and nephews inside the Descalzas, where they sometimes took up residence for weeks and even months.[9] Focusing on Palma's *Vida*, Eleanor Goodman has located Sor Margarita's engagement with images of the infant Jesus within the contexts of Franciscan tradition and feminine devotion.[10] Ana García Sanz, the curator of the Descalzas, has turned to the sculptures and paintings themselves, providing a detailed analysis of the myriad sixteenth- and seventeenth-century images of the Christ Child that are still housed in the convent.[11] In different ways, each of these scholars has provided a rich picture of Sor Margarita's life inside the cloister. Yet the significance of living children in her devotional practice remains to be understood.

This essay explores how the royal children helped Sor Margarita to bridge the boundaries between her worldly status as a Habsburg woman, raised for childbearing, and her vocation as a nun bound to Christ. In my analysis, I consider texts such as Palma's *Vida* and writings by Sor Margarita. I also examine the visual culture of the Descalzas, which played a central role in structuring the nun's religious practice. Focusing on images rarely studied by scholars, I argue that the portraits of the royal children and images of the Christ Child displayed throughout the Descalzas at once reflected and reinforced Sor Margarita's belief in the status of her nieces and nephews as living pictures of the infant Christ.

'The Office of Mother'

Through her bonds with children, Sor Margarita fulfilled many of the maternal obligations of a Habsburg woman.[12] She forged a close relationship with the young Philip III, who assumed the throne in 1598, and was instrumental in negotiating his marriage to her kinswoman, the Archduchess Margarita of Austria (1584–1611). Before her marriage, the young Queen Margarita had apparently aspired to assume religious vows, and she and Sor Margarita developed an intimate friendship based on shared piety and familial ties.[13] The queen bore eight children in ten years (six of whom survived infancy) and she attended closely to her sons and daughters, at least by the standards of early modern European courts.[14] Hoffman has shown that Queen Margarita's children, unlike their royal counterparts in France and England, 'spent considerable time together and with their parents' and were often nursed by their mother during their many illnesses.[15] Consistent with her own piety, the queen took particular care with her children's religious education. She prayed that they would be 'great servants of God',[16] ensured that they attended mass regularly and encouraged them to imitate her devotional practices and charitable activities. Like her children, Queen Margarita sometimes lodged in the Descalzas's royal apartments, and she enjoyed papal dispensation to enter the enclosure of the convent. The king and queen also entrusted their children to Sor Margarita's care when they were traveling and during times of disease. For example, when Prince Philip (1605–65; the future Philip IV) was suffering from a contagious illness in 1609, his older sister, the Infanta Ana (1601–66; Fig. 2.2), spent two months in the Descalzas before it was deemed safe for her to return home.[17] (In Spain, the term 'prince' refers to the heir to the throne, whereas 'infante' and 'infanta' refer to the other children of the king and queen.)

Sor Margarita's correspondence highlights her deep affection for the children of Queen Margarita and Philip III. In a letter to the king dated 1 November, 1606, the nun describes a night caring for the nineteen-month-old Prince Philip who, she reports, 'ate his soup very well' and 'did me the mercy of playing with me until it was time to nurse'; when night fell, the nun 'rocked [the prince] for a long while', and he 'slept like an angel'.[18] Sor Margarita characterizes the day as 'lovely', but 'confesses' that she 'sorely missed' the five-year-old Ana.[19] She also inquires about the newest addition to the royal family, the six-week-old Infanta María Ana (1606–46) who, she has been told, is 'very beautiful, with her arms already out [of her swaddle]' and 'will be brought to see me soon'.[20]

After Queen Margarita died from problems following the birth of her last child in 1611, Sor Margarita assumed an increasingly vital role in the lives of her nieces and nephews. According to Palma, the royal children stayed with Sor Margarita in the days after the queen's death, and Philip III asked the nun to assume the 'office of mother for them'.[21] Palma contends that the children thereafter 'looked upon their aunt as a mother', an assertion supported by surviving correspondence.[22] In a letter of 1618 to his daughter, Ana (by then the Queen of France), Philip III writes that her siblings had danced a masque at the Descalzas specifically so that Sor Margarita 'could see it'.[23] That same year, Philip wrote to the nun to thank her for sending 'congratulations' on María Ana's twelfth birthday and promising to 'bring the prince with [him]' to the Descalzas upon his return to Madrid the following week.[24] Offering a glimpse into the visual arts as practiced by the royal children, the king also mentions 'the image that the prince painted for your Highness [i.e., Sor Margarita] ... of the [Immaculate] Conception', a doctrine of key importance at the Spanish court and one ardently supported by the nun and the Franciscans in general.[25] Sor Margarita also maintained strong relationships with her nieces and nephews as they assumed adult roles and responsibilities. Letters reveal her interest in the ten-year-old infante Fernando's (1609–41) acceptance of a cardinalate and the fifteen-year-old Prince Philip's betrothal to Isabel de Valois.[26] Toward the end of her life, she helped to arrange the marriage between Ferdinand, king of Hungary (and future Holy Roman Emperor), and María Ana, whose previous betrothal to the Protestant Prince of Wales she had opposed.[27] In celebration of the engagement, Sor Margarita presented María Ana with enormous trunks laden with extravagant gifts: writing desks, clothing, portraits, relics, rosaries, 'dressed dolls' (perhaps sculptures of the Christ Child) and myriad other sacred objects.[28]

As suggested by these examples, visual and material culture played integral roles in the expressions of affection and kinship between Sor Margarita and the royal children. The children danced and painted for her, and she showered them with lavish presents, in particular objects of religious significance. Through her sacred gifts, the nun demonstrated the extraordinary wealth and exemplary Catholicism of the Habsburgs. By giving holy objects, she also encouraged her younger relatives to uphold the pious practices embraced by the family.

Sor Margarita continued to send religious presents to her nieces and nephews – and eventually to their own children – until the very end of her life. In late January of 1633, María Ana wrote to Sor Margarita and confessed her suspicions of pregnancy;[29] in fact, she gave birth early the following September. According to Palma, the confirmation of María Ana's pregnancy delighted Sor Margarita, who correctly predicted the birth of a male heir and vowed 'to make the first clothes the prince wears' (see fig. 2.5 for María Ana and her firstborn).[30] Although ailing and blinded by cataracts, Sor Margarita ordered two infant-sized monastic habits, one Franciscan and the other Conceptionist (a branch of the Poor Clares), 'had them blessed', demanded that 'many masses be said for them' and placed them for 'nine days on an altar dedicated to Our Lady' before dispatching them to Vienna.[31]

With this pious offering, Sor Margarita also paid tribute to María Ana's late mother, who had professed a strong devotion to the Franciscans. Queen Margarita had commissioned portraits of her children in religious habits, among them a poignant image in the Descalzas (fig. 2.1), a work in which court artist Juan Pantoja de la Cruz depicted the two-month-old Infanta María lying dead in her coffin and clad in Conceptionist garb.[32] In baby María's death portrait, the habit functioned as a means of inscribing the child in the Catholic religion and of encouraging prayers for her and her family.[33] Through her own present of religious habits, Sor Margarita similarly offered protection for María Ana's unborn child by bestowing objects meant literally to cloak him in the faith. The sacred gift was one of Sor Margarita's last; as she supposedly predicted, she died before the prince was born.[34]

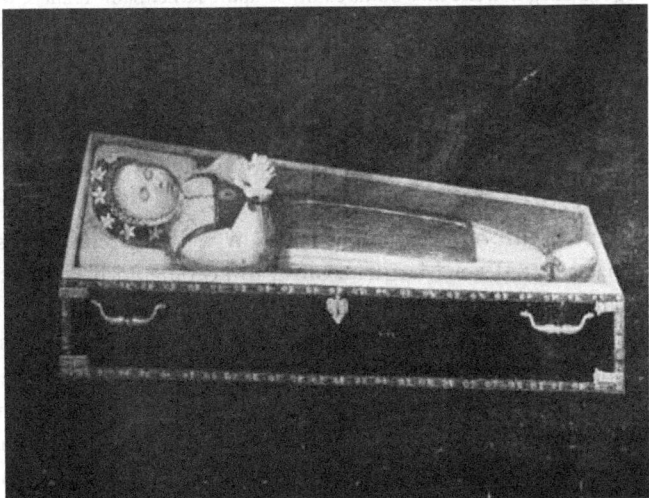

Figure 2.1: Juan Pantoja de la Cruz, *The Infanta María in Her Coffin* (probably 1603). Madrid, Monasterio de las Descalzas Reales. Photograph in the public domain: image taken from E. Tormo y Monzó, *En las Descalzas Reales: Estudios históricos, iconográficos y artísticos*, 2 vols in 3 (Madrid: Blass, 1917–45), vol. 2, part 1, *Treinta y tres retratos más*, figure XXIV.

Children, 'Little Idols' and Devotion

From the perspective of her hagiographer, Sor Margarita's affection for the royal children was fully in keeping with her religiosity. Palma contends that Sor Margarita's attachment to the infantes, and to children in general, constituted a form of devotion to the baby Jesus. In a chapter on 'the love and devotion that [Sor Margarita] had for the infant Christ', Palma writes that 'it was remarkable to see the tenderness she showed' toward her 'very little' nieces and nephews; he argues that this tenderness 'was in keeping with the spiritual feelings she had for the memory of the Christ Child'.[35] Palma emphasizes the exceptionality of such exalted piety by explaining that Sor Margarita's maternal behaviour was sometimes misunderstood by other nuns at the Descalzas, who perceived the royal children as dangerous distractions from the contemplative life. By Palma's account, 'some of the nuns' would tell her to beware, saying 'that these children are little idols who take your heart and dry up your soul'.[36] To these rebukes, Sor Margarita would patiently reply that 'the very opposite occurs ... with their beauty and grace, [the children] help me to remember the Christ Child; I feel that each of them represents him, that they are his living images, and I serve them as such'.[37] Highlighting Sor Margarita's status as a Poor Clare and his own as a Franciscan, Palma argues that the nun's practice of remembering the Christ Child through small children exemplified the lessons of Francis himself:

> Like a good daughter, she thus imitated my seraphic father Saint Francis, who could not stand to see lambs slaughtered, because it reminded him of the lamb of God; in this way, just as my father Saint Francis loved the mystical lamb in real lambs, her Highness loved the Christ Child in children.[38]

Through his emphasis on Sor Margarita's love of the infant Jesus, Palma also inscribes her within a broader tradition of Franciscan devotion to Christ's humanity and especially his infancy.[39]

Like Francis with his slaughtered lambs, it was apparently the suffering of children that affected Sor Margarita most. In keeping with Franciscan vows of poverty, Palma tells us that Sor Margarita 'loved poor children most of all' (her nieces and nephews notwithstanding) 'because, she would say, they most resembled the Christ Child' and in them she found 'the innocence of Christ, humble, and poor'.[40] Impoverished children were brought to the Descalzas in order to 'please' Sor Margarita, who 'would give them lots of affection' and practice Catholic charity by 'order[ing] that clothing be found for them'.[41] According to Palma,

> Sometimes the children would be made to cry, so that [Sor Margarita's] reaction could be seen. And when she would hear [their cries], she felt such great compassion that she would weep too, saying: My God, why must they make this little angel cry? Thus the Christ Child would cry in the manger.[42]

With this anecdote, Palma contrasts the tenderness of Sor Margarita's piety with the callousness of the other Poor Clares. Whereas the other nuns carelessly provoked the children's tears, Sor Margarita heard the voice of Jesus himself echoed in their cries.

Although Palma's account is highly idealized, it is deeply rooted in the portrait that Sor Margarita herself presented of her religious sentiment and practice. In her *Exercicios de devoción*, Sor Margarita wrote that during Advent, real children would inspire her to contemplate the mystery of the baby Jesus: 'all the children whom I see or hear weeping will awaken my emotions, so that I do not neglect to praise [Christ,] the one who weeps for me'.[43] Sor Margarita thus characterized her love of children as not only compatible with – but as integral to – her religious calling. In so doing, she accommodated the maternal conduct, expected of a Habsburg archduchess and infanta, to her vocation as a nun.

Children and Visual Culture at the Descalzas

For Sor Margarita, the role of the royal children as reminders of Christ would have been reinforced by the visual culture of the Descalzas. As a royal foundation, the convent was filled with portraits depicting generations of Habsburg children; the three-year-old Infanta Ana, 'dressed in green', even had her portrait painted by Pantoja within the convent walls.[44] The nuns also saw myriad paintings and sculptures of the baby Jesus – many of them acquired by Sor Margarita – along with images comparing the Habsburg children to Christ himself. Indeed, images displayed throughout the Descalzas proclaimed the close resemblance between the Habsburgs and key figures in Christian history. In keeping with pictorial conventions prevalent in the Habsburgs's German-speaking dominions, a number of portraits in the convent depicted illustrious members of the dynasty with the attributes of particular saints. Among other examples, Sor Margarita's father, Maximilian II, was portrayed in the guise of Saint Valerius of Trier; her brother, Rudolf II, appeared as Saint Victor; and her aunt, Princess Juana of Portugal (the convent's foundress), became the Virgin herself in an inventive copy of Raphael's *Madonna of the Fish*.[45]

Sor Margarita's confidant, Queen Margarita, likewise commissioned works depicting herself and her family as witnesses to key events in the infancies of Christ and the Virgin. In 1603, the same year that the Infanta María was born and died (Fig. 2.1), Pantoja included portraits of the queen's relatives and of the monarchs themselves in a *Birth of the Virgin* and an *Adoration of the Shepherds* destined for the queen's private oratory in Valladolid (both works are now in the Museo Nacional del Prado in Madrid). Around 1605, the year of Prince Philip's birth, Pantoja also portrayed Queen Margarita as the Virgin Annunciate, accompanied by the Infanta Ana as the winged angel Gabriel (the painting, Pantoja's *Annunciation*, is now in the Kunsthistorisches Museum in Vienna). As María

Cruz de Carlos has shown, the queen used these works in locating her pregnancies, and the births of her children, within explicitly sacred contexts.[46] Although commissioned for spaces outside the Descalzas, Pantoja's *Birth of the Virgin*, *Adoration of the Shepherds* and *Annunciation* epitomize the tradition, embraced by Sor Margarita, of comparing the births of royal children to the Advent of Christ.

Through her sculptures of the Christ Child, Sor Margarita gave further material expression to the perceived resemblance between her nieces and nephews and the infant Jesus. Like other nuns at the Descalzas, Sor Margarita would have ornamented sculptures of the baby Jesus with jewels and seated them on thrones, offering visual demonstrations of Christ's status as divine king.[47] Palma writes that Sor Margarita dressed her sculptures in elaborate finery,[48] and she doubtless placed them in doll-sized cribs, cradles and beds, many examples of which are still in the convent. Not surprisingly, those objects were close imitations of the real clothing and furniture used by royal and aristocratic children. Garments for sculptures of the Christ Child, housed inside the Descalzas, were fashioned from expensive, embroidered fabrics, like those worn at court, and the figures' beds were modelled on types used by the royal family and members of the upper classes.[49] Moving between sculptures and real children, Sor Margarita would have cared for her Niños Jesús (as the sculptures were called) and placed them in cribs, much as she played with Prince Philip and 'rocked' him 'in his cradle'.[50]

In the Descalzas, two paintings from Sor Margarita's lifetime gave explicit visual form to the idea that the royal children were 'likenesses' of the king of heaven: a portrait of the Infanta Ana, signed and dated by Pantoja in 1602 (Fig. 2.2), and an anonymous painting, *The Christ Child with a Bird* (Fig. 2.3), probably also dating to the early seventeenth century.[51] In both works, a fair-haired, rosy-cheeked baby sits on a red velvet cushion, an allusion to earthly and divine royalty. Both children gaze at the viewer, and their wide eyes and luminous skin provide strong contrasts to the plain, dark backgrounds behind them. Each child is clad in white – Ana wears a gown, with a fashionably stiff collar, and Christ a diaphanous tunic bordered with lace – and is accompanied by objects of sacred and worldly significance. An enormous jewelled crucifix covers Ana's chest and, hanging from her gown, are another crucifix, two reliquaries (containing relics of Saint Anne and the crown of thorns, respectively) and various apotropaic objects that testify to early modern fears of infant mortality. Little Ana clutches a branch of coral: a material that was sometimes used for teething and one especially valued for its ability to ward off evil and illness.[52] In the painting of the Christ Child, the artist employed an iconography strikingly similar to that of Ana's portrait. The baby Jesus wears a crown of thorns, a coral necklace and a coral bracelet. In his right hand he carries a goldfinch – a protector against disease as well as a symbol of resurrection – and in his left, he holds an orb with a crucifix, a reference to his kingly status.[53] A comparison between these paintings is especially significant because the iconography used in both (the baby clad in white and seated on a red cushion) was repeated in numerous portraits of Philip III and Queen Margarita's children.[54] By extension, each of those portraits would have similarly established a comparison between the Spanish infantes and the infant Christ.

Figure 2.2: Juan Pantoja de la Cruz, *The Infanta Ana as a Baby* (1602). Madrid, Monasterio de las Descalzas Reales. Photo Credit: Album / Art Resource, NY.

Figure 2.3: Anonymous, *The Christ Child with a Bird* (early seventeenth century). Madrid, Monasterio de las Descalzas Reales. ©PATRIMONIO NACIONAL.

Like most portraits of her children,[55] Queen Margarita may have commissioned *The Christ Child with a Bird*, but it is also worth entertaining the possibility that it was Sor Margarita who charged the anonymous artist with painting the work. At the very least, the image corresponded precisely to the nun's claim that her nieces and nephews encouraged her to remember the Christ Child. García Sanz has suggested that the painting is a literal portrait depicting one of Philip III's children,[56] but the Child's features seem, instead, to represent idealized versions of those shared by almost all the children born to the king and Queen Margarita (and indeed Habsburg children more generally): reddish-blond hair, blond lashes and large, bright eyes. For Sor Margarita, the image could have stimulated devotion in various ways. When looking at the painting, she would have seen visual evidence of the practice of valuing children because they were 'living images' of the baby Jesus.[57] She may also have found the image compelling precisely because it reminded her of the real children she knew, whose cries, as she claimed, helped to return her thoughts to the Christ Child.

María Ana and Sor Margarita's Legacy

After Sor Margarita died in 1633, the nuns at the Descalzas maintained strong associations between royal children and the Christ Child. Throughout the seventeenth and eighteenth centuries (and well beyond), they continued to dress their Niños Jesús in regal clothes, to place the sculptures in miniature thrones and to lay them upon meticulously crafted beds. The nuns also began acquiring and ornamenting ever-more elaborate Nativity scenes, which consisted of tiny sculptures representing the Holy Family and throngs of extravagantly dressed onlookers: all set against fictive landscapes festooned with coral.[58] At the same time, the nuns gazed upon a growing collection of portraits commemorating new generations of royal offspring.[59]

One painting in the Descalzas, created not long after Sor Margarita's death, would have functioned as a particular tribute to her spirituality and her practice of 'lov[ing] the Christ Child through children'.[60] In the painting (Fig. 2.4), the Christ Child stands holding an orb, gazing out at the viewer and offering a gesture of greeting and benediction. Although the image has been identified as Christ dressed in the regal manner of a Spanish infante,[61] a close examination indicates that it, in fact, portrays a specific Habsburg boy. The child depicted bears the unmistakable features of María Ana's son, the future Emperor Ferdinand IV (1633–54), whose impending birth Sor Margarita had honoured with her gift of two religious habits. Indeed, the child's features are identical to those of Ferdinand as he is portrayed, together with his mother, in a portrait of 1634 (Fig. 2.5), where he is shown with a long nose, round lips, wide hazel eyes and a prominent Habsburg chin.

Figure 2.4: Anonymous, *Prince Ferdinand as the Christ Child* (c.1635). Madrid, Monasterio de las Descalzas Reales. ©PATRIMONIO NACIONAL.

Figure 2.5: Anonymous, *María Ana, Queen of Hungary, with her Son Ferdinand* (1634). Vienna, Kunsthistorisches Museum. Photo Credit: Kunsthistorisches Museum, Vienna.

The identification of the painting as *Prince Ferdinand as the Christ Child* is especially significant because it sheds new light on the lasting relationship between María Ana and Sor Margarita's convent. After arriving in Vienna, a homesick María Ana had written to Sor Margarita, describing a visit to the convent of Poor Clares, founded by the nun's sister, Queen Elisabeth of France, where the nuns reminded the infanta of the Descalzas (*'me dieron aires de las Descalzas'*).[62] María Ana also described various sites in Vienna, wondered whether Sor Margarita remembered them and speculated that the city had changed so much that the nun would 'recognize very little' of it.[63] Vienna is seemingly the city represented in the background of *Prince Ferdinand as the Christ Child*, and the image would have given the nuns at the Descalzas a glimpse of the imperial capital as María Ana and her firstborn knew it.[64] More importantly, the painting paid homage to the devotional practice of Sor Margarita, who had joined her love of Christ and her love of children in prayers for María Ana's pregnancy.

As suggested by María Ana's continued association with the Descalzas, Sor Margarita had maintained close relationships with her royal nieces and nephews until she died. In grandmotherly fashion, she chided María Ana for not writing with sufficient frequency and the young queen responded with assurances of love (and protestations that her letters had gone astray). Writing to Sor Margarita the day after the nun's birthday in 1633, María Ana described the 'sadness I always feel on this day, for not finding myself at the celebration ... in the Descalzas', and expressed gratitude for a gift of sacred objects.[65] Within the Descalzas, Sor Margarita cherished the regular visits and letters she received from Philip IV and, after she lost her sight entirely in 1625, she affirmed that one of her only regrets was her inability to see his face.[66] Upon her death, some of her most treasured sacred objects were bestowed upon her nieces and nephews; María Ana inherited a rosary that Sor Margarita had received from her own mother and the Cardinal-Infante Fernando (the child who had assumed the cardinalate at age ten) was bequeathed the nun's favourite Niño Jesús.[67] In turn, Sor Margarita's nieces and nephews worked to honour her memory. It was Philip IV who commissioned not only Palma's hagiography, but also her eulogy from the eminent preacher and poet, Fray Hortensio Paravicino.[68]

Conclusion

By the time Sor Margarita died, the children of the Spanish king were no longer portrayed in monastic garb or in the guise of the infant Jesus. As far as we know, Philip IV's court painter, Diego Velázquez, never depicted the royal children covered in crucifixes and relics, and he never gave them the attributes of saints.[69] This departure from earlier convention exemplified Velázquez's interest in naturalism and broader changes in artistic taste, but it also reflected political and cultural concerns. By abandoning the pictorial traditions embraced by Philip III and Queen Margarita, Philip IV emphasized his departure from the previous reign, whose policies and ostentatious displays of grandeur he sought, in large, to repudiate.[70]

Yet we have already seen that distinctions between images of secular and sacred personages, and especially between earthly and divine children, remained blurred in the visual culture of the Descalzas. A key example, from late in Philip IV's reign, exemplifies the continued connections between the worldly and the heavenly in the convent: a life-sized group portrait, painted in fresco, which crowns the Descalzas's grand staircase. Probably painted around 1660, the portrait depicts Philip IV, Queen Mariana (his second wife and the daughter of his sister, María Ana) and their two children at the time: the short-lived Prince Felipe Próspero and the Infanta Margarita, who was given the same name as the king's mother and aunt.[71] An assemblage of religious figures also adorns the staircase walls, among them the Crucified Christ, Francis, Clare and the seven archangels, who were often compared to Habsburg rulers – and to whom Sor Margarita had expressed ardent devotion.[72] In the portrait, the monarchs and their children gaze outward, drawing the beholder into the secular and sacred realms depicted on the walls. Together with his young family, the aging Philip IV presides over the space where he, along with his brothers and sisters, learned some of his earliest lessons in the piety that he continued to project throughout his reign.

3 *E RILUTTANTE RAGAZZOTTI*: YOUTHS AS HESITANT PARTICIPANTS IN THE CRUCIFIXION

Margaret Flansburg

Children began to appear with some regularity in Italian narrative painting in the late 1200s, where their energetic presence added interest to the subjects and religious instruction for viewers. In an expansion of narrative story telling, especially of the Passion of Christ fostered largely by the Franciscan movement,[1] figures of children served to energize the newly humanized experience of faith. Italian artists and patrons drew on both northern Italian, Romanesque tradition and a more adventurous Byzantine style, with illusionary settings and naturalized form. In scenes of Christ's Passion, small children join the followers of Jesus to Jerusalem; however, they appear less frequently at the Crucifixion. The presence of children in biblical events is not supported scripturally. The New Testament briefly cites them as models of innocence and goodness[2] and the Old Testament occasionally cites misbehaving or troublesome children.[3] In her 1990 essay, on wicked children on Calvary,[4] Amy Neff discussed the sources and lessons of wicked children in Passion scenes very thoroughly. She notes that the mocking children, in the Passion scenes of the 1295 *Supplicationes variae*, appear for the first time on Calvary and represent the Jews of childish understanding.[5]

In this chapter, I will review some depictions of children at the Crucifixion that serve as examples beyond the 'wickedness' which is the subject of Neff's study. A primary source for the figures of children is the *Supplicationes variae*, where some children are innocent and sometimes sympathetic observers. They observe the hostility of the abusers of Jesus but hesitate to join. And I will discuss examples from the School of Rimini, a less often studied group of artists, whose expressive imagery often produced narratives that encouraged sympathy for Christ and his followers. I will also include the unusual figure of Stephaton, the sponge bearer, who is presented as a child in some Crucifixions produced in mid-century riminese painting.

Already in the eleventh century, the *Christus patiens* appeared in Byzantine art and became popular in Italy, in the early Trecento, where the image of the crucified Christ encouraged viewers to identify with his sufferings. In the late 1200s, owing in large part to the rise of the mendicant orders, especially Franciscan and Dominican, a more sympathetic understanding of the suffering Christ arose.[6] Such empathic attachment was spread widely in humanized meditative literature including the *Meditatio pauperis in solitudine* (1282–3), the *Dialogus de Passione Domini* (sometimes credited to Anselm, after 1250), the *Supplicationes variae* (c.1295), the mystical *Lignum Vitae* and *Itinerarium mentis in Deum* (Bonaventura who died in 1274) and the *Mediationes vite Christi* by a Friar Minor for a Poor Clare (probably in the last half of the thirteenth century). The influence of Aristotelian nominalism and attention to the specific and the individual (also found in Franciscan thought and other sources) combined to produce new perspectives expressed in written and artistic work.[7] The fullest meaning of the suffering of Christ could be translated into the experience of the faithful individual. The *Mediationes vite Christi*, for one example, tells the faithful that one is 'cleansed of vices and clothed with virtues' by contemplating 'Jesus crucified' and 'contemplation of Christ's humanity'.[8]

In depictions of the Passion, happy children appear along with both Christ's followers and his enemies in the *Entry into Jerusalem*. However, in the journey to Calvary and certainly at the Crucifixion, their cheerful mood has changed. They display curiosity and reluctance to join in the abuse demonstrated by the hostile crowds of armed and mocking centurions and Jews. Instead they appear innocent – hesitant and unwilling to join the abuse – openly sympathetic to Jesus and his mourning followers.

A major source for figures – and a primary conveyer of models to artists – the *Supplicationes variae* is an illustrated manuscript probably produced in 1293 in Genoa and known to Italian artists.[9] It was probably a gift to the Franciscan convent of the Clares at Vallechiara, a community of Poor Clares.[10] It provided many basic models for the figures of children. In her 1977 dissertation study of the manuscript, Amy Neff discussed the naturalistic trends in Italian narrative scenes, derived from French Gothic figural style, with its sense of anatomical realism, including three-quarter drawing of heads.[11] In the *Supplicationes variae*, small boys appear in four scenes: Christ Teaching in the Temple, the Entry into Jerusalem, the Via Crucis and the Ascent to the Cross. Their proportions are slender and they take a limited variety of poses – frontal, side, back and frequently a dorsal view as they converse, with one facing forward and one back.

When required by the narrative (as in the *Entry into Jerusalem* and the Via Crucis), they stoop, climb trees, drop palm branches to the crowd and lay down their cloaks on the ground before Christ. They wear short belted tunics under voluminous robes and high-topped tight-fitting boots. In the Entry, one of the six boys, with short muscular legs, spreads his cloak on the roadway. Two in long draped robes stand side by side in conversation, facing forward. In the Via Crucis (Fig. 3.1) one centurion and five Jews (one wearing a short tunic who may be an adolescent) mock Christ. Two boys join them with sticks and rude hand gestures. These wicked children are dressed in ornamented robes with ruff collars that are symbolic displays of finery and pride. However, a small drama seems to be in progress. The centurion appears to drop back in dismay and attempt to move away from the mockers. Eight children behind the struggling Christ appear in a variety of very active poses and different viewpoints. Four have climbed palm trees to watch the procession and have shed their cloaks. One watches the Jews and three more cling to branches above the five mourning followers including the Virgin and three Maries and John the Evangelist. Five or six sympathetic children, including one pair in back view, accompany the grieving followers. These paired boys, in their great cloaks, occur many times in narrative scenes among the several works related to the *Supplicationes*. Their frequently repeated presence, as well as other figures and groupings in Trecento narrative scenes, indicates the proliferation of sketches and motif books in use by well-traveled and informed artists. Two taller youths walk behind Jesus; one carries his arm in a sling and leans on a walking stick as his companion looks back with interest at the mourners. Their curly hair is cut short and they wear long cloaks and fitted boots. This group of children demonstrates a subdued interest in the progress of the procession surrounding Jesus. In the *Supplicationes* Ascent to the Cross, only two cloaked boys stand at the base of the Cross and seem to discuss the activity. They wear the fine collars marking elevated status and stand before a jeering centurion, but are discussing the event and not participating – as if hesitant in the midst of the dangerous activity around Christ.

Figure 3.1: *Via Crucis*. Miniature in the *Supplicationes variae*. Florence, Biblioteca Medicea Laurenziana, Ms. Plut. 25.3 (c.375v).

Other children, whose figures are closely related to those in the 1293 *Supplicationes* and its sources, appear in the work of early Trecento artists Simone Martini, Duccio and a related but unknown designer of the fresco cycles at the Clarissian convent church of Santa Maria Donnaregina, in Naples, from the 1320s. In the Naples cycle of the life of St. Agnes, the Saint is led to a brothel, where two boys stand with their backs to us and show interest but do not openly threaten her – although they may have come armed with stones in their tunic skirts. But the Passion fresco program features only wicked children whose positions, figures and costume are very like those in the *Supplicationes*. In the Via

Crucis, two boys pick up rocks or mud to hurl at Christ as he passes. In the Preparation of the Cross which includes the stripping of Christ and his ascent to the Cross, four energetic barefoot little boys stand before the Cross with a group of labourers and several Jewish figures with evil faces. The boys' faces also show threatening expressions of hatred and contempt.[12]

Giotto includes three pairs of boys whose poses and activities echo the *Supplicationes* children in *Entry into Jerusalem* in the Arena Chapel (although the Crucifixion there does not contain children). Two boys have climbed trees to collect branches. In front of the donkey, one lays down his garment and another offers the little animal a palm branch while a third takes off his garment – another hails Jesus with a palm branch. There are also no children in Duccio's Maesta Crucifixion (1308–11) but the Entry into Jerusalem includes about sixteen celebrating young people of mixed sizes whose figures and activities are similar to those of the *Supplications* model.[13]

Simone Martini's Orsini polyptych, of about 1335, also shows knowledge of the *Supplications* figural style. In the Via Crucis, three richly dressed boys are armed with stones or mud that they prepare to throw; their finery marks them as proud and vain. One is poised with his back to us and holds stones in his tunic skirt. But in the Crucifixion (Fig. 3.2), six sympathetic boys are among the observers, talking and gesturing with interest in the activity. On the right, one is staring intently but not with malice at the figure of Christ. On the left, one small child is pushing his way past Longinus, who is in the act of piercing Christ's side. His arm is around his friend as he draws attention to the grieving mourners on the left. Behind the mourners one small boy looks down with interest at the grieving women. Three others look up at Christ at the moment that the Longinus' spear pierces his side. The entire crowd is in movement but the one child's hand is raised in a halting gesture and all three look up with expressions of concern.

Figure 3.2: Simone Martini. Piercing with the lance (Crucifixion from the Orsini Polyptych). Koninklijk Museum voor Schone Kunsten.
Photo Credit: Bridgeman-Giraudon / Art Resource, NY.

In her 1990 study of wicked children at the crucifixion, Amy Neff included a list of twenty-three Italian works that contain children in Passion scenes with brief indications of the numbers and activities of children included.[14] Among these, sixteen are Crucifixions dated in the Trecento, including the *Supplicationes variae*, the Naples fresco and Simone Martini's Orsini Crucifixion. She indicated the numbers of children and made note of some which were not obviously 'wicked'. Several stand so that their expressions are observable but there are over fourteen children who grieve or watch as well as others who are 'apparently innocent'.

I have two Trecento paintings to add to this list from Genoa and Fabriano in Rimini that include an additional interesting character for Crucifixion imagery. In the Indianapolis Museum of Artist, a panel of *c.*1374 by Barnaba da Modena (Fig. 3.3) shows design relationships to Giotto's Arena Chapel Crucifixion and figural parallels to the *Supplicationes* tradition. Barnaba was active between *c.*1330–86 in Genoa which, in those years, was an outpost of Siena. He left a number of signed works, including several Crucifixions. The boy in the foreground is the only child present among the crowd of over thirty enemies and followers. He is barefoot and carries a bucket rather carelessly in his left hand and rests a long pole on the ground, showing that he does not actively participate in the Crucifixion. He is Stephaton the sponge bearer. He walks toward the cross, but looks beyond the Magdalene at the foot of the cross toward the mounted figure of the centurion Longinus. Longinus' spear is propped on his shoulder and he makes a gesture with his hand to his face (perhaps as a mocking sign, but occurring just before his miraculous healing and moment of enlightenment). Jesus looks down upon Longinus and toward the fainting Virgin. Neither Stephaton nor Longinus are participating in the abuse of Christ.

Figure 3.3: Barnaba da Modena, *Crucifixion* (*c*.1374). Source: Indianapolis Museum of Art, James E. Roberts Find, 24.5.

The pairing of Stephaton and Longinus is a motif developed early in sixth century Byzantine literature. The earliest known image of the sponge bearer appears with the centurion Longinus in the Rabula Gospels in 586.[15] In the Gospels, the sponge bearer is not named, although Longinus is labeled; his name is probably derived from the Greek word 'lonka', *longche* or *longke*, meaning lance, lancer and commander of a troop of lancers. In the fifth and sixth century *Acta Pilati*, a centurion below the Cross, was labeled Longinus. According to later legend, Longinus suffered from a disease of the eyes and became a Christian when he was cured by Christ's blood, flowing from the lance wound, as he delivered the stab wound to Christ's side. He is frequently positioned beside the Cross and directs the viewer toward the body of Jesus as a reminder of the meaning of the event. In St John's account of the last moments of the crucifixion, Jesus said, 'I thirst ... [and] there was set a vessel full of vinegar: they filled a *spunge* with vinegar, and put it upon hyssop, and put it into his mouth'.[16] We do not know when a particular soldier became associated with the vinegar sponge and came to be known as Stephaton,[17] however, the name may derive from the Greek 'spong', *spongon* meaning 'sponge'.

The second additional Crucifixion dates from *c.*1360 and also features a barefoot boy walking away from centurions and toward the Cross (Fig. 3.4). It is from Fabriano and by an unidentified artist from the School of Rimini. This group of artists, from the environs of the Marches and Umbria, was based in a strong Byzantine tradition but absorbed the influence of the international schools of Siena and the North and also knew the illustrations of the *Supplicationes variae*. Giotto was present in Rimini where he produced the great cross in 1300 (for the *Tempio malatestiano*) and frescoes at the church of San Francesco, between 1313–18. His program at the Arena Chapel in Padua was well-known to these artists through direct exposure and through sketches and motif books. The riminese response was an adjustment to their tradition of Byzantine style by incorporating his naturalistic and humanizing influence in a distinctive body of works, with sensitive and emotional figural style. Art historians including Bernard Berenson, John White and, more recently, Italian scholars Mario Salmi, Miklos Boskovits, Alessandro Marchi, Carlo and Alessandro Volpe and Federico Zeri have noted the uniquely expressive qualities in imagery of the Trecento school of Rimini.[18] However a major problem in riminese scholarship has been insufficient documentation and political, ecclesiastic and military turmoil in the region during the Early Modern Era.

Figure 3.4: Master of the Urbino Coronation, *Crucifixion*. Boston Museum of Fine Arts. Photo Credit: Boston Museum of Fine Arts.

In 1995, Alessandro Marchi verified over 104 extant works of *la famiglia de depentoris* of Rimini[19] although not all of his attributions are accepted. There are many attributions in studies and in collections, including the Galleria Nazionale delle Marche in Urbino (which holds a number of the riminese works credited to the Master of the Coronation of the Virgin, Master of St. Emiliana, Master of Compodico, etc.). Giovanni da Rimini (contemporary of Giotto) is documented in 1292 at the Ospedale of San Lazzaro in the Rimini. He signed and dated the great cross for the Augustinian abbey of Poggiolo in Montefeltro. His brother Giuliano da Rimini signed and dated the 1307 *Enthroned Madonna with Saints* for San Francesco, in Urbana, that is now in the Isabella Stewart Gardner Museum in Boston – although James Stubblebine doubted the veracity of the date and placed it in the second quarter of the Trecento – and signed a great cross for San Francesco at Mercatello that is documented in the *Verification of the Stigmata*, in the Upper Church of San Francesco in Assisi.[20] A second generation of riminese painters include Pietro da Rimini, Francisco da Rimini (not of the family of Guiliano and Giuliano) and, a better documented painter, Giovanni Baronzio, who died in 1362. He produced a polyptych for the Franciscan church of Macerata Feltra, dated 1343, and has other undocumented works attributed to him.

Among riminese paintings of the Crucifixion, Stephaton the sponge bearer makes his appearance as a child. The ragged boy is present in the detached fresco showing the Crucifixion (Fig. 3.4) from the Dominican church of Santa Lucia del Mercato in Fabriano, now in the Boston Museum of Fine Arts. The artist is not documented although attributions have been made to the ubiquitous Master of the Urbino Coronation (it is so designated in the Boston Museum of Art) or to Giovanni Baronzio.[21] The fresco is eleven feet high with imposing life size figures. A barefoot child in a tattered tunic walks away from soldiers, who are busy with the dividing of Jesus's garment. He ignores the activity behind him and focuses on the figure of the dead Christ. Shown in a back view and profile head (recalling the *Supplicationes* children), he walks calmly toward the Cross and exhibits no evil intention, although he carries a bucket, presumably filled with vinegar. Several elements in the design show knowledge of the ubiquitous Arena Chapel Crucifixion – grieving Marys and John, with the Magdalene at the base of the Cross on the left and soldiers preparing to divide Jesus' robe on the right. In the Fabriano scene, a centurion holds one side of Christ's robe but his companion is lost due to surface damage. Longinus stands to Christ's left wearing a grey robe with red sleeves and cloak (a uniform common in Trecento riminese painting). He raises his hand to draw attention to the Cross in a gesture borrowed from Giotto's haloed King. Giotto's adult Stephaton is a minor figure at Padua, almost hidden by the raised arm of the King; he is barefoot and wears a long ragged brown tunic as he steps forward to gaze up at Christ. G. W. Constable, in his 1941 documentation for the Boston Museum of Fine Arts, written at the time of the acquisition of the fresco, interpreted its boy walking slowly toward the Cross as Stephaton.[22] However, another reading of the scene suggests that the almost-lost figure is the sponge bearer in his traditional position beside Longinus. His right hand (now lost) gripped the sponge rod midway down the shaft. I suggest that the ragged boy in the foreground is a helper or apprentice to the sponge bearer, who stands beside Longinus. He is walking away from the now lost group and indifferent to the soldiers behind him, as he focuses on the body of Christ on the Cross. He is not participating in the abuse of Jesus and but, like Longinus, is becoming a converted follower of Jesus.

Other boys in riminese Crucifixions are related to this figure.[23] An artist or patron who had seen the Fabriano boy, or possessed sketches of him, designed a small pinnacle, now detached from its altarpiece and in the Galleria Nazionale de Marche of Urbino (Fig. 3.5). In the painting, perhaps by Pietro da Rimini,[24] a child standing in front of Stephaton is the same type as the Boston figure, who wears the ragged brown tunic and looks soberly up at the body of Christ. Mary Magdalene kneels and embraces the foot of the cross in both paintings. The sponge bearer and centurion wear silver grey uniforms with red cloaks; the child watches and Longinus prays before the bleeding side of Christ. The cross beams of both Crosses are made of pruned limbs.[25] The small child is pressed in the group of mourners and mounted threatening soldiers, but appears oblivious to the turmoil. He carries a bucket that contains the vinegar for the sponge bearer standing behind him. He dangles it carelessly before him and seems to have not remembered its purpose, as he looks up at the Cross in the same thoughtful and hesitant mood as the Fabriano boy.

Figure 3.5: Pietro da Rimini, *Crucifixion*. Urbino, Galleria Nazionale delle Marche. Photo Credit: Matthew Knox Averett, author.

The substitution of a young man for a boy, for Stephaton, using the same poses, gestures, costume and attitude, appears in similar Crucifixion scenes. One such example is the foreground figure of the sponge bearer in the centre of a Crucifixion fresco from San Marco in Jesi. It has been credited to Giuliano da Rimini and dated *c*.1325 although it may actually date from the second quarter of the century.[26] The striding figure of Stephaton, in the centre front, walks into the crowded scene holding his sponge rod before him, with his gaze directed to the face of Christ and the hands of the converted centurion. He tilts his head far back as he strains to see Christ's face. He has bent his neck so far back that we can see his brow, nose and cheeks over the top of his head.[27] He wears the short yellow tunic of the *Supplicationes* children and bears no malice toward Jesus. A small detached pinnacle in the Urbino Galleria[28] shows that the artist borrowed and compressed elements from the Jesi Crucifixion scene. The sponge bearer, again a gawky young adult wearing a plain yellow tunic and carrying his rod and bucket, is an awkward copy of the Jesi figure, with his small head at an even more extreme angle. Longinus on horseback, whose spear is not present, reaches up with both hands to touch the blood of Christ that healed his disease.

Another boy appears in a short tunic in the foreground of the pinnacle of an altarpiece in Rimini (Fig. 3.6), that is credited to Giuliano da Rimini and dated 1340. He appears in back view with most of his face hidden and holds a bucket at his side, stepping forward as he looks up at the body of Jesus. Stephaton, holding his sponge rod away from the Cross, looks down into the boy's face. The two are not part of the hostile spirit of the group of soldiers and Jews but are withdrawn and appear to communicate their shared sympathy. Another juvenile (both are slightly shorter than the adults) stands behind the cross and reaches out to comfort one of the weeping women. While assumed to be part of the enemies of Christ and his followers, the boys (and perhaps Stephaton) reject active roles in the death of Christ.

In the Crucifixion tympanum (Fig. 3.7), of the 1340[29] triptych by Giovanni Baronzio, from the convent of the Friars Minor in Macerate Feltra (now in the Galleria Nazionale de Marche in Urbino), a barefoot young man wears the same short drab brown tunic as the boys in the Boston fresco and in the Urbino polyptych. However, rather than a companion or assistant, he is clearly identifiable as the sponge bearer himself carrying his bucket, and a sponge rod that is propped on the ground and not pointed toward Jesus. He looks up at the Cross, head tilted uncomfortably far back, with a grieving expression that is like that of John the Evangelist beside him. As one of the front figures, he directs the viewer to the figure of the dead Christ. In fact, there seem to be no openly hostile figures in this little group – all is sorrow and sympathy.

Figure 3.6: Giuliano da Rimini, *Crucifixion* pinnacle. Polittico dell'Incoronazione della Vergine, Santi e scene della Passione (1315–c.20), tempera e oro su tavola, Rimini, Fondazione Cassa di Risparmio, on deposit in the Museo delle Commune.

Figure 3.7: Baronzio, Giovanni (d.1362), *Crucifixion*. pinnacle Polyptych, Madonna, Saints, and Scenes from the Life of Christ. 1345. Tempera on panel, 143 x 221. Urbino, Galleria Nazionale delle Marche.
Photo Credit: Mondadori Portfolio / Electra / Art Resource, New York.

The Barnaba da Modena painting (Fig. 3.3) with its Stephaton that is very close to the Fabriano boy, is dated in the last quarter of the Italian Trecento. With its crowd of almost forty figures, it is an example of large crowd scenes at the Crucifixion that appeared in a number of frescoes and panels in the Trecento as early as Pietro Lorenzetti's fresco, in the Lower Church of Assisi in *c*.1320. Andrea di Firenzi, at the Spanish Chapel in Santa Maria Novella in Florence (*c*.1366–7), and Altichiero, in the Oratory of St. George in Padua (completed in 1374), produced Crucifixion paintings filled with many participants. Andrea di Firenzi's scene, that includes a Via Crucis, contains a crowd of several dozen people in procession with horsemen. Two boys walk in the procession toward Jerusalem while two others talk and point, but show no rancor, and two standing and talking before the Cross are seen from the back as one gestures upward. In a crowd of more than three dozen onlookers, the Crucifixion at the Basilica del Santo in Padua, Altichiero placed the barefoot sponge bearer in the now-familiar plain tunic carving his way through the crowd of onlookers with Longinus who is above/behind him in the crowd. One small boy in rear view in the foreground stands outside the mob. Quietly and hesitantly, he awaits the outcome of the gathering.

A final riminese work will complete this review of children at the Crucifixion. The riotous, clamorous, noisy crowd surges around the hill of Golgotha in the Crucifixion fresco painted in 1416, by the brothers Lorenzo and Jacopo Salimbeni for the Franciscan Oratorio di S. Giovanni, in Urbino. At least a dozen small children are scattered among the participants and a number of young adults on horseback join the armed men whose spears and lances point toward Jesus. A distraught mother with her hair flying runs to retrieve her small, bare-bottomed son. A pair of boys watches an episode on the rocky road up the hill, in which a bad boy kicks at the head of a companion. A child dressed in a gaudy spotted costume looks out from a group of Jews. The supporters of Mary and John the Evangelist writhe and gesture wildly in their grief. Only the figure of the Virgin, who has collapsed with her body cradled by the three Marys, is at rest. Isolated in the centre, a barefooted Stephaton mounts the rock of Calvary and lifts the vinegar sponge to Jesus.

In summary, children appeared infrequently in Italian painting before the Trecento, but soon began to take on a clearly moral purpose in Calvary scenes, to assist in readings of the event. With figural types and poses drawn initially from the 1293 *Supplicationes variae*, based largely on the biblical story of the bald Elisa, a group of narrative Crucifixion paintings developed in which children sometimes appear as hostile and even wicked but, simultaneously, other children become hesitant participants – often sympathetic and watchful – at the foot of the Cross. In riminese paintings, the unusually expressive style produced imagery that encouraged sympathy for the suffering characters and helped to develop the character of Stephaton the sponge bearer and his companion Longinus. Young Stephaton developed from a child watching the crucifixion, as a casual follower of the armed men and Jews, into an enlightened companion of the followers of Christ. He may still carry the vinegar and sponge rod that were assigned to him in his role as an abuser of Jesus, but he is a hesitant participant on his way to enlightenment and conversion.

4 'THESE STORIES ARE NOT FOR CHILDREN': MISBEHAVING CHILDREN IN 'WORLD UPSIDE DOWN' PRINTS AND THE ORIGINS OF FOLK TALES

Rachel L. Chantos

Prints from the early modern era were some of the first works of art to fully develop themes of the secular world, and often these prints expressed social concerns and tensions. Images of the *World Upside Down* typically depict scenes of peasant life and inversions of animals and men, men and women and children and their parents, such as the version published by Nicolò Nelli and Ewout Cornelisz Muller in the late sixteenth century (Figs 4.1 and 4.2). The primary subject in these prints is role reversal, such as women doing men's work or beating their husbands. The theme of the *World Upside Down* has been discussed in art historical scholarship in regards to gender conflicts and social hierarchies, yet little attention has been given to children.[1] In *World Upside Down* prints, the children, typically boys, are often depicted whipping their fathers with the assistance of their mothers and rebelling against other established authorities, such as their teachers and masters (Figs 4.3 and 4.4).

Figure 4.1: Nicolò Nelli, *Il Mondo alla Riversa* (c.1575–90), etching, New York Metropolitan Museum of Art.

Figure 4.2: Ewout Cornelisz Muller, publisher, *De verkeerde wereld* (c. 1595), broadside.
Source: Cotsen Library, Princeton, New Jersey.

Figure 4.3: Detail from Nelli, *Il Mondo alla Riversa*.

Figure 4.4: Detail from Muller, *De verkeerde wereld*.

The role reversal of boys and their patriarchal authorities in *World Upside Down* prints reveals an alternate and undesirable reality, a reality often featured in early folk tales, and both were used to teach a moral, cope with hierarchic anxieties and relate to the civilizing process. In this essay, I discuss the humour and moral of violent children in *World Upside Down* prints and the development of popular folk tales through the stories of folklorists Giovanni Francesco Straparola (1480–1557) and Giambattista Basile (1566–1632). Similar to the emergence of folk tales, the role of the genre print theme of the *World Upside Down* will be explored, in order to gain an understanding of the potent social message of unruly children in the early modern era, including the original audience and similarities to the function of Carnival and the development of a civilizing process in Renaissance Europe. The violence by children in these visual and literary narratives will be our focus and it is my goal to establish that the dark humour present is aimed at an adult audience wary of a threat to the paterfamilias.

The World Upside Down

Prints dedicated to the theme of the *World Upside Down* were ubiquitous types of broadsheets that emerged in the middle of the sixteenth century. The print type exists in at least sixty different versions from seven various countries, almost all of which use the title *World Upside Down* in their respective languages,[2] such as the Italian *Il Mondo alla Riversa* and the Dutch *De verkeerde wereld*. The broadsheet was a popular form of printmaking that utilized multiple images over a single long sheet of paper, arranged in narrative panels with accompanying text below, similar to contemporary comic strips. These narrative prints were sold in public fairs and streets, and posted in taverns, workshops and homes for the sake of amusement and edification.[3] In the case of the *World Upside Down*, David Kunzle has argued that these broadsheets were perhaps aimed at the intermediate urban classes such as tradesmen and craftsmen.[4]

In the developing early modern capitalist economy, prints dedicated to the *World Upside Down*, as well as their folk tale counterpart, offer consolation to the discontented, particularly to those of less economic means. The theme of *World Upside Down* was so prevalent that the same woodblocks were often reused over generations, regardless of changes in styles of art, indicating a universally marketable subject.[5] The popularity of the *World Upside Down* broadsheet type, as well as the emergence of the folk tale, began its commercial ascent twenty years after the Peasant's Revolt of 1525, concurrent with the reform and suppression of carnival celebrations.[6] Religious and political authorities feared village carnival celebrations as a breeding ground for organized opposition, heresy and dissidence,[7] and *World Upside Down* prints and folk tales offered a visual and literary solution to the censorship of public pageantry of Carnival.

Carnival was suppressed by Protestants during the Reformation, but not before the tradition was used as a catalyst for the Reformation itself. In Bob Scribner's important study on Carnival, the author traced twenty-four incidents in which Reformers staged carnival processions to ridicule and revolt against the Catholic Church. The earliest incident dates from December 1520 when Martin Luther burned a papal bull condemning him, after which roughly one hundred students set up a large float with a giant papal bull affixed to the stage like a mast to a sail. An important detail in these carnivalesque revolts against Catholic authorities is the role of young men, which appear in almost sixty percent of the incidents.[8]

The theme of youth in carnivalesque play parallels the role of children in *World Upside Down* prints and folk tales, as these occasions gave license to display unrestrained behavior and invert established roles of authority. One of the primary tropes of *World Upside Down* prints is the inversion of parent and child; second only to the inversion of male and female.[9] Natalie Davis has demonstrated, in her study of youth groups, that youth behavior is not anomalous but rather a manifestation of the social and cultural values of the communities in which it is found.[10] The rebellious spirit of youth in Reformation demonstrations, seen as a test to their established authorities, is in fact a reflection of the values of adult society, which these youths are expected to ultimately integrate.[11]

Although characterized by youth performers, Reformation carnival play, *World Upside Down* prints and folk tales are in fact a representation of adult concerns cast as youthful folly and rebellion. In these contexts, the irreverence of the young and the impotence of age are revealed as stock themes of comedy, aimed more at the old than the young.[12] In Muller's *De verkeerde wereld*, a narrative panel feature a humorous scene of young girl rocking her father in a cradle and another young girl feeds her mother like an infant; both panels are designed to highlight the folly of adults, not the power of children (Figs 4.5 and 4.6).

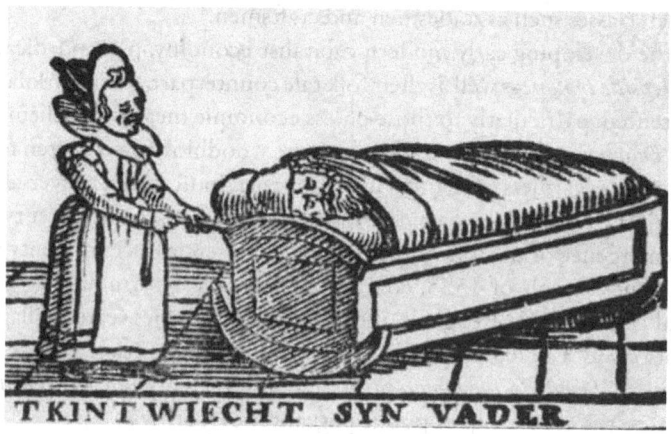

Figure 4.5: Detail from Muller, *De verkeerde wereld*.

Figure 4.6: Detail from Muller, *De verkeerde wereld*.

The Origin and Context of Folk Tales

Scholars have long identified the important role of popular prints as a means of transmitting ideas of social conventions and behaviors, particularly in their inversion and the resulting humour.[13] Much like the recent attention given to genre prints, folk or fairy tales have only garnered scholarly attention in the last thirty years.[14] Although a contemporary audience is most familiar with German folklorists Wilhelm and Jacob Grimm, modern analysts have traced the origins of many of the Grimms Brothers' tales to Renaissance and Baroque Italian authors, Straparola and Basile. It is paramount to our study of popular prints and their depictions of family relationships, particularly that of children and parents, to address the parallels between the literary and visual genres.[15]

The catalyst for early modern Italian tales was Boccaccio's *Decameron*, which set the precedent by creating a frame tale, in which a series of tales are told by a group of courtly individuals who gathered each evening over the course of ten days. Giovanni Francesco Straparola's *Le piacevoli notti* (*The Pleasant Nights*), c.1550, marked a significant turn from the courtly nature of Boccaccio and engaged in a variety of rural and urban social experiences, similar to those depicted in popular *World Upside Down* prints. The early modern Italian press, dominated by Venice, began to produce a large number of books, pamphlets, prints and broadsheets, responding to a broader buyership who desired leisure reading. Similar to the humour of *World Upside Down* prints, the stories of Straparola were intended to make their audience laugh and are generally considered to be embellishments of actual events and relationships. Straparola's success lay in his combination of a humble protagonist, a feature of urban stories and the magical nature of courtly tales.[16] By 1558, Straparola's first tale of Salardo, his ingrate wife and their adopted son was transformed into chapbooks and presented as if it was current events or news.[17]

Both the plot and language of Straparola's tales suggest that his writings appealed to a wide audience, much like the audience of popular prints of the *World Upside Down*. The narratives share much in common with high literature, of such authors as Boccaccio, Petrarch and Dante, but *The Pleasant Nights* was written in the vernacular Italian.[18] Straparola's folk tales had been first cultivated in oral form by the common people in order to express their views of nature and social order, although it is clear that each community altered the original folk tales in order to satisfy their own particular needs and desires. In mid-sixteenth century Italy, the folk tale represented a change in values and ideological dissension during the highly transitional shift of the economic systems of feudalism to capitalism.[19] Much like the agrarian themes prevalent in the *World Upside Down*, folk tales of the early modern era most commonly feature humble protagonists and demonstrate critical views of power struggle with a lack of moralistic preaching.[20] Multiple panels in the Italian, Dutch and German broadsheets feature animals hunting humans and the reversal of agricultural tasks between the two, such as plowing, pulling carts and carriages, slaughtering and butchering.

Similar to the widespread popularity of the *World Upside Down*, which can be found in almost every region from Italy to the Low Countries, from the sixteenth to late seventeenth centuries, Straparola's *Pleasant Nights* was published twenty times between 1550–1600.[21] The popularity of Straparola's *Pleasant Nights* was followed by the work of Neapolitan poet Giambattista Basile, whose collection of folk tales, known as *Lo cunto de li cunti overo lo trattenemiento de peccerille*, or *Il Pentamerone*, was published in two volumes in 1634 and 1636. Basile made prominent changes to the previous literary structure of folk stories, helping to form the understanding of the fairy tale genre for later centuries. *Il Pentamerone* contains the earliest versions of such tales as *Rapunzel, Cinderella, Puss in Boots* and *Sleeping Beauty* in which the author takes great pleasure in minimizing the differences between social classes, creating a truly carnivalesque atmosphere.[22] Additionally, Basile's collection contains a higher percentage of tales about love and marriage,[23] and much like the domestic emphasis in *World Upside Down* prints, *Il Pentamerone* often features the emotional involvement between parents and children.

A clear and present danger in *World Upside Down* prints and folk tales by Straparola and Basile is the presence of women, typically in the role of a maternal figure, reflecting the patriarchal values of early modern society. In *World Upside Down* prints, the women depicted are usually unruly wives and conspirator mothers, using their feminine wiles and their children, typically male children, to usurp the father's authority. The struggles of the peasantry, particularly in relation to women and children, are a common denominator shared by *World Upside*

Down prints and the early modern folk tale tradition. In Nelli's *Il Mondo alla Riversa*, the wife/mother holds the husband/father over her back while their young son whips the father's back. Images such as these personify the societal and patriarchal fear of the mother's authority over her children, particularly her male children, and the concern that she may use the child as a weapon against the patriarch.

A prominent example from Basile's *Pentamerone* is *Nennillo and Nennella*, from Day Five, Tale Eight, which is an early version of the more popular German tale, *Hansel and Gretel*.[24] In the story, a widower takes a second wife to provide care for his house and children, although she rejects the latter, demanding her new husband choose between herself or his children.[25] Pressured by her ultimatum, the father takes the children to the woods with food and drink, instructing them to eat and be merry, leaving them a trail of ashes to follow back home should they need anything. The father is portrayed as innocent, the victim of the cruel stepmother, and the children are abandoned to care for themselves.[26] Essential stories such as these are historical documents which provide a rare illustration of the illiterate masses and the authentic reality of stepmothers, orphans and peasants in their brutish and often short existence.[27]

Children are often the focus of these narrative strategies and it has been theorized that folk tales became a manner in which to reconcile children to the hierarchical structure of daily lives.[28] The central focus of bread or *bran*, the hard outer layers of cereal grain, stresses the simple meal of the peasantry and illustrates the social realities of the household.[29] Although the narrative focus appears to be the children, the true struggle lies between the husband, his new wife and his preexisting family.

A clear and present theme in folk tales and the *World Upside Down* prints is the role of violence. In particular, the common motif of boys whipping their fathers with the aid of their mothers demonstrates, through humour, the reality of domestic abuse within the early modern household. In Nelli's *Il Mondo alla Riversa* and Muller's *De verkeerde wereld*, the father is held onto the mother's back and his breeches have been pushed aside so he will suffer the beating on his bare flesh. If we reverse the alternate reality, the boy would be in the position of the victim, illustrating the role of violence as a daily occurrence and tool for childrearing. Domestic abuse was omnipresent in the early modern household and, whether it be aimed at the wife or children, the use of force was ultimately at the father's discretion.[30] While the inversion of the male child whipping the father, with the aid of the mother, may have brought humour to a society fraught with change and revolt, the scene fundamentally appeases an adult male audience.

The Carnival Tradition

It is this author's belief that popular prints of *World Upside Down* and the emerging tradition of folk tales share an inherent connection with the carnival tradition. The prints and tales similarly convey a world of inversion, particularly that of 'ordinary people', and their resulting 'culture of laughter' represent the radical fact of carnival.[31] A common feature in *World Upside Down* is the pairings of seemingly opposite sets: mother and baby, father and child, master and servant, etc. Likewise in folk tales, the story often begins with parent and child relationships within a socio-economic structure; i.e. the pauper shall become a prince, the servant girl, a princess.[32] Parallel to the humour found in the *World Upside Down*, justice is only found in folk tales when the fallen prince or princess has been recovered to their rightful social position. This particular tradition of tales has been categorized as 'restoration tales',[33] popularized by such well-known classics as 'Beauty and the Beast', in which the prince, turned into a hideous beast by a curse, is restored to his former self once he earns true love through his own humility and self-sacrifice.

The very nature of carnival, *World Upside Down* prints and folk tales is to turn everything on its head, earning the nickname of a 'World Upside Down'. Although it has been described as a social revolution, carnival is in fact an embodiment of everyday life experiences, which itself manifests in visible pairs of opposites: high and low, rich and poor, pretty and ugly.[34] A common motif shared in all three traditions is that of cross-dressing and mimicry, a tradition used to understand the opposite's experience through imitation and parody. In carnival tradition, men often dressed in women's clothes, and vice versa, while in the *World Upside Down*, wives beat husband's over the men's trousers or sons whip their father's backsides, a reversal of the patriarch's authority in the family. In folk tales, characters often dress in disguises to usurp authority and use deception to enact righteous results.

The ostentatious pageantry of Carnival predates both *World Upside Down* prints and the literary tradition of folk tales, but it has been theorized that carnivalesque tradition, which had waned after the Protestant Reformation, was restored with the rise of the folk tale.[35] Although Protestants had abolished Carnival, Catholics maintained a logistical toleration of the celebration while establishing a sacred separation from the festivities, such as banning the use of any liturgical vestments or rites in parody.[36] However, elements of the humour and inversion present in this festivities were noted, by such famous Protestant pastors as Martin Luther, as being necessary to elicit public attention in sermons.[37]

Though Carnival was one of the most famous of religious festivals, lesser known feasts, such as the Feast of the Fools (December 28), connect our themes of *World Upside Down* and folk tales to that of the world of children.[38] The Feast of Fools is the religious festival associated with the Feast of the Innocents, or

Holy Innocents Day, marking the Massacre of the Innocents by Herod. The feast falls within the Christmas season, which itself is considered carnivalesque because the Son of God was born in a manger, an excellent example of the 'world upside down'.[39] As early as the Middle Ages, the Feast of Fools involved a role reversal between children and adults in which the children were allowed to take over the community, extending as far as boy bishops presiding over church services.[40] After the Reformation, the Feast of Fools was suppressed, leading the way for a second, secularized tradition in which boys became a king or prince for a day, rather than a clergyman or bishop.[41]

The Feast of Fools and the carnivalesque theme of Christ's birth resonate in a typical scene from *World Upside Down* prints. Nelli's *Il Mondo alla Riversa* and Muller's *De verkeerde wereld* features a depiction of a child teaching professors (Fig. 4.7). Although the illustration adheres to the same type of inversion present in the other vignettes, the child teaching is a direct correlation to the Gospel accounts of Christ's life. Often referred to as *Christ Among the Doctors*, Luke 2:41–52 recounts Christ at the age of 12, who stays behind in Jerusalem, from his parents' pilgrimage from Nazareth, to converse with the religious elders in the temple. The wise teachers are in awe at the wisdom of Christ, and when his parents ask why he has strayed from them, he matter-of-factly states that he was naturally to be found in His Father's House.

Figure 4.7: Detail from Nelli, *Il Mondo alla Riversa*.

In Muller's broadsheet, two *doctoreen* present open books to an enthroned young boy, indicating their deference to his knowledge, much like the story of Christ (Fig. 4.8). The importance of inversion in a Biblical context lends legitimacy to *World Upside Down* prints and folk tales and is not only apparent in the story of *Christ Among the Doctors*, but also present in the theatrical carnival traditions. The Feast of Fools can be considered a meditation on a line from the *Magnificat*, 'He has put down the mighty from their seat and exalted the humble,'[42] and appears to directly illustrate the scene from the two broadsheets. In Matthew 19:30 it states that the 'last shall be first and the first last', and the parable of Lazarus and the rich man epitomizes an essential economic and spiritual inversion.[43] Of course the most cogent form of inversion present in Biblical context was that of the Antichrist, who embodied the complete reversal of everything that Christ represented.[44] The powerful use of inversion stemmed from Scriptural sources and thus validated its role in Carnival, *World Upside Down* prints and folk tales, all of which utilized the role of children as an important vehicle for these metaphors.[45]

Figure 4.8: Detail from Muller, *De verkeerde wereld*.

Children, Folk Tales and Popular Prints: Actor or Audience?

A common misconception with folk tales is that the children of the stories were the targeted audience, in the early modern era: a notion that can be easily dismissed through the comparative analysis of the *World Upside Down* print tradition. Early modern prints of the *World Upside Down* were widely disseminated in streets and at fairs, often ending up in private collections of middle and upper class buyers, or publicly displayed in taverns for the edification of the lower social strata. Although it is arguable that children, who shared these public spheres with their parents, were likely exposed to the world of prints, they were clearly not the intended customer. Why then, would we assume that children were the likely audience for folk tales as well?

It is this author's contention that prints such as *World Upside Down* and folk tales were not marketed for children because children in the early modern era were not recognized as a separate developmental stage from adults. Costume historians have long noted that children were typically dressed as miniature adults and often expected to act as such. Church doctor St Augustine stated that children's innocence lies not in their soul, but rather in the frailty of their bodies, and that evil establishes dominion over the growing child.[46] Similar to the Feast of Fools, humour was to be found in the mimicry of children aping adults' behavior, such as in Pieter Bruegel's *Children's Games* from 1560 (Kunsthistorisches, Vienna). In the painting, young boys are depicted drinking, fighting, smoking and gambling and it is arguable that children were clearly not censored from the vices of adults.

Carole Collier Frick has observed that the costume of young boys in the mid-sixteenth century are vital signs in recognizing that childhood was not viewed as a separate stage of life from adulthood. Between 1530 and 1580, the codpiece was an article of male clothing at the summit of its popularity, appearing in official portraits of noblemen as well as young nobility in their early teens. Although codpieces first appeared as simple triangular flaps to cover the male genital area, as tunics became shorter in the fifteenth century, by the early sixteenth century codpieces had developed into a grand display of aristocratic dress. The commanding spectacle of the garment has elicited much speculation among historians, although the general consensus is that the codpiece illustrates a desire to assert overt masculinity.[47] First associated with soldiers, codpieces in depictions of young men illustrate the concerns of adults, not children, including sexuality and political allegiance.[48]

As previously stated, the origin of folk tales derived from the literary tradition of scholars, and early 'folklorists' Straparola and Basile were in fact well-educated members of courts, as well as their patrons. The sixteenth and seventeenth centuries witnessed the expansion of the literary genre into the aristocratic arts of ballet, opera and court festival. It was not until the late eighteenth and early nineteenth centuries that what had essentially been adult reading material was then transformed into narratives for children.[49] During the early modern era, for all sakes and purposes, the perspective of children in *World Upside Down* prints and folk tales was a mere afterthought and, if they were considered, it was as miniature adults, not the independent stage of life we understand childhood in a contemporary context.

The Civilizing Process

The ultimate impact of *World Upside Down* prints and the popularity of folk tales can be seen in their contribution to the civilizing process in the early Renaissance, although again it was a process largely aimed at adults, not children. In 1939, German sociologist Norbert Elias coined the expression 'civilizing process' to describe the historical development of manners and etiquette in early modern society, which addressed social standards regarding violence, bodily functions, sexual activity, table manners and forms of speech.[50] The evidence for an increased interest in refinement is witnessed by the numerous books dedicated to courtly manners, first produced in Italy, correlating with the rise of literacy and the domination of print culture.[51] Much like popular broadsheets and folk tales, given the reading practices of the time, many of these books were, in all probability, read aloud, and writers can be understood as also tellers in the sixteenth century.[52]

The process of civilization, evident in *World Upside Down* prints and folk tales, is not aimed at children in the early modern era, but rather the adults of an artisan class, and the carnivalesque inversion of their behavior seeks to normalize certain acceptable behaviors and hierarchies. In Basile's *Il Pentamerone*, the author often minimizes the differences between coarse peasants and high aristocrats, emphasizing a universal desire for good manners. The long, intricate narratives address issues of decorum and behavior in European society and question the disbursement of power between classes and sexes. *World Upside Down* prints and folk tales reveal strategies of invention that exposed abuse of power and authority through the guise of humour, violence and carnivalesque inversion.[53]

Much of our perceived notions of folk tales and *World Upside Down* broadsheets, as a genre for the edification of children, were not codified until the eighteenth and nineteenth centuries in France and Germany. Some of the earliest adaptors of Italian folk tales include Charles Perrault (1628–1703) and Madame d'Aulnoy (1650/51–1705), French authors who were concerned with serious commentaries on court life and cultural struggles in Versailles and Paris. Perrault and d'Aulnoy made significant changes from the Italian models to demonstrate French social mores that were particularly focused on the roles of women and power at court.[54]

In Germany, the Grimm Brothers carefully selected and altered tales for the publication of their 1812 collection, *Kinder- und Hausmärchen (Children's and Household Tales)*, which was one of the first folk compilations to be specifically addressed to children as the primary audience. Folk tales also became a popular staple of Victorian English society, whose cultural emphasis on morality and the corruptions of adulthood helped establish the belief of the innocence of childhood, a doctrine not shared with the early modern European era.[55] Similar to folk tales, the tradition of *World Upside Down* broadsheets did not enter into the so-called 'children's market' until the nineteenth century, first appearing in English markets, in which chapbooks depicting satirical inversions manifested in the form of nursery rhymes, merging the traditions of folk tales and *World Upside Down* prints into a cohesively whimsical children's fancy.[56]

Conclusion

The predominant conclusions previously drawn from the tradition of *World Upside Down* prints in academic scholarship have focused on the role of male and female inversions, as political and religious motifs, during the Protestant Reformation. Although these scholarly assessments are just, the important role of the depiction of children has been largely overlooked, particularly when one considers that children were not the primary audience of the prints. This essay has investigated the meaning of the role of children in *World Upside Down* broadsheets and folk tales to ascertain the connection of these artistic and literary types with Carnival tradition and the development of a civilizing process in early modern Europe. These various artistic and theatrical forms, ripe with tropes of inversions, particularly that of parent and child, were not aimed at children but rather appealed to adult sensibilities, contrary to our modern conception. The often violent role of early modern children in *World Upside Down* prints, folk tales and Carnivalesque play, are lessons in civility, and the inventions of courtly poets and scholars, adapted from peasant tradition and morphed into children's genres in later centuries. In the Renaissance, however, it is clear that *World Upside Down* prints and folk tales were not, in fact, child's play.

5 DYNASTIC IDENTITY IN RENAISSANCE COURT LIFE: DYNASTIC PRIVILEGE IN PORTRAITS OF CHILDREN

Jasmin W. Cyril

Late Quattrocento and early Cinquecento portraits of Renaissance court family life, at the same time, both underscored the significance of the dynastic legacy of the family, implicit in the heraldry and placement of images of privileged children, and introduced an element of familial association that determined the future of the court itself. Painters and sculptors, in the employ of the dukes and counts of central and Northern Renaissance courts, utilized the trope of the interconnectedness of an extended privileged family, as introduced by Augustus in the Ara Pacis Augustae, 13–9 BC, Rome.[1] Andrea Mantegna, in the environmentally frescoed Camera Picta, Ducal Palace, Mantua, 1465–74, framed the minor family members of the family of Ludovico Gonzaga and Barbara von Hollenzollern in a setting that emphasized their dominion over both the physical space of the palazzo and the contado under their political control, and through the portrait of Cardinal Francesco Gonzaga, their entry into the principate of the Church hierarchy.[2] Federigo da Montefeltro, singular in his emulation of the antique in his Humanistic court and support of scholars and philosophical inquiry, had his heir, Guidobaldo, included in every artistic commission from his regency as Duke of Urbino.[3] Notably, as a youth, Federigo was a hostage in the courts of Northern Italy, in Mantua itself. Although most of their dynastic portraits follow the elevation of a private family to noble status in 1523, when Alessandro de' Medici was created Duke of Florence, the newly ennobled Medici had practiced in the fifteenth century, in the Cappella dei Magi, Palazzo Medici-Riccardi (*c.*1459), by the hand of Benozzo Gozzoli.[4] Their established role in Florence and their children's portraits supporting this idea were also made public in the Sassetti Chapel, St Trinità (1483–6) by Domenico Ghirlandaio, commissioned by Francesco Sassetti, and not the Medici themselves.[5] Just as Augustus had employed a public monument in a sacred setting to legitimize the privilege and principium of his family, so also did the *nobili nuovi* seek status and recognition of dynastic privilege in portraiture.

John Pope-Hennessy defined the basic impetus for Renaissance production of portraiture, on the whole, in his Bollingen series of lectures published first in 1966.[6] He used cult of personality, Humanism, the mental processes of the subject, court portraiture, emblems and donor and participant as the subject headings for his discussion of Renaissance portraiture. The Renaissance artists were responding to the interests of their patrons, the *uomini nuovi* – that the great families were founded on wealth and commerce, the Florentines, including the Medici, or the aristocratic lineage of a specific geo-political entity, and *nobili nuovi*, the Gonzaga of Mantua or Montefeltro of Urbino. The connection to the Roman origins of dynastic portraiture is consistent with the emphasis on family, the prosopography that underlaid, first, the Roman Republic and, later, underscored the Roman Empire.[7]

This concerted effort to stress the importance of the family as an entity in social, political and economic realities is the shared sentiment that clearly demonstrates the similar mechanisms used to present dynastic identity and privilege in both the Roman context and the Renaissance. Augustus, the progenitor of the Empire and the initiator of the tradition of Imperial portraiture in Rome, employed a sanctified space, as the Medici and Sassetti would do later in the Quattrocento, to publish his identity as the *paterfamilias* of the Julio-Claudian imperial dynasty, and the legitimacy and access to power for his heirs, including his adopted heirs through his wife, Livia. Augustus adopted the children of his daughter, Julia, with Agrippa, Gaius and Lucius, in 17 BC, and Agrippa Postumus in 12 BC.[8] The natural sons of Livia, Tiberius and Drusus represent the other line of descent in Augustan portraiture.[9] After the deaths of Gaius and Lucius, Augustus adopted Tiberius as heir, on the precondition that he likewise adopt Germanicus in addition to his natural son, Drusus II, thus setting the stage for the Julio-Claudian succession that followed the demise of Augustus.[10] In the frieze from the Ara Pacis Augustae, dedicated on 30 January, 9 BC, the procession of the Imperial family follows the togate Augustus and the college of priests, Augures and Flamines, on the south side of the altar. Although the identifications vary, most scholars agree that both the Julian heirs and the Claudian heirs are depicted with the maternal origins of each, initiating the individualized portraits of each child or youth (Fig. 5.1).[11] Pollini suggested, as did Toynbee, that the Aeneas panel included Iulus, the son of Aeneas, participating as *camillus* in the sacrifice, just as Augustus included his heirs in the imperial frieze to enhance the strength of imperial legitimacy with Troy and Venus, and the dynastic legitimacy based on sacral representation.[12] Although the frieze was first excavated in the Cinquecento, the traditions of representation, and the connections between sacral activity and the legitimacy of dynastic lineage, were persistent characteristics of the Imperial construction of identity that were transmitted to the Humanist scholars of the Quattrocento, through their study of ancient texts and authors.

Figure 5.1: *Ara Pacis Augustae* (13–9 BCE), Rome. Source: Wikipedia Commons.

In the Introduction to Chapter One 'The Allure of Rome', in *Locating Renaissance Art*, Carol Richardson quoted a dialogue between two travellers, between Florence and Rome in 1497, from the poem by Girolamo Porcari.[13] Richardson follows with a discussion of Quattrocento art and artists, and the profound influence on their development that comes from Rome and antique Roman influences. The conjunction of Humanist writers and literature and Renaissance artists intersects with the propagation of portraiture of children that defines, visually, the inherent prestige of their family line and the placement of their true images in a sacralized space.

Most representations of children in the fourteenth century, in central and Northern Italy, have a predominantly sacred meaning. Children in art are represented as the Christ Child or infant saints, like infant St John the Baptist, or as examples of piety and witnesses to sacred events.[14] Secular contemporary images of children occurred in the fourteenth century as recipients and avatars of communal beneficence. For example, the fresco of children from the façade of the Bigallo in Florence from 1386, by Niccoló Gerini and Ambrogio di Baldese, show the Capitano della Misericordia setting out orphans to be fostered (Fig. 5.2).[15] The same foundational ethic, Christian charity to orphans, engendered the Spedale della Scala frescoes in Siena, in the Sala del Pellegrinaio 1439–44, by Domenico di Bartolo, Vecchietta and Priamo della Quercia.[16] Children in the fourteenth century, in Italian art, are the avatars of their parents and guardians and, with the exception of those like the Christ Child or youthful saints who represent the presence of the Holy Spirit, do not appear as individuals in portraiture.

Figure 5.2: Niccoló Gerini and Ambrogio Baldese, *The Brotherhood of the Mercy Receiving the Orphans* (1386), Loggia di Bigallo, Florence. Source: Alinari; Art Resource, NY.

The child portraits by Desiderio da Settignano, while they are generic juvenile images that display the tenderness and melting innocence of early childhood, have not been identified as portraits of specific individuals (Fig. 5.3).[17] Coonin cites the influence of images of the Christ Child and infant or juvenile St John the Baptist as exemplars, especially for young boys, of the virtues they should cultivate and practice in life. He also references the writing of Matteo Palmieri and Leon Battista Alberti, noted Humanists, on the importance of children in the civic context and their necessary education and nurturing in the domestic environments.[18] In Book One of *Della Famiglia,* Alberti presented a scenario at the passing of his own father, Lorenzo Alberti, with himself and his brother receiving last words of wisdom and instruction in paternal responsibility from the *paterfamilias*. Alberti had studied with a Humanist scholar in Padua and attended the University of Bologna.[19] His knowledge of Latin history, prosopography and ancient literature informed his sense of the duties of the head of household to his progeny. In Book One, Alberti has a passage delivered by Lionardo Alberti, a relative also present, who extols the merits of education for children, and states:

> A father delights in making his offspring well read and learned. You, young men, you should work hard at the study of books. Be assiduous ... Try to make your civil life shine by your splendid character. Seek to know human and divine things which, with good reason, are entrusted to writing.[20]

The focus of Book 1 is Alberti's reasoned explanation of the importance of children in both the domestic and civic continuum. His principles for raising children entreat the readers to value each child for her/his own talents and nurture them accordingly. He also praises physical activity and games, and mentions Gaius Caesar as an example.[21] Roman examples of the merits of education are visible in reliefs on sarcophagi, such as an historiated one with a youth learning to read.[22]

Figure 5.3: Desiderio da Settignano, *Laughing Boy*, marble (*c.*1430), Vienna, Kunsthistorishes Museum. Source: Wikipedia Commons.

Desiderio's *Laughing Boy* in the Kunsthistorisches Museum, Vienna, while not identified by name, clearly seems to reflect the particular spirit of an individual child. More securely identified as images or works based on children of noble families are three marble portrait busts, with one in New York at the Metropolitan.[23] Stephanie Miller has also surmised that some tin-glazed terra cotta busts by the della Robbia are similarly unidentified members of noble or wealthy families in Florence.[24] There appear to be several examples of sculpted busts of children deprived of a context that might identify the subjects' names. Miller relied on John Lydecker's study of Florentine inventories that placed such busts, some specifically of children, over the doors of bedrooms or in bedrooms.[25] This suggests that Quattrocento households cherished the moments of childhood in a manner that created a desire for more permanent and lasting reminders of the fleeting stages of childhood and youth, as Desiderio so winsomely captured in his marble busts. This also demonstrated the realization that childhood was a stage of life deserving of celebration and reflection.

The Medici, who emerged as the most prominent family in the fifteenth century and went on to hereditary nobility in the sixteenth century, were consistently involved in identity construction through dynastic association and privilege. Contexualizing the use of sacral space in constructing dynastic identity, the Medici commissioned Benozzo Gozzoli to represent the origins of the family in the chapel inside the Palazzo Medici-Riccardi, in 1459 (Fig.5.4). Their engagement in civic and religious processional display and the procession of the Magi in the guise of the *Compagnia dei Magi* resulted in an emblematic association that endured throughout the fifteenth century.[26] Hatfield provided the documentation that the procession and theatrical presentation were so popular that they appeared, not only on the feast of Epiphany, 6 January, but were included by decision of the Signoria of Florence to also perform at the Festa di San Giovanni, held on 23 June, in honour of the patron saint of Florence, St John the Baptist.[27] Trexler has described the education, both religious and secular, of grammar school, for middle and lower class youth in Florence, under the tutelage of the confraternities, such as the *Compagnia dei Magi*.[28] He quotes from Ambrogio Traversari's missive to Eugenius IV about the nature of the activities of the youthful members of the confraternities.[29] The Medici confirmed their prodigious participation and conspicuous position in both civic and religious experience. The *Compagnia dei Magi* was also quartered in the monastery of San Marco, not coincidentally under the patronage of the Medici.[30] In their private chapel in their palazzo, the entire dynastic lineage is depicted. Cosimo il Vecchio in black on a mule looks towards his son Piero, on a white horse that is in lock step with another white horse ridden by the Medici scion, impersonating the youngest magus; a highly idealized portrait of Lorenzo de' Medici.[31] Lorenzo embodies the hope and flower of the Medici family and every design element used by Gozzoli made him the emblem of both his family and civic virtue. Much as Augustus presented his heirs and dynastic ambitions on the sacral space of the Ara Pacis Augustae, in the processional relief, the Medici family similarly confirmed their ambitions, and celebrated the future leadership role they hoped to achieve through their progeny. Lorenzo is crowned with a laurel.[32] While it is a word play on his *name* Lorenzo, the laurel crown was also worn to signify imperial honours in the Augustan images. The sacerdotal element was acted out by the priests who performed the Eucharist before this scene, an almost Byzantine extension of the votive portrait. As an adult, Lorenzo would have impressive *boti* or *fallimagini*, the wax votos that recreated the veristic image of the commissioner in wax, with silk and false hair placed in important shrines in Florence, especially Santissima Annunziata.[33]

Figure 5.4: Benozzo Gozzoli, *Procession of the Magi*, Medici Chapel, Medici-Riccardi Chapel, Florence (1459). Source: Erich Lessing; Art Resource, NY.

The passage of Alberti quoted above is aptly illustrated in the frescoes in the Sassetti Chapel, in Santa Trinità in Florence, commissioned by Francesco Sassetti, in 1483–86, for his own funerary chapel from Domenico Ghirlandaio, yet featuring the youthful members of the Medici family and their Humanist tutors.[34] The Albertian construct of the nexus of education and civic humanism fostered in Book One of *Della Famiglia* was evident, in the Sassetti Chapel frescoes by Domenico Ghirlandaio, in the middle scene on the altar wall; the Confirmation of the Rule of St Francis (Fig. 5.5). In this scene, the actual meeting of St Francis and Pope Honorius, in San Giovanni Laterano in Rome, takes place in deep space while the foreground is given over to a portrait gallery that includes, on the extreme right, Francesco Sassetti and his son Federico standing next to Lorenzo de' Medici and Sassetti's brother-in-law, Antonio di Puccio Pucci. To the extreme left, Sassetti's other sons Galeazzo, Teodoro and Cosimo stand as pendants to the right side group. In the lower foreground, arising from the steps into view at the edge of the painting are Lorenzo's sons: Giuliano, Piero and Giovanni, as an adult Pope Leo X follow their tutor, Angelo Poliziano, up the staircase. Ghirlandaio replaced the Roman setting with the Piazza Signoria in Florence and the Loggia dei Lanzi. Rubin has suggested that Ghirlandaio constructed this new image of a traditional iconographic scene, in Italian painting, to create a new view of this event, in which the present day and contemporary Florentines are engaged in creating a new urban environment, sacralized by the events they are witnessing and thereby expunging the violence of the Pazzi conspiracy and the turbulence engendered by it.[35] In the view of this study, the Humanists Poliziano, Lorenzo and the Gonfaloniere Antonio di Puccio Pucci, embody and represent that nexus described by Alberti in the education of youth, intense study under the direction of the tutor Poliziano, parental supervision under the watchful eye of Lorenzo de' Medici and the civic life luster by the Gonfaloniere Antonio de Puccio Pucci.[36] The magical realism of the painting is enhanced by the verism of the portrait types. They are consistently recognizable, unidealized and concrete. The stage craft of the *Compagnia dei Magi* procession is replaced with sober Florentine quotidian stability. Francesco Sassetti employed Ghirlandaio to reframe the sacred text in the new civic context of Florence as a new Rome.[37] His penchant for prosopography resulted in the inclusion of at least twenty-two recognizable portraits, that later were transcribed from the remembrances of a member of the family.[38] In terms of dynastic identity and privilege, Lorenzo de' Medici and his sons, as Francesco Sassetti and his nuclear and extended family inhabit a new urban landscape constructed according to the Albertian model from *Della Famiglia*. As discussed, that provided a context for familial authority in all fields, scholastic, civic and religious. Their permanent position as leaders and exemplars was expressed directly in the Sassetti Chapel frescoes with respect to that Albertian focus as here.

Dynastic Identity in Renaissance Court Life 93

Figure 5.5: Domenico Ghirlandaio, *Confirmation of the Rule of St. Francis*, Sassetti Chapel, Santa Trinità, Florence (c. 1480-5). Source: Wikipedia Commons.

Andrea Mantegna, in the environmentally frescoed Camera Picta, Ducal Palace, Mantua, 1465-74, framed the minor family members of the family of Ludovico Gonzaga and Barbara von Hollenzollern in a setting that emphasized their dominion over both the physical space of the palazzo, the contado under their political control and, through the portrait of Cardinal Francesco Gonzaga, their entry into the principate of the Church hierarchy.[39] Andrea Mantegna was both a skilled portraitist and a student of Classical art and architecture. Elegaic poems about his portrait abilities were written in Padua, as well as one praising his recreation of Classical art, especially in portraiture.[40] This knowledge of antique prototypes and skills of representation resulted in the prodigious verism of the panoramic portraits in the Camera Picta. The illusionism of the room, like the anomalous setting of Florence exchanged for a Roman one of San Giovanni Laterano in the Sassetti Chapel by Ghirlandaio, created that magic setting, contrasting with the true to life likenesses of Duke Ludovico, Barbara of Brandenburg, their children, courtiers and, notably, at least one portrait of a Humanist scholar, if not two, directly connected to the court and embedded with the children (Fig. 5.6). Ludovico, in the court panel on the window wall, is seated holding a letter and looking back up at a man, likely his secretary, Marsilio Andreasi Raimond or Lupi di Soragna. Under his chair, a curule throne, lies his dog, Rubino, a symbol of fidelity. Above his left shoulder is third in birth order, Gianfrancesco with his hands on the shoulders of, possibly, Ludovichino. The marchese Barbara von Brandenburg sits next to him and, likely her youngest daughter, Paola leans over her mother's lap with an apple. Behind the marchese

Barbara stands their son Ridolfo, behind whose shoulder is Barberina Gonzaga, her nurse. The man in the black hat, between Gianfrancesco and Ridolfo, is Vittorino da Feltre, one of the most important Humanist scholars of Northern Italy and responsible for the educations of many aristocratic youths of important families in the mid to late Quattrocento.[41] Vittorino was well-known to take interest in all aspects of his pupils lives and deportment and civic participation. Vittorino seemed to have embodied the precepts set out by Alberti concerning the proper embrace of serious study, physical activity and training in riding and martial arts, as well as games, and decorous behavior that responded as service to others and the commune, and not to satisfy appetites for novelty or enjoyment.[42]

Figure 5.6: Andrea Mantegna, *Court scene, Camera Picta*, Ducal Palace, Mantua (*c.*1465–74). Source: Wikipedia Commons.

The other man wearing a similar black hat, in the background between Ludovico and Gianfrancesco, is a possible portrait of Alberti himself. If this is indeed the case, then Duke Ludovico has included the actual Humanist tutor for his children, Vittorino da Feltre, with the philosophical Humanist author, Leon Battista Alberti, who framed the process of Quattrocento education in his writings. Vittorino and Alberti appear as branches off the tree behind Gianfrancesco, possibly an allusion to the fruit of their labors as pedagogues.

On the adjacent wall, between the window and the door, is the panel usually called the Meeting, where Ludovico and his younger sons and nephews meet Cardinal Francesco Gonzaga, with embedded portraits of Emperor Frederick III and King Christian I of Denmark, a relative by marriage.[43] Cardinal Francesco

Gonzaga holds his younger brother Ludovico's hand, who is, in turn, held by his cousin Sigismondo (Fig. 5.7). Christiansen has made the connection to the Imperial children on the Ara Pacis Augustae holding hands, whose poses, like the ones here, create the interlocking dynastic lineage visible through gesture.[44] Therefore, Mantegna, under the direction of his patron Ludovico Gonzaga, Duke of Mantua, has constructed a reality that melds contemporary events, references to ancient history of Rome, in the portraits of emperors and classical mythological events in the gilded stucco ceiling trompe l'oeil, as well as the need to carefully record dynastic lineage and privilege with the attendant Humanists, Vittorino da Feltre and possibly Leon Battista Alberti in attendance. This codifies all the elements presented so far in this study.

Figure 5.7: Andrea Mantegna, *The Meeting, Camera Picta*, Ducal Palace, Mantua, (*c.* 1465–74). Source: Wikipedia Commons.

In the last example, Federigo da Montefeltro, singular in his emulation of the antique in his Humanistic court and support of scholars and philosophical inquiry, had his heir, Guidobaldo, included in every artistic commission from his regency as Duke of Urbino.[45]

Federigo, who although born illegitimate, succeeded his brother Oddantonio as first Count of Urbino and later Duke of Urbino, is wearing all the attributes of his station (Fig. 5.8). He wears armour, a nod to his primary occupation as condottiere – the order of the Ermine, the order of the Garter – and the prominent placement of a tiara given by Persian ruler, Uzan Hazan.[46] Next to him wearing a jewel encrusted robe and holding a gold scepter with PO(N)TIFEX inscribed on it, his small son Guidobaldo rests his arm on his father's knee.[47] Federigo is seated at his scholar's desk and holds an open manuscript in his hands. Federigo was the true Renaissance man. He had studied under Vittorino da Feltre in Mantua when he was a child hostage there in his youth. That early Humanist education inspired his collection of antique manuscripts. He acquired the largest collection of antique manuscripts in the Quattrocento. The library he built in the Ducal Palace at Urbino became the essence and core of the Vatican Library. In his Studiolo, this portrait was hung with a collection of the greatest Humanist writers of the fourteenth and fifteenth centuries. Federigo worked to expand his territory and confirm the dynastic lineage of his family through Guidobaldo, whose birth brought about the demise of his beloved Battista Sforza. The scepter confirms the papal legitimization that allowed Federigo to leave the duchy to Guidobaldo. By touch, as in the previously mentioned dynastic image in Mantua and the similarity to the Ara Pacis Augustae, Federigo and Guidobaldo's pose visually communicates that dynastic privilege. The tiara from the Persian ruler is suspended over Guidobaldo's head in an obvious reference to his future growth into the future role of Duke of Urbino and internationally renowned ruler. The books are also visually placed over his head, again the notion of wisdom is being suggested here as an allusion to the future erudition of the young heir. In the Altarpiece of the Confraternity of the Corpus Domini, Justus of Ghent included a woman and baby, likely embedded portraits of Battista and Guidobaldo, between Federigo and the Persian ambassador.[48]

Dynastic Identity in Renaissance Court Life 97

Figure 5.8: Justus von Ghent or Pietro da Spagna, *Federigo da Montefeltro and Guidobaldo Montefelto*, **Galleria nationale delle Marche , Urbino (*c.*1475).**
Source: Wikipedia Commons.

The infant in the painting goes back to the early Quattrocento representations of children first examined here. Guidobaldo's shining locks and soft contours could be the painted equivalent of Desiderio's cherubic portrait busts. Overall, Federigo's double portrait with Guidobaldo sustains the interests in dynastic portraiture to enhance the allusions to dynastic legitimacy and privilege addressed in previous examples examined here. The constricted space is an inner construct that limits the consideration of the elements of meaning which is emphasized to the viewer through the restricted view. There is no other focus possible in the space of the painting and the intent of the portrait is startling in its clarity and potent message of dynastic provenance. The Humanist element, as described by Alberti, is present in the setting, the study and the activity of 'assiduous' study – as seen in the passage above. The tiny stature of Guidobaldo is at once supported and enshrouded in the pearl-encrusted ducal robes, much as Lorenzo wore brocade in the Gozzoli Procession of the Magi in the Medici Chapel. Both function as literally shining examples of familial dynastic ambition and privilege. Federigo and Guidobaldo's portrait encapsulated the dynastic goals of the Renaissance courts, embodied in the portraits of children of privilege while alluding to the Humanist philosophy and civic participation required to maintain both power and privilege and the transmission to a new generation.

In summation, the portraits of children linked to dynastic practice seem to share common sources, Humanist writing and philosophy, economic and social mechanisms and political and civic presence. These sources were all examined in the child portraits evident in the Ara Pacis Augustae, important symbols of Augustan Imperial propaganda. It effectively sacralized the dynastic lineage of the Julio-Claudian family. The early Renaissance portraits in marble and tin-glazed terra cotta added to the idea of child portraiture as an interest in the stage of childhood in the life of the family. The Medici portraits in the Medici Chapel and the Sassetti Chapel further extended the sacral aspectm, yet added to it an immediate presence cemented in the urban context. Notably, the Albertian construct of Humanist principles of education and familial obligation in nurturing children in civic responsibility, as well as scholarly endeavor, was evident with the inclusion of portraits of the Humanist pedagogues with their students. The Gonzaga frescoes only amplified and codified that connection of dynastic power and privilege, and Humanist education and training. The subtelty of interlocking gestures that seemed casual or merely familial reinforced the dynastic lineage of each family. Finally, from the Montefeltro portraits, all of the previously outlined mechanisms were not only present, but emphasized through compositional and descriptive methods in the actual painting of the portrait. Renaissance court portraits of children were carefully constructed to preserve, not only the likeness and personality of the future ruler, but to encode the image with multivalent indicators of the dimensional identity required to participate on the level of international courtly conversation.

6 'YOU WILL BE A MAN, MY SON': SIGNS OF MASCULINITY AND VIRILITY IN ITALIAN RENAISSANCE PAINTINGS OF BOYS

Fabien Lacouture

These words are from Federico da Montefeltro, Duke of Urbino and Count of Montefeltro, on the occasion of the birth of his son, he wrote the following words in a letter to Lorenzo di Piero de Medici: 'Tell your wife that she has done much better than my wife, who made eight girls before she made my son'.[1]

Though such words offend our sensibilities today, they reveal how important having a boy was in the Italian Renaissance. Indeed, numerous means existed that were thought to guarantee a boy and thus make the result of the pregnancy 'successful'.[2] Even if we do not see the birth of a girl as the catastrophe some Renaissance testimonies describe, families feared having a girl, in particular due to the increase of the dowries in the fifteenth and sixteenth centuries.[3] Generally, the birth of a girl immediately put a strain on the family's finances, which was not the case with a boy. Furthermore, the marriage of a girl led to the loss, or at least the disappearance, of the girl's family name for the benefit of the husband's. The family that had a male heir had an advantage over the family who had a girl.

The essential place of boys within families is clearly highlighted in the treaties about the art of ruling a house. Written by urban elites – humanist merchants in the fifteenth century, noblemen and gentlemen during the sixteenth century – those textbooks developed in Western Europe and, particularly in Italy, on the basis of Xenophon and Aristotle's rediscovered texts.[4] The Family was seen as a vital structure of human life, a sphere that connected the individual and the political community and, therefore, should be controlled and run according a set of rules and precepts. This knowledge, culturally accepted, was a bridge between individual expectations and convictions, and civic rules and values. The themes tackled in those treatises were varied: politics and its links with domestic life, games, hunting, religion, the importance of literature, choice of women and of course the care and education of children. *I Libri della Famiglia*, written between 1440 and 1450 by Leon Battista Alberti, is today the most famous treatise about these questions. Its first book is dedicated the care and education parents have to bring to their descendants.[5] A quick listing of the words designating the progeny reveals that in Alberti's mind the most desired child is, above all, a boy. The words 'fanciullo' – the child – and especially 'figliuolo' – the son – are used by the author throughout the text and, although they could actually refer to the child generically,[6] their recurrent combination with words from the lexical field of manhood does not leave much doubt about the greater importance given to the male child.[7] Thus, the word 'child' designated above all the boy.

The image of the boy also recurs frequently in the visual culture of the Italian Renaissance. Even if the Christ-Child – the boy *par excellence* – is with no doubt the figure that immediately comes to mind, in this study I will content myself with talking about the representations of secular children. In this article, I would like to study the signs of masculinity and virility, which appear in the pictorial representations of boys. More than a simple inventory of every boy in the Italian Renaissance painting (which could only lead us to notice that they are more numerous than girls), this analysis will focus on the signs (attributes, clothing, possessions, etc.) that point out the social and anthropological importance of the gender of a child.[8]

Although the underlining of the signs of masculinity could be considered as a constant and usual tool in depictions of boys, this observation has to be moderated according to the age of the model, which is why this exposé will follow the categorization of the ages of life most common since the seventh century.[9] Moreover, a distinction will be drawn between masculinity and the virility of manhood. The former will relate to the set of specific characteristics normally associated uniquely with men. Virility, if we refer to the works of Georges Vigarello, does not only represents the male but the man, in his most noble and complete part. 'Virility would be virtue ... with its qualities, clearly stated: sexual qualities, those of the 'active' husband, sexually powerful, procreator, but also well balanced, vigorous and reserved, brave but with the sense of proportions'.[10]

The first stage, *infanzia*, is commonly depicted in art, particularly in the painted birth tray – *desco da parto*. In these decorated objects, we notice that the male child is essentially defined as a boy through the emphasis of his genitalia in order to emphasize the plenitude of his masculinity.[11] During the *puerizia*, every sign of sexualization disappears and the superiority of the males in the family can be seen in the command of double portraits between fathers and sons, a way to display the importance of men and their role in the perpetuity of the *casa*. Finally, during the *adolescenza*, we will see how the virility of the model as a social process is underscored by the physical and intellectual.

I Deschi da parto and the Display of Genitalia.

The birth of a child during the Renaissance, fraught as it was with fears and risks, was an important moment for the family and society. The infantile mortality was high as recurrent epidemic of plagues had decimated the children population in numerous cities of northern and central Italy.[12] The population needed to participate in a demographic regrowth, so much so that in 1420s, Bernardino da Siena, in one of his sermons, beseeched couples to marry so that they could procreate.[13] Having children was an accomplishment and a source of honour, and a great emphasis was put on the perpetuation of the lineage, which could only be seen assured by the birth of male heirs.[14] Boys kept the family alive and secured its heritage and its social position. That is why boys were more desired than girls, whose marriages could bring financial difficulties, such as their future dowries.

The birth of a child, and more particularly of a boy, was celebrated according to an established ritual, during which specific objects were normally offered, both practical and apotropaic.[15] Among those gifts was the *deschi da parto*, which had a central place in the domestic rituals surrounding birth. They were used to bring food, drinks or linens to the wives during their containment.[16] After this period, the trays were kept as structural elements of the memory and the identity of the family.[17] That very few *deschi* survived could have led to the belief that only rich people own some; but they were frequently listed in inventories. Therefore, families belonging to any social background could own a tray.[18] They were quite small – most often between 55 and 75 cm in diameter, had a polygonal form and were most often painted on both sides. The topics they are decorated with vary, but generally involve the same repetitive themes: biblical or mythological scenes that represent birth scenes or post-partum scenes. *Deschi* can also be decorated with the heraldic arms of the family, and often depict naked male children. This limited spectrum shows that this iconography linked to the child was not only decorative but also symbolic and meaningful. A particular meaning and agency can explain the recurrence of each topic.[19]

Even if they were made for a feminine audience, these trays were nonetheless often ordered by male patrons, and made and painted by men. This is an important element in understanding the choice and the reiteration of little naked boys. Additionally, the absence of little girls compared to the presence of little boys can also enlighten us. If we keep in mind that the birth of a male child was much more celebrated than that of a female child, then this motif of little naked boys could have been chosen either to provoke or to celebrate the arrival of a little boy. Moreover, their nudity raises another question. Divine or secular, the nudity of male children is visible in numerous scenes, painted, engraved and sculpted. But there is no trace of such nudity for a female child of any kind. The feminine nudity must stay hidden, whereas the masculine one must by displayed.

The emphasis placed on the masculinity of these boys through the displaying of their *genitalia* is particularly obvious in the *deschi da parti*, the only kind of works of the fifteenth century that show sexualized secular children. Two birth trays made by Bartolomeo da Fruosino are decorated on their backs with a seated and smiling naked little boy who is wearing around his neck a branch of red corral attached to a golden chain (Fig. 6.1).[20] The boy is holding in his hands two traditional toys: a windmill and a stick used as a wooden horse. The two other boys have their legs open, a pose that allows the audience to view his genitals. These images of the naked boys are also decorated with the coat of arms of a particular family, likely the one who commissioned the tray.[21] The combination between an element allowing the audience to identify a particular family and the displaying of the sexual attributes of a little boy, underlines the will of the patron to insist on its own capacity to father a boy, a new man who will keep alive the family's name and reputation.

Figure 6.1: Bartolomeo da Fruosino. Desco da parto (1428).
Photo Credit: Matthew Knox Averett, author.

Sometimes it is through displays of sports that masculinity is displayed. In a *desco* by Giovanni di Ser Giovanni, called Lo Scheggia, its recto depicts a game of *civettino* in the streets of a Tuscan city (Fig 6.2). This game consisted of avoiding the slaps of the other players while having a foot caught by the foot of an opponent. In these images, there are three opponents, already teenagers, wearing doublets and stockings, clothes perfectly fit to this kind of activities. On the other hand, the little boys' masculine attributes are visible due to their restlessness in playing the game. On the back of the *desco*, however, two very young boys completely naked are also playing this game, pulling each other's hair and penises. The grasping of penises has no purpose in the game and appears here only to highlight the masculinity of the little wrestlers.[22] One last example is even more interesting. On the back of a birth tray attributed to the workshop of Appolonio di Giovanni two naked boys appear again, this time with three coats of arm above them.[23] The boy on the right leans forward, legs spread and prominently displaying his genitals. He holds a receptacle in which the boy on the left is urinating, the other boy's penis also quite visible. In every case, the clear visibility and legibility of the coats of arm with the displaying of genitalia demonstrates the *desco's* patrons' desire to illustrate not only the strength of his fertility, but also his continuity with the birth of a boy.

Figure 6.2: Recto– Giovanni di Ser Giovanni, called Lo Scheggia, *Desco da Parto with the Game of Civettino* (1455). Source: Wikimedia Commons.

Figure 6.2: Verso – Giovanni di Ser Giovanni, called Lo Scheggia, *Desco da Parto with the Game of Civettino* (1455). Source: Wikimedia Commons.

Those *deschi* had a practical goal related to the birth ritual, specifically the transport of food and drinks. But once this was past, the *deschi* were kept and displayed within the houses.[24] One of their purposes was to show to certain audiences – friends, relatives, or important guests – the strength of the family, a strength that can engender virile and masculine sons. The *desco da parto* was a unique medium for the representation of naked male children and the display of their *genitalia*. So, from the sixteenth century when majolica bowls replaced wooden trays in birthing rituals, the iconographical topics were transformed. The demand had turn to smaller objects in which the images were meant for a more restraint and intimate audience and no more for a public exhibition. Whereas confinement scenes were still represented, the *mostratio genitalium* had no more sense. If naked boys were painted on trays and not inside bowls – except in the form of *putti* – it was because the birth trays offered a much broader visibility and transcended their initial function and their initial – feminine – audience.

Father and Son Portraits: Displaying the Seminal Masculinity of the Family

The nudity of boys is limited to this first age when families – and above all fathers – had to display their ability to perpetuate the lineage and their powerful fertility through their son.[25] But as the child grows, the display of boys' genitals ceases to fit with social and moral norms or with the etiquette that governs representations of the family. Depicting a boy older than seven naked is absolutely forbidden by moral authorities. The *puerizia* is an age where sexuality – and so the signs of sexuality – are banned and banished. During the *infanzia*, boys and girls could play together, but the age of seven marked the end of their lives in common and the beginning of a gendered division of children. From that age, children could not be submitted to any possible desire by the other sex.[26] The display of the masculine importance and domination within the family, however, continue through other kinds of signs and images, notably with the portraits of fathers and sons. This association by gender is clearly visible in a diptych by Veronese (Figs. 6.3 and 6.4).[27] Today held in two different museums, the two paintings were undoubtedly meant to decorate the *portego* of one of the family's houses. The two parts of the work are distinct and the division is even more obvious in that it is based on the gender of the characters. On one side are Livia and her daughter Porzia; on the other, Iseppo and his son Adriano. Porzia is hidden behind her mother's dress and shyly peeking out at the world outside. In contrast, Adriano, the heir who will continue to bear the family name, is in front of his father. In the foreground, he wears the same exact clothes and attributes of his father. Moreover Iseppo, was a knight (evidenced by the sword at his belt), and young Adriano already carries his own little sword. Unlike the little girl hidden behind her mother, the male child is presented to the public as the bold heir, both social and pictorial, of the family. This kind of work is a symbol of the system of cultural transmission. Role models and values, both aristocratic and bourgeois, are transmitted from father to son. As Alberti describes the transmission of the family patriarchal model:

> It is natural for the fathers, I do not know how, to have a broader necessity, a certain appetite to have and raise children, and then to be pleased to see in them the reproduction of their own image, and the resemblance with themselves: they put in those children all their hopes, then expect to have in them, in their old days, a strong defence and support for their age now tired and weak.[28]

Figure 6.3: Paolo Veronese, *Portrait of Iseppo Da Porto and His Son* (1551). Galleria degli Uffizi, Florence. Photo Credit: Scala, Florence.

Figure 6.4: Paolo Veronese, *Portrait of Livia Da Porto Thiene and Her Daughter* (1551). Walter Art Gallery, Baltimore. Photo Credit: Scala, Florence.

Let us take another example. The *Portrait of Alfonso d'Avalos* was painted by Titian for Alfonso himself, *condottiere* for the Emperor Charles V and one of the most famous warlords in Italy.[29] Titian presented him in ceremonial armour and a traditional position of glory. The man strikes a pose, looks out boldly and faces a crowd of his soldiers as though he were addressing them. Alfonso's son Fernando is also painted with him, full-length, on the platform and he, too, wears ceremonial armour. He holds his father's helmet, which in the boy's hand becomes a symbol of the future transfer of power between the two leading men of the family. The boy once again is in front of his father, in the foreground, as if he were presented both to the troops and the audience.

More than the accessories and the attributes those young boys are equipped with, it is through their depictions with their fathers that displayed their masculinity and their inclusion in the male part of the family. The father and son portraits show the male child, the most important part of the family, the masculine one. This masculine inheritance is both civic (because it is a product of a well-accepted power struggle) and moral (by presenting the audience a honourable tradition the young children – boys – should admire and aspire to). As Francesco Valori, *gonfaloniere* of the Republic of Florence put it:

> Your sons, being virtuous in their behaviours and their customs, learn virtuous and good habits that, once acquired during this softest age, will be theirs forever.[30]

The children, and above all the sons, should imitate their ancestors' behaviours and replicate their achievements, beginning with their father's. The masculine familial resemblances, that they have been true or created, were disavowal for changes, tools of perpetuation of the masculine model of domination.

The path from the *puerizia* to *adolescenza* can be seen by the transformation of the double-portrait of father and son to an individual portrait. The assertion and exhibition of the masculine perpetuation of the family is replaced by the display of the virility of a soon-to-be man. But this moment of transition takes time: a young boy, even one accustomed to wearing a little sword at his belt and an outfit which looks like his father's, cannot become, *in ictu oculi*, a declared and virile young man. For all that, the fragility which characterizes the period is rarely represented by the painters, who do not take into account the slowness of this process and transform the young men to fully formed adults.

In something of an exception, Titian succeeds in rendering every state of this transition in the *Portrait of Ranuccio Farnese* (Fig. 6.5). Ranuccio's portrait, painted in 1542, marks the start of Titian's association with the Farnese family.[31] The new characteristic of this portrait rests on the way Titian managed to give a pictorial definition of this transitional period where a child is almost overwhelmed by his life and his body. In this portrait, Ranuccio is barely twelve or thirteen. Grandson of Paul III, he has just been nominated prior of San Giovanni dei Furlani of the order of Malta, a title indicated by the cross visible on his coat. Three years later, his grandfather will appoint him to the college of the cardinals.[32] Ranuccio is painted in bust with a sword and gloves and wearing a heavy dark coat. All of these details are related to the model of gentlemen that also applies to portraits of teenagers and young men.

Figure 6.5: Titian, Portrait of Ranuccio Farnese (1542). Photo Credit: The National Gallery of Art, Washington, DC.

Son of one of the most powerful Italian families, Ranuccio has great responsibilities, but he is not absolutely ready to take them all on, as symbolized by his oversized heavy coat. Indeed, it is interesting to notice that everything in this painting is too large or too heavy for him: the coat, but also the gloves and of course the sword. The straps that tie the sheath to his waist are weighed down due to the heaviness of the sword. On his face, adolescence can be discerned: his hair is cropped neatly and the curls of the *infanzia* are no more. Still beardless, though, he is too young to pretend to mature virility. As Philippe Ariès said, 'there is in the teenager an ambiguity due to puberty and an accent put on the effeminate aspect of a young boy who just go out of childhood. The boy was still beardless. The feminine aspect is related to the transition from childhood to adulthood: it reveals a state for a certain time, the time of the budding love'.[33] Ranuccio concentrating, careful to seem as tall as possible. His look is steady, his cheeks pinkish. His senses are about to wake, as Titian reminds the audience of this via the red of his shirt. This is the sanguine humour: 'Blood is the liqueur of vitality: when the blood spills out of a body, life is also spilling out'.[34] Nevertheless, through the composition and the framing he used, Titian tempered this passion: the lower part of the frame cut the figure exactly at the place of the *genitalia*. Ranuccio is still too young; sexuality is not a part of his life yet.

For this commission, Titian has used every traditional attribute of the state portrait, but he adapted these stereotypes to a character who has neither the shoulders nor presence to bear them yet. The signs of potential virility are there, but the boy – even if he tries so – cannot take on this display of power. Titian understood perfectly what was happening in the life and body of this boy and, rather than painting a usual state portrait, he painted Ranuccio torn between a still youthful body and a social virility he has to, but cannot yet, assume.

Adolescenza: From Masculinity to Manhood

The third age of childhood, *adolescenza*, is marked by the exhibition of virility. The boy is not shown and characterized by his belonging to a male world, he becomes the incarnation of values that make up the concept of virility. As Georges Vigarello underlines, 'the *vir* is not only *homo*, he is not only man, he is more than a man: an ideal of power and virtue, of assurance and maturity, of certainty and domination.'[35]

Virility must not be thought of according to the meaning we give it today, as a concept based on displayed physical force and sexual power. On the contrary, virility as it is perceived and conceived in the fifteenth and sixteenth centuries, is a pursuit of Baldassare Castiglione's recommendations in *Il Cortegiano*. Authors at the end of the sixteenth century and the beginning of the seventeenth century, such as Le Tasse or Giovan Battista Assandri, took great care to synthesize those ideas.[36] As Vigarello said, the *vir* is not only the man, the male. He is an ideal, cultured, graceful, expert on literature and philosophy but also on arms drilling and interested in elegant clothing. This is what differentiates the double portraits of the *puerizia* from the portraits of youths. Admittedly, as already visible in father and son portraits, attributes such as swords, letters or open books, when associated with an older boy are full of significance. They are no longer mere symbols of the social rules of masculinity, simple toys that 'look like dad's' and maintain the present and future predominance of the male part of the family. In youth portraits, these attributes are much more eloquent: they become signs of virility, a virility understood and assumed by the sitters.

One of the essential qualities of virility is of course proficient drilling with arms, and this is visible in numerous portraits of male teenagers. Pontormo, in his *Halberdier* for example, represents a young man (perhaps Francesco Guardi) at around the age of fifteen years old.[37] The model, standing up straight, leans on his halberd, which gives the painting its title. He wears a red breech and a yellow jacket tightened at the waist. His narrowness is emphasized by a thin leather belt holding the weight of a sword. The boy is staring at the audience and puts his left hand on his hip, just above the blade. This gesture, which will become a distinguishing characteristic of ceremonial portraits, gives a form of nobility to his pose and stresses the assurance of the sitter. This halberdier is everything Ranuccio Farnese was not, or not yet. The belt that holds the weapon is perfectly fitted and does not sag; the same is true of his clothes. His face is no longer that of a child; the cheeks of the young boy painted by Titian still showed the fleshy curves of childhood, whereas those of the halberdier are hollow and his face angular and much more mature, though he is only three of four years older than Ranuccio. Another physical detail, his hands are much bigger, and they seem almost already worn out, maybe due to the handling of the heavy axe. These features and specific representations of virility, and can be seen in the *Boy with a Greyhound* by Veronese (Fig. 6.6).[38] This boy presents to the spectators a harsh face, proud and self-assured. He is wearing clothes made-to-measure, with a puffed out breech and a perfectly fitted belt holding his sword. Finally, he goes with a big greyhound he seems to have trained, the dog being a symbol of his ability to rule.[39] This young man is not yet an adult, but he is no longer a child, he has to take his responsibilities, which he does with great self-confidence.

Figure 6.6: Paolo Veronese, *Boy with a Greyhound* (1570s). Photo Credit: Metropolitan Museum of Art, New York.

The use and the mastery of the literary and cultural structures are important characteristics of virility in sixteenth-century Italy. As Paolo Caggio observed,

> There is no doubt that it is necessary that boys should be taught, because today you say the same of a man who is not cultured as a statue; and the difference between a living man and one who would be painted is equivalent to the one between the essence and the habits of a man who knows and a man completely deprived of literary abilities.[40]

It is important to give boys the traditional tools of knowledge, the methodological basics to face the practical and social demands of their future life. So, the individual portraits of young men must stress, as it was done with the arms drilling, the necessary interest for letters. Bronzino's *Portrait of a Young Man* represents this obligation (Fig. 6.7).[41] Standing, seen from thighs to head, the young man wears a dark hat and outfit. As with the halberdier, Bronzino's sitter places his left hand on his hip and, with his right hand, marks his page in a book he holds on a table decorated with a grimacing *mascaron*. Behind him can be noticed a partial door and some architectural details. Finally, in the bottom right angle of the canvas is a chair, the armrest of which – decorated again with a grotesque head – is the only visible part. This young man stares at the audience, proud and self-confident, aware of the nobility of his pose and of his beauty and virtue. This painting is clearly a pictorial and social construction which has nothing left to do with the representations of young boys previously studied. Cultured and belonging to the scholarly elite, this young man presents, among other items, a perfectly lit and conspicuously held book, which demonstrates his attraction and attachment to Florentine literary circles.[42]

114   *The Early Modern Child in Art and History*

**Figure 6.7: Bronzino, *Portrait of a Young Man*, 1530s.
Photo Credit: Metropolitan Museum of Art, New York.**

Books and arms are the two attributes a young man has to possess and display. On the ceiling of the Barbaro Villa at Maser, near Venice, Veronese managed to create a synthesis of the precepts of virility. On one side, there is Giustiniana Giustiniani-Barbaro, wife of Marcantonio – the owner of the villa, along with his brother Daniele – attended by her last son Alvise and an old servant. On the other panel, the two eldest sons (who flank a space where there absent father should be, but is now occupied by a monkey) are depicted, each one holding an attribute of virility. Francesco Barbarbo holds a book in his hands to show his knowledge and the good education his parents – his father – offered him and which would allow him to pretend to a good social position.[43] His brother, Almoro Barbaro, is painted holding a hunting dog by the collar. Let us remember that hunting is a metonymy for war (as, for example, Castiglione repeatedly states), in time of peace or within the home or the civil society. Being trained to the rudiments of hunting is the same as being trained in arms and it is a proof of the physical abilities of the young man. These two boys form the synthesis of the necessary requirements in order to fully embody the concept of virility.

One last important point is the issue of clothing. According to Castiglione, the clothes of a courtesan must always tend 'a bit more to something solemn and serious than to something vain; this is why I think the colour black is best for the garments that any other else; and if it is not black, at least it must be verging on a dark colour'.[44] Some years later, the authors of treatises would make a summary of clothing conventions to respect for the young nobles and gentlemen, but these precepts can also be noticed through some portraits. This is the case with Bronzino's young man with a book, as well as the Florentine master's portrait of Ludovico Capponi. Ludovico's sitter wears a black doublet that shows a white sleeve, picturing in this way the family colours.[45] But his portraits also depict an element which brings back the initial question of the displaying of the *genitalia* as a sign of masculinity: the codpiece. In southern Europe, particularly in Italy, codpieces were physical displays of virility, and were often highlighted by colors of paint, contrasts of light and dark or elements of the painting, such as thigh-high framings.

In Bronzino's portrait of Guidobaldo della Rovere, a handsome boy of eighteen years and old known for his romantic fervour, is pictured with a grand bearded and highlighted codpiece.[46] What is called in Italian the *cazzaria* emerges from the armour with an amazing relief. The effect is accentuated by the play between complementary colours: embroidered satin with golden threads, the *cazzaria* is bright red, which contrasts with the grey-green and the green, respectively, of the armour and of the background curtain. The sexual potential of the sitter is obvious: what an historian has called 'his *vis generativa*, his ability to perpetuate his lineage'.[47] The displayed codpieces in individual portraits notify the audience of sitters' sexual potency, realized or potential.[48]

These portraits belong to a precise period of time; they can be put into context by the links they have with some of the contemporary social rules, stated in several treatises. Their interaction comes from a global cultural atmosphere, due to the diffusion of these books but, above all, to the diffusion of the ideas they expound. These precepts – arms drilling, literary learning and attention to garments – were widely distributed, as proven by their ubiquitous presence in didactic treatises. But we must not see in these portraits a plain illustration of these writings. The paintings did not act as illustration of a treatise that had already been read. Instead, they act in parallel with these books, in a pedagogic manner. *Adolescenza* was seen as a time of outburst of passions, leading to an excessive violence. These works of art, without denying their sexual dimension, both showed to the young men of northern and central Italy an ideal of virility, an example of good appearance and good behaviour and presented to audiences that the sitters were able to attain these goals.

Conclusion

While girls appear in great number in Italian Renaissance painting of children, boys are overrepresented in certain kinds of paintings. Masculine effigies prevailed because the Renaissance society was, before all, a patrilineal one. Of course, masculine representations must not be studied as an homogeneous whole, but nuanced according to the sitter, his social group and his age. Studying the issue of the representation of boys and young men in the early modern period enables us to observe that the western tradition of the masculine model was not the plain illustration of a natural 'état de fait', but a language of exchanges and representative strategies aiming at some definable agencies. The presence of little naked boys on *deschi da parto* was a way to celebrate the birth of a new male. Their nudity come under the will of displaying to the audience, relatives, friends and close ones, but also honourable guests, the sexual power of both the husband who managed to father a son and of the son, a perfectly well-proportioned boy and already a man in the making. During the *puerizia*, the predominance of the boy compared to the girl is put, in form, through the presence in ceremonial portraits of the son along with his father, as the heir. The boy must perpetuate the lineage still personified by the father. In those paintings, the association of father and son and the resemblance between one and the other, serves to reaffirm the present and future existence of the *casa*. *Adolescenza* shows a change since we move from the affirmation and exhibition of the masculinity of the boy represented to his incarnation of virility. The attributes do not serve to underline his essence as a *homo*, a male, but to stress the *vir*, the ideal man, the one who has interiorized the numerous precepts of education and formation in force at the time. Obviously, and particularly with the exhibition of the codpiece, it is possible to find some signs of pure masculinity. But these details are always associated with other physical elements in order to present the model of a perfect young man, sexually vigorous, physically accomplished and intellectually sharp. Becoming a man was becoming an adult male, able to engender and perpetuate the lineage thanks to sexual power, but it was also achieving an ideal of civility and education, both physical and intellectual, so that the family, as embodied by the young man, should in addition be considered as exemplary.

7 DRESSING THE PART: PICTURING AND PROMOTING THE EARLY MODERN CHILD

Parme Giuntini

With few exceptions, American girls between the ages of five and twelve wear clothing styles that closely approximate mainstream adult fashion.[1] Like adult styles, the preferred look for young girls is predicated on popular culture and current fashion trends. Everything from the latest movie and music videos to Paris runways and urban street chic is fair game for children's designers. Advertisements for these fashion forward styles reverberate with notions of creativity, individuality and youthful exuberance – all the necessary buzzwords for the juvenile market and modern parenting alike. There are style exceptions to this and they reside primarily in the realm of special occasion clothing, the garb worn for holidays, weddings and formal portraits. These are the moments when children are particularly on display and when young girls are asked or compelled to wear classic clothing presented to them as more appropriate. For these occasions and the photographs that document them, the classic style is grounded in an eighteenth-century model. This was the pictorial moment when western childhood was philosophically and materially reconceptualized, visualized in portraiture dominated by Sir Joshua Reynolds, and popularized through Royal Academy exhibitions, the London press and a burgeoning print trade.

Reynolds was the architect of English eighteenth-century children's portraiture. He had rivals; primarily Thomas Gainsborough, George Romney and John Hoppner, but they were not peers for that category.[2] His biographer James Northcote recounted the artist's easy way with children, his interest in their gestures, his belief that all children were naturally graceful.[3] Such anecdotal evidence has often supported the belief that Reynolds's fondness for children was the reason he painted so many of them, a persistent claim that art historians were citing as late as 1985.[4] Although Marcia Pointon criticized Reynolds, along with his contemporaries Thomas Lawrence and George Romney, for their sexual and infantilizing representations of girls, she did not dispute that Reynolds successfully popularized an ideal of English childhood.⁵ Whether Reynolds liked children is a moot point. He never married or fathered any offspring, although he did have a niece whom he painted and exhibited. His contact with children was primarily professional: their portraits were a source of income and artistic prestige. His pre-eminence as a portrait painter was undisputed and, by the time that he turned his attention to children's portraiture, he had already successfully reconfigured new models for male and female adult portraits. Children's portraiture was a sub-genre that was ripe for the taking and Reynolds had a reputation as an aggressive professional.

In the contemporary world of digital cameras, Facebook and Instagram, the reliance on pictorial documentation of children is a foregone conclusion. Parents, friends and relatives photograph everything from the ritual to the mundane. Children are documented at their outstanding moments as well as their most awkward. Their pictures are on walls, tables and counters, in digital frames that change regularly, in cell phones, on iPads and they make regular appearances on Facebook postings. Professional photographs range from annual school pictures to individual photographs against stock backgrounds shot in discount department stores to costly studio renditions affixed to canvas mounts that approximate the texture of an oil painting. There are no right or wrong poses; the spontaneous silly gesture is treasured as much as the orchestrated professional composition.

The proliferation of pictorial documentation of children today is as much a testament to contemporary notions of parenting, domestic life and the sanctity of childhood as in eighteenth-century England, when changing philosophies and practices of parenting profoundly influenced the aristocracy and gentry. The deluge of print information ranged from the discourses of Rousseau and Locke,⁶ to practical books penned by working physicians like Codogan and Buchan.⁷ There were essays in the *Spectator*, novels like *Pamela II* and *Amelia*, periodicals and advice books, some of them written by women where the discourse of childcare, maternal power and influence would prominently figure.

Whether grounded in philosophical positions, medical observation or driven by the alarmingly high infant and child death rates among gentry and aristocratic families, the writers stressed a common checklist of childrearing practices taken for granted today. Tight swaddling from birth to six months was abandoned in favour of long loose gowns called 'carrying frocks' that extended past the feet. Once believed to be the best way to ensure straight limbs, philosophers and physicians now advocated against swaddling, and it fell out of favour with the English although the French and Germans continued the practice well through the eighteenth century.⁸ Harsh physical punishment was condemned, and demonstrable parental affection highly encouraged. In particular, fathers were admonished to pay as much loving attention to their children as they did to their hounds and horses.⁹ Mothers were to supervize their children's activities personally during the nursery years rather than leave them to the care of servants. They were strongly encouraged to breastfeed their own infants at home rather than send them out to be wet-nursed, which was a long-standing practice and could last for up to two years.[10] Daily bathing was enthusiastically suggested and boys were advised to bathe in cold water to reinforce their physical stamina. Corseting was discouraged in favour of looser, more comfortable clothing that allowed greater physical activity. Rather than rich, highly spiced foods, parents were advised to feed children simple diets of bland, plain fare. Parents who followed these instructions were to be rewarded with children who regularly lived past infancy, grew into healthy adolescence and were obedient out of love rather than fear of physical punishment.

By mid-century, a fashionable new domestic ideal was emerging. Childhood was constructed as a unique and privileged moment presided over by a patriarchal, but affectionate, father and a loving mother who oversaw her children's upbringing, although most of the actual responsibility and physical labour was relegated to servants. This was a common theme of advice manuals authored by upper class women such as Lady Egarton[11] and the Honourable Juliana Susannah Seymour[12] who aimed their books at gentry class women who had servants, but did not run great houses.[13] As domestic life was increasingly conflated with private life, architects revamped space planning to accommodate new notions of private family rooms and childrearing activities.[14] Participation in the ideal carried with it more than the promise of reciprocal love and obedience, domestic bliss and healthy children; it also augured economic security, bespoke a genteel life and effectively circumscribed appropriate fields of male and female parental power.

The most striking visual evidence of the English commitment to a new childhood ideal was the significant change in clothing and the rise in commissioned and publicly exhibited portraits of children wearing those new fashions. Portraits were the most avidly commissioned genre, providing the steadiest employment for British artists and the least risk.[15] The most significant innovation in family portraiture was the increasing trend toward commissioning pictures of young children, alone or with their parents. The popularity of these portraits was so pronounced that the Earl of Fife noted that it was not just those of great families or great service but everybody 'who can afford twenty pounds, has portraits of himself, wife and children painted'.[16] Portraiture dominated all eighteenth-century English exhibitions, especially the Royal Academy, the premiere exhibition venue in London, and they offer an intriguing ground where new domestic ideology, professional practice and fashion merged.[17]

We are accustomed to rapid style changes today, especially in fashion and particularly for females. Stylistic change is scheduled, reported, advertised and retailed in a consumption cycle that is ongoing and intimately related with a multi-billion dollar clothing industry. In the eighteenth-century, there was nothing approximating a fashion industry. Stylistic change was the prerogative of the upper classes, accomplished through custom orders or done in-house, often led by royals or prominent aristocrats. It was gradual and incremental, dependent on social acceptance as well as material resources. This is critical to keep in mind since the abandonment of one set of long established practices for dressing children and the adoption of another quite different set, communicated a new ideology that redefined childhood. Fashion may be about style, but style is always a cultural symptom.

Prior to the eighteenth century, children were customarily dressed in the same styles and fabrics as their parents, according to their means. Gentry and aristocratic girls wore gowns made from luxury fabrics with stays or stiffened vertical welting which reconfigured a natural childlike torso into a miniature edition of an adult female corseted body, allowing their fashionable clothing to maintain the same lines and contours. Like swaddling, corseting was believed to reinforce good posture and, while it restricted physical flexibility, it increased the visual associations with parental status. By the 1740s with the trend for small scale, full-length portraits called 'conversation pieces', an increasing number of English patrons begin commissioning paintings of their children alone and in family groups (Fig. 7.1). These paintings demonstrate how the physical depiction of children was changing. Young children were painted with more anatomically correct proportions, fuller more rounded limbs, shorter necks and plumper faces. As patrons increasingly opted for domestic settings, that reinforced the intimacy of the family group rather than the stock column and drapery backgrounds of the previous century, their children were often shown playing and they shared canvas space with toys, games, dolls and pull carts. Children's dress, however, still remained a modified version of adult dress with gowns stiffened with stays or welting (Fig. 7.2).

Figure 7.1: Anonymous, *A Family Group in a Landscape* (c.1750). Source: The Tate Collection.

**Figure 7.2: William Hogarth, *The Graham Children* (1742).
Source: The National Gallery of Art, London.**

These were private commissions with very little, if any, public visibility beyond visitors to the home or servants, but that situation changed in 1769. The founding of the Royal Academy established a hierarchy of painters and held a juried, public venue for artists to show their work and compete for dominance in all genres. Emerging from the contentious disagreements and leadership battles that characterized the earlier Society of Artists,[18] the founding members of the Royal Academy secretly approached George III and secured his exclusive patronage. Joshua Reynolds was elected the first president, a position that he held until his death in 1792, and given an honourific title. London newspapers immediately familiarized the public with the Royal Academy, dubbing it an 'instant institution' already experienced with the exertion of genius and a testament to the prestigious artists who were the first members.[19] Although bitterly criticized for furthering their own reputations, splintering the professional community and permanently dividing working artists into two groups that the public was encouraged to perceive as unequal,[20] the Royal Academy found immediate and lasting success, much to the chagrin of the other two competing organizations. The Free Society of Artists held its last exhibition in 1783 and attributed its declining audience to 'the fascinating charm of a Royal Exhibition'.[21] Facing the same dwindling numbers, the Society of Artists collapsed in 1791, leaving the Royal Academy unchallenged as the official authority on art and the premier exhibition venue.

Upwards of twenty thousand people a year visited the Royal Academy month long exhibition offering an annual opportunity for the largest public audience to see the most prestigious contemporary art.[22] It was in the careful orchestration of exhibition that specific artists and models were tested, found successful or wanting, promoted or ignored.[23] This is the arena in which Reynolds presided as President and chief art theorist, where he crafted and exhibited a new model for childhood in which fashionable dress was complicit. For the most part, he did this in maternal portraits and those of children alone or in small groups, and these two categories constituted the largest percentage of domestic portraits exhibited in the eighteenth century.[24] Pictures of children attracted little negative attention and, although rarely the subject of lengthy reviews, their popularity with artists, patrons and a growing public was reflected in the steady rise of numbers annually exhibited. Within thirty years of the establishment of the Royal Academy, over one thousand portraits of children had been shown. The most prodigious exhibitor of children in any category was Sir Joshua Reynolds, who showed thirty-five portraits during his Royal Academy career, establishing the idealization of the English child.[25] His closest rivals were John Russell with twenty-eight portraits, John Hoppner with seventeen, John Francis Rigaud with thirteen and Thomas Lawrence with eleven, but all four were strongly dependent on models and compositions popularized by Reynolds, and they all began exhibiting well after Reynolds had established a reputation as the foremost painter of children.

Reynolds routinely represented children with stereotypical beauty, endearing innocence and refined gentility. They are plump, pink cheeked, curly haired and well dressed; they are 'pre-eminently English children'.[26] These characteristics may bear no relation to the individual persona of the sitter – Northcote readily acknowledged that Reynolds sometimes lost likeness in the portraits, but those deficiencies were compensated by the beauty of the painting.[27] Much like contemporary photographic retouching and Photoshop, these corrective practices were consistent with Reynolds's well-known position on idealization and client expectations, especially when the paintings were headed for public exhibition and wider circulation as prints. Parents and artists negotiated the representation of childhood, speaking for the child no more, or less, than modern parents do today when putting children into the hands of professional photographers, who are often selected for their distinctive styles. Ironically, Reynolds was not a favourite of the royal family. They preferred Thomas Gainsborough, who did a series of individual portraits of the royal children exhibited at the Royal Academy, cited as a courtesy to their status, but not reviewed. Gainsborough did not disguise their elongated faces and necks, thin lips and limp hair. Gainsborough's routine idealization of his adult female sitters did not extend to children, even his own. The portraits of his own daughters were probably closer to their actual appearances, which may have been his primary consideration, but they are plain and unflattering by comparison to Reynolds's approach (Fig. 7.3).

Figure 7.3: Thomas Gainsborough, *The Painter's Daughters* (1756).
Source: The National Gallery of Art, London.

In painting the aristocratic and gentry children, Reynolds navigated around the artistic theories that he presented in his Discourses, popular domestic ideologies, parental preferences and new fashions for children.[28] By the 1770's that meant painting toddlers or very young children of both sexes[29] in white dresses, made of lightweight fabrics with scooped necklines, natural bodices, short sleeves, coloured sashes and tucked skirts, what we would call today 'age appropriate clothing'.[30] By comparison to mid-century gowns that were silk or satin and still featured lace and trims, the new style was relatively simple, devoid of decoration and distinguished by fabrics that were modest in cost. The poses of Reynolds's young sitters clearly show that stays or welting had been discarded. These children are represented casually, bending over, reaching up or in active and playful poses that establish their ability to move easily in new, comfortable and fashionable clothing that is now unencumbering. Between the ages of four and six, boys were breeched and shifted to juvenile modifications of adult male suits. Depending on the stylistic changes, modern boys' suits were cut with shorter and less fitted jackets, looser trousers rather than tight breeches and shirts with soft or ruffled collars. On the other hand, girls continued to wear the same style of child's dress until they reached puberty. These dresses were designed with back lacing and deep rows of tucks near the hem that were let out as needed. While a very young girl's dress would have several rows of tucks, an eleven- or twelve-year-old, like Sarah Moulton, better known as *Pinkie* from the 1794 portrait by Thomas Lawrence, would wear a gown with all the tucks let out. The reconfiguration of dress in the eighteenth century ensured that girls from toddler to puberty wore the same style; they all dressed like little girls. Only at puberty did girls adopt more adult styles along with welted or corseted bodices, more costly fabrics and trimmings.

Reynolds's position on portraiture and its ennobling potential were well established through his *Discourses*, and he was particularly concerned about women's fashions. Always worried that changing contemporary styles – which in the eighteenth century could be anything from the number of feathers in a bonnet to the trim on a bodice – would make portraits look out-of-date too quickly, he preferred to paint women in quasi-classical or vaguely historical costumes. It was a battle that he frequently lost. Most of his female clients, like Lady Elizabeth Delmé insisted on fashionable styles for their portraits, and he increasingly demurred to their requests. However, in re-conceptualizing the image of girlhood, Reynolds found his own artistic theories dovetailing with the fashion preferences of his clients for their daughters. Both children are wearing newly fashionable dress, with the young girl attired in the favoured portrait uniform of a white dress with its short sleeves, rows of tucks and coloured sash which fit the artist's preference for simple, generic, fashionable and consistent styles. Although there were minor deviations, generally in the cut of a sleeve or shallowness of neckline, the wholesale adoption of the white dress and its repeated appearance in portraits, exhibitions and prints successfully shifted the fashionable dress into the classic dress ... at least in paintings (Fig. 7.4).

Figure 7.4: Sir Joshua Reynolds, *Lady Elizabeth Delmé and her Children*.
Source: The National Gallery of Art, London.

From eighteenth-century diaries, household accounts, fabric orders and letters, it is fairly apparent that while white dresses were rapidly becoming the preferred garb for formal portraits, everyday dress for girls was less circumscribed. The growing abundance of colourful printed cottons and muslins from India, as well as textile manufacturing in England, ensured a ready supply of lightweight fabrics that were cheap, durable, washable and available in a variety of colours and patterns. In portraits, little girls were often posed in landscapes wearing lightweight white dresses, and oblivious to the weather. This was a typical compositional choice that reinforced their health and delight in nature. In lived experience, those girls wore a broad range of coloured or sprigged fabrics. The cold, damp English climate necessitated the inclusion of underskirts and layered petticoats for warmth, as well as jackets, bonnets, gloves and short coats. Nevertheless, the portrait model for girlhood was grounded in the uniform of the simple white gown with all its connotations of innocence and purity as well as the contemporary associations of fashion and enlightened parenting.

Reynolds's paintings enjoyed even wider visibility because so many of them were engraved and printed, including portraits of young girls. Northcote noted that there were more prints after Reynolds's portraits than any other single artist.[31] Between 1754 and 1792 Reynolds authorized about 400 different engravings from his portraits, but the total was considerably larger if all the duplicates, piracies and book illustrations were considered. By comparison, less than 50 works of Gainsborough appeared as prints. Most of the engravings were made soon after the commissions were completed and exhibited pictures were generally engraved the same year while they were still fresh in the public mind. Two of his most popular portraits of little girls were exhibited at the annual Royal Academy show but published as prints with the titles *Innocence* (Fig. 7.5) and *Simplicity* (Fig. 7.6) rather than the sitter's name. Such generalized titles linked popular ideological associations of girlhood with the fashionable new dress and expanded the portrait model from the exhibition space into a wider sphere of public consumption.

Figure 7.5: Sir Joshua Reynolds, *The Age of Innocence* (c. 1788).
Source: The Tate Collection.

Figure 7.6: Francis Bartolozzi after Sir Joshua Reynolds, *Miss Theophilia as Simplicity* (1989). Source: Yale Center for British Art.

While eighteenth-century concern over child rearing dramatically influenced the redesign of children's dress and established fashion guidelines for girls' clothing, any reliance on a singular style was abandoned in the nineteenth century. Industrialization, cheap manufacturing and advertising fed the desires and demands of a growing consumer base. As Enlightenment notions about childhood crystallized into modern assumptions and practices, it was less necessary to restrict girls to a uniform style. The simple garb that hallmarked eighteenth-century girlhood was a mere memory by the 1870s, supplanted by changing dress styles that took their cue from adult fashion trends again. Mid-century advertisements in popular magazines, like *Godey's Lady Book*, featured illustrations of young girls wearing the same lavishly trimmed, wasp-waisted dresses as their mothers. When pouter pigeon bodices and bustles dominated late nineteenth-century high fashion, girls' clothing featured the same silhouette and that practice continued through the twentieth century. From high-end clothing to mail order catalogues, the mantra remained the same: 'The little miss will look just like the grownups'.[32] That pattern continues through the present: mainstream girls' fashions mimic contemporary female styles and that includes cut, fabric, colours, patterns and trims.

Changing consumer demographics further complicates the situation. Children are now recognized as an independent consumer group with parents and their children in the five- to twelve-year old range spending upwards of $30 billion annually. Children's overall influence on their parents' general spending patterns has been estimated as high as $126.1 billion and growing.[33] Advertising has reacted accordingly, shifting from a focus primarily on parents to that of the child buyer who enters the store already familiar with popular culture and peer pressure. Consequently, mainstream clothing for little girls today is dependent on brand consciousness and trendy styles, incredibly sensitive to peer pressure and increasingly provocatively sexual. Girls can and do wear rhinestones and leather, clingy fabrics and cutouts, thigh high skirts and halter tops ... most of the time. This is where the category of classic clothing with its stylistic and semiotic links to the eighteenth-century portrait model reappears, generally in special occasion clothing worn for major holidays, formal portraits and ritual events. Parents customarily select special occasion dresses in anticipation of a wider audience and fully aware that their children will be the subjects of formal and informal documenting photography. Irrespective of current trends, generally purchased with a specific event in mind, often worn only a single time, classically designed, special occasion dresses share little resemblance to everyday styles or preferences. Besides their aesthetic, they serve a twenty-first century purpose that echoes that of the eighteenth.

The Florence Eiseman Company established the standard for contemporary classic girls' clothing with their first collection in 1945. Initially, these were custom made designs sold at Marshall Fields. Unique silhouettes, high quality fabrics and signature appliqués rapidly made Eiseman clothing highly recognizable and, despite their expense, the line attracted a large and loyal following with collections sold nationwide in high end stores such as Saks Fifth Avenue and Neiman Marcus, regional department stores such as Bullocks and I. Magnin, as well as numerous smaller boutiques and children's specialty shops.[34] Within ten years, Florence Eiseman had been singled out for the prestigious Neiman Marcus Award for Outstanding Contributions to fashion, the first children's clothing designer to be so honoured. In 1984, the Denver Art Museum presented a retrospective of her work, made possible because so many people had saved Eiseman clothes. Sixty-eight years after that first collection, Eiseman styles have expanded but maintain the founder's original directive and company mantra that clothes should 'let children be children'. Eiseman dresses for girls are classic in design, simple and understated with silhouettes that cover the body rather than reveal it. They are modestly embellished, often with signature appliqués and scalloped hems, and manufactured with high quality fabrics, under-stitching, linings, generous hems and extendable straps. Although there are design changes from year to year, these are subtle, often only a different colour or fabric.[35] By comparison to fashion forward girls' clothing, Eiseman special occasion dresses are expensive, but their classic style and high quality construction means they can be worn, passed down and worn again.

The range of fabrics and trims today far outstrips eighteenth-century choices, and often includes luxury fabrics, but the most popular body style for girls' special occasion clothing is still characterized by common design elements that Reynolds and his clients would recognize: easy fit, mid-calf or ankle length dresses with natural or raised waistlines, sashes, sleeveless bodices or puffed sleeves and white is often the dominant colour.[36] Unlike fashion forward clothing that can be worn for a variety of occasions and activities, and is valued for its currency with contemporary style, comfort and easy care,[37] classic dresses are blatantly conservative in cut,[38] generally much more expensive because of fragile or luxury fabrics and trims and usually require special cleaning care. Often designed, purchased and intended for a specific occasion or event, they are commonly associated with prime retailing seasons such as Christmas and Easter or ritual events such as Bar Mitzvahs, First Communions and weddings. These are the hallmarked moments when parents are willing, if not expected, to spend considerably more money on dresses whose design and fabric bear little resemblance to everyday clothing. That cost and stylistic shift is more than compensated for by the pictorial documentation that these occasions generate. Girls dressed in classic styles commonly dominate formal wedding pictures and professional studio portraits, as well as amateur family pictures on holiday occasions, lending the same sense of elegance and timelessness as their eighteenth-century portrait predecessors and garnishing the same kind of attention. Regardless of the trendy styles or ubiquitous jeans that girls wear on a daily basis, it is the classic dress that most often defines them in large, framed photographs that hang over countless mantles and march up staircases.

Synthetic fabrics, mass production and Internet retailing mean that classic designs are readily available in virtually every price range regardless of seasonal preferences or geographical location. At the high end, there are the prohibitively costly dresses of Joan Calabrese, often running into hundreds of dollars (Fig. 7.7). Focusing exclusively on girls' special occasion clothing, Calabrese has signature designs in the costume collections of both the Metropolitan Museum and the Philadelphia Museum of Art.

Figure 7.7: Girls' dress designed by Joan Calabrese (*c.*2015).

Although made in luxury fabrics and often embellished with pearls, crystals and re-embroidered lace, Calabrese designs remain heavily indebted to the eighteenth-century model and its associations of girlish innocence and simplicity. They invariably feature the same signature elements that redefined childhood materially and pictorially: high waistlines, sashes, scooped necklines, mid-calf hemlines, full skirts and easy fit. Internet advertising for these dresses reinforces both the timelessness and elegance of the classic style, but also their association with portraiture, a subtle reminder to prospective buyers that these are dresses with a celebrated design history. A typical Calabrese ad features a single young girl against a pale background and, ironically, that background generally remains the same for a toddler model as well as a tween, reinforcing the continuity of desirable and ideal girlhood qualities. At the low end are retailers selling similar designs in inexpensive synthetic fabrics to parents who want the classic look and associations for a fraction of the cost. Because the classic style dress accommodates such a wide variety of body types, the majority of classic styles are sold in sizes that accommodate toddlers to tweens, offering a generalized configuration of female fashion identity, even though it is highly improbable that a twelve-year-old girl would normally wear clothing identical to a two-year old.[39]

Derived from an eighteenth-century model that was widely circulated through exhibition and print distribution and which remains highly visible in museums and on the internet, today's classically designed special occasion clothes construct a palpable but momentary simulacrum of historical innocence and youthful elegance for the wearer and deliver a comforting message of stability and security for the viewer. In this they share a common bond with eighteenth-century girls, patrons and audiences. For contemporary parents whose young daughters daily resemble miniature versions of fashionably dressed adults ranging from jeans and tee shirts to thigh high dresses and spandex tops, the classic dress offers an appealing, and justifiable option despite the cost and limited opportunities for repeated wearing. Overlaying its conservative style with the seductive veneer of fabrics and trims that echo both costume and fantasy dress, these special occasion clothes reinforce a popular belief that every little girl is a princess and that special occasions automatically command different styles. As the favoured garb for holidays and ritual events, as well as the accompanying formal and informal photography that both documents and celebrates their significance, classic dresses demarcate a fashion terrain of an unchanging ideal girlhood, innocence and upper-class aspiration, successfully re-creating the same timelessness that Reynolds established with his reconceptualization of the eighteenth century child in portraiture.

8 PRINCELY PORTRAITS OF ADOLESCENCE IN THE HABSBURG COURT OF PHILIP II IN THE MID-SIXTEENTH CENTURY

Lisa Tom

In the Spanish court of Philip II (1527–98), between 1559 and the late 1560s, three Habsburg princes were raised and educated together: Don Carlos (1545–68), the king's son and heir, Alessandro Farnese (1545–92), the king's nephew and heir to the Italian dukedoms of Parma and Piacenza and Don John of Austria (1547–78), the king's illegitimate half-brother. These youths were close in age, Alessandro and Don Carlos were born only two months apart, and Don John was younger by two years. During their time together at court, the likenesses of the young princes were frequently recorded to take note of their development, to assess their viability in marriage negotiations and to be displayed in emerging portrait galleries in European courts. This was in line with the practice of the Habsburg rulers to cultivate the production, reproduction and distribution of high quality portraits of members of their royal household, to maintain a sense of presence over their subjects and with family members across the expanse of Europe. Both Philip II and his sister Juana of Portugal (1535–73), who served as regent for Philip in Spain, avidly commissioned works for their portrait collections in their respective palaces, El Pardo and the Descalzas Reales. In a recent monograph, Maria Kusche analyzes the patronage of and formal influences between original paintings, copies and adaptions of portraits by the court artists Anthonis Mor (1517–77), Alonso Sánchez Coello (1531–88), Sofonisba Anguissola (c.1532–1625) and Jorge de la Rúa (act.1552–78).[1] Kusche explores the formal, semi-private, familiar and genealogical functions of the portraits and acknowledges almost all early portraits of Don Carlos, Alessandro and Don John fit within a broad schema of depictions of youths.[2] This article further explores the concept of adolescence through these representations. Examined individually, the paintings of the princes appear to emulate those of Philip II and sometimes his father, Emperor Charles V (1500–58). Considered as a group, this mimicry of forms does not merely set out to depict a child or adolescent as a miniature adult. These princely portraits also present an understanding of early modern adolescence as youthful promise that was observed and illustrated by their evident physical growth between images and the attributes that indicate the titles and roles they were expected to fulfil as adults.

The Adolescent Portraits of Alessandro Farnese: Emulation, Fealty and Youthful Promise

Before 1559, Alessandro's portrait program appears to have been more formally developed than the other two princes' and had a more direct message of Habsburg fealty (Figs 8.1 and 8.2). Until Don Carlos's early death at the age of twenty-three, the prince was Philip's only son and heir apparent, born to the king's first marriage with Princess Maria Manuela of Portugal (1527–45). Philip's second marriage to Mary I of England (1516–58) bore no children and his third marriage to Isabel of Valois (1545–68) produced only two daughters. Don John's very existence had been a secret until the death of Charles V, in 1558, when it was revealed that the emperor had sired an illegitimate son with the daughter of a Regensburg burgher. The following year, Philip brought his half-brother to Spain, to recognize him officially and to integrate him into court. The earliest extant portraits of Don Carlos and Don John are intimate and informal, such as the miniature of Don Carlos in the Museo Lázaro Galdiano in Madrid, or the small panel of Don John with mussed hair in the Art Institute in Chicago. These works were meant primarily to convey the facial likenesses of the princes to other family member in the Habsburg courts of Vienna or Brussels. In contrast, Alessandro's position in Philip's court was less certain, and his portraits attempt to reinforce more tangible ties to the Habsburg rulers to whom the Farnese owed their allegiance.

Figure 8.1: Anthonis Mor, *Portrait of Alessandro Farnese* (1557). On the concession of the Ministero dei Beni, delle Attività Culturali e del Turismo -Galleria Nazionale di Parma.

Figure 8.2: Anthonis Mor, *Portrait of Alessandro Farnese* (1561). Meadows Museum, SMU, Dallas. Algur H. Meadows Collection, MM.71.04. Photography Michael Bodycomb.

Alessandro was the only son of Ottavio Farnese (1524–86), the grandson of Pope Paul III (1468–1549) and Margaret of Parma (1522–86), the illegitimate daughter of Emperor Charles V (1500–58). When he was born in 1545, the duchies of Parma and Piacenza had been scarcely established by the pope, who had sought to create a ducal dynasty for his Farnese descendants.[3] Alessandro's very existence as heir gave the family a crucial sense of stability through succession and continuity. However, Charles V refused to ever acknowledge the new duchies. When the emperor abdicated, in 1555, Philip II became the king of Spain and agreed to recognize the Farnese's claims to Parma and Piacenza on certain conditions, including that the eleven-year-old Alessandro would attend and be educated in Philip's court until the age of twenty. This arrangement became a mutual opportunity for Philip to try to instill a sense of Habsburg loyalty in his young nephew and for the Farnese to win favour with the Spanish king. Thus several of Alessandro's youthful portraits were commissioned to demonstrate or possibly even to encourage the Farnese family's allegiance to Habsburg rulers.

Prior to Alessandro's departure from Parma to his uncle's court at the end of 1556, his mother Margaret commissioned an elaborate, full-length portrait of her son, painted by Girolamo Mazzola Bedoli (c.1500–69).[4] The allegorical painting celebrates Alessandro as the heir to the Farnese dynasty beside a female personification of Parma, which suggests a thematic semblance to Parmigianino's *Allegorical Portrait of Charles V*, painted twenty-five years prior, in 1530.[5] Parmigianino had meant to impress the emperor with an inventive composition, by depicting the ruler sitting or kneeling before a female allegory of Fame or Glory, who holds in either hand a branch of laurel and palm, symbols of victory.[6] In the lower left corner, a baby Hercules presents, to the emperor, a globe of the world. Bedoli adapted Parmigianino's vision of mature triumph into an image of youthful promise. In the later painting, Alessandro sits on the globe of the world, that was metaphorically conquered by his grandfather, and looks forward to accomplishing great deeds of his own. He steadies himself with a baton of command in his right hand and one arm thrown around the neck of an allegorical female figure of Parma. In an ornamental *all'antica* breastplate and helmet, the figure of Parma kneels by the prince's side and embraces him with her right arm, while she cradles the coat of arms of Parma in her left arm. The young prince wears a set of etched and gilt cavalry armour with bright red stockings and slippers, his helmet sits at the ready on the floor to his right and a sword hangs from his left hip. The age of ten, as Alessandro appears in the painting, is about the time a boy would begin his martial training and receive his first suit of armour. Judging by the high degree of detail, the painting possibly reflects an actual piece owned and worn by the prince. In the upper left corner, behind Alessandro, a small bronze figure of Fame blows her trumpet, heralding the future glory of the next Duke of Parma. Alessandro never met his imperial grandfather and would have only known him through deferential images such as that by Parmigianino. Bedoli's painting was the first of many such portraits of the young prince that were meant to evoke the Habsburg rulers as exemplars, to whom Alessandro and the Farnese family owed their allegiance.

An example that explicitly illustrates Philip II's influence over Alessandro's youthful development and allegiance is a medal produced by Gianpaolo Poggini (1518–c.1582) at the bequest of the Farnese in 1559.[7] On the obverse, the prince's left facing profile is depicted in armour and the legend along the edge identifies him at thirteen years of age. The reverse reveals a horse rearing up on its hind legs, gazing up to the right at a flaming torch or a stylized thunderbolt, bearing a crown and a pair of wings. This image was based on the proposal of an *impresa* by the poet Annibale Caro (1507–66), who was commissioned by Margaret, in 1557. Caro imagined the young prince as an untamed horse, gazing upon the light of a torch that bore wings.[8] According to the poet, the light represented Philip II, who had the power to elevate Alessandro from being a humble horse into a splendid Pegasus. An inscription above the horse reads: HVIVS AVRA (By his wind), referring to Alessandro and the glory that might be bestowed upon him by Philip. The medal evidently impressed the king, as he commissioned several medals of his own from Poggini over the next decade.

The motif of flight and elevated greatness also appears in the earliest extant formal representation of an apparently twelve-year-old Don Carlos, painted by Coello, in about 1557. The prince is shown wearing a golden yellow ensemble with a heavy coat lined with lynx fur. A window in the upper left corner of the painting reveals a distant mountainous landscape and an eagle carrying aloft a column towards the heavens, where a figure sits enthroned in the clouds. The eagle was an imperial emblem of the Habsburg family and Kusche suggests that the column evoked the legend of Hercules, thereby presenting Don Carlos as a successor to the heroic figure from antiquity.[9] The painting was probably once a more commanding full-length depiction, but it was later cropped just above the knees, which would have conveniently masked part of his deformity. Don Carlos had been born with severely uneven shoulders and legs, and a letter from the Venetian ambassador Federico Badoaro describes the prince as having a sickly, pale countenance and an oversized head.[10] Coello obfuscates these defects in his painting with a voluminous furred coat and a large black cap. Kusche proposes that the frontal pose with his hands on his hips is reminiscent of the various full-length portraits of Charles V from the 1530s. While the image itself does not immediately bring to mind that of the emperor, it does share a relatively stark simplicity that emphasizes an authority seemingly inherent in the figure itself.

In a similarly unadorned manner, the less elaborately allegorical portraits of Alessandro, produced during his time in Philip's court, were equally emphatic in their display of Habsburg loyalties. A few months after Margaret and her son arrived at Philip's court in Brussels, the duchess commissioned Anthonis Mor to paint a portrait of Alessandro (Fig. 8.1), probably based on a 1554 painting of the king from Titian's workshop.[11] The painting of Alessandro is signed by Mor and dated to 1557. In both full-length portraits, the subjects stand within a nondescript interior and are dressed in cream colours and dark furred coats. Their poses mirror one another with one leg extended, one hand on the hilt of a dagger or sword and the other hand holding a pair of gloves. Despite relatively minor differences, such as Philip's lavishly embroidered blue and gold sleeves, his gaze off to the side, Alessandro's fuller fur coat and his engaging gaze towards viewers, the two overall compositions share a strong resemblance, with comparable colour palettes and the same basic pose. Letters sent to Ottavio from Brussels indicate that Philip took a personal interest in his nephew's portrait, and that the painting was meant to present him as a prince 'refined by the judgment of a king'.[12] Joanna Woodall notes Alessandro's distinctly Habsburg appearance in Mor's portrait and interprets it as a sign of the Farnese family's lack of political autonomy as they were beholden to Philip.[13] Conversely, molding the young prince into the model of Habsburg portraiture could be understood as a privilege and a sign of his acceptance as a part of the royal *familia*, as the king himself had taken an interest in Alessandro's portrait and had served as its exemplar.

Mor's portrayal of Alessandro served as a model for Sofonisba Anguissola, when she painted a half-length portrait of the prince in about 1560.[14] The painting was one of her first works upon arriving at the Spanish court and may have been an early test of her skills.[15] Kusche suggests that Anguissola may have been chosen to paint Alessandro because she herself had spent some time in Parma.[16] The young prince is portrayed in almost the exact same three-quarter stance as Mor's painting, with his head turned to look at viewers. The arrangements of the costumes are also similar, with a fur-lined coat jauntily hanging over his shoulders and a feathered cap perched at an angle on his head. In Anguissola's painting, Alessandro is more lavishly attired in an eye-catching, sable-lined, silvery-white and gold brocade cape, the richness of which Anguissola depicts with as much clarity and attention as the prince's young face. His slashed and beribboned breeches are visible just below the expensive cloak. Anguissola enlivens the image by showing Alessandro reaching across his body to pull a single glove onto his left hand, showing the young prince in the act of assuming the noble trappings of authority. The portrait was probably intended as an updated likeness recorded for posterity and to inform his parents of their son's growth and progress. It marks his early years upon arriving at the Spanish court, before he began his studies at the University of Alcalá (now known as the Complutense University in Madrid). There exists at least one copy of Anguissola's painting by Coello, who converted the composition into a full-length portrait.[17] One of these works, if not a lost third copy, must have been sent to Italy, because Taddeo and Federico Zuccari incorporated the exact likeness and costume into a fresco panel in the *Sala dei Fasti Farnesiani* in the Villa Farnese in Caprarola.[18]

In the sixteenth century, copies of portraits of the king were sent throughout the Spanish empire, to make his royal presence felt, even in the absence of his physical presence.[19] According to Kurt Johannesson, Philip II promoted his likeness and those of his courtiers as models that, through their frank simplicity and uniformity, rhetorically cultivated a royal aura.[20] These paintings were not necessarily military in nature, but were of particular importance when displayed alongside the portraits of his viceroys and representatives in the colonies abroad. Thus, fantastical images of symbolic allegory were eschewed in favour of more literal images that might evoke a greater sense of reality. Rosemarie Mulcahy suggests that portraits in Philip's courts are 'striking in their simplicity and directness. There is an absence of allegory ... Allegory would have broken the illusion of royal presence'.[21] Philip perpetuated a powerfully direct and exemplary program of portraiture that had been established by his father. Although Charles V had complimented the inventiveness of Parmigianino's portrait, he had not taken the work into his possession or commissioned any others similar to it. Instead, the emperor preferred the simple grandeur of Titian's portraits, which became recognizable as his standard likenesses as authoritative copies were commissioned and circulated. Miguel Falomir points out that the emperor had admired the opinions of the Dutch humanist Desiderius Erasmus (1466–1536) and had probably adopted the scholar's dislike of allegorical imagery in portraits.[22] In the treatise *On the Education of the Christian Prince* (1516), Erasmus criticized portraits as mirrors of vanity but subscribed to them as promoting exemplary individuals, upon whom others might model themselves. He advocated against 'noisy displays of privileged rank' and suggested that rulers' virtues should be revealed by the force of their character alone. Portraits, such as Alessandro's, furthered Philip's royal presence through a visual echo that resonated in a portrait made at court, while under his uncle's guardianship.

Emulation may also be associated with fealty, such as in the painting of Alessandro by Mor in 1561 (Fig. 8.2).[23] This somber, full-length painting shows the sixteen-year-old prince in a suit of armour, a short ruff and white hosiery. It appears to be modelled on a similar portrait of Philip II, of which Mor had completed two copies, one while in Brussels in 1557 and another in 1560, during the artist's stay in Spain.[24] In turn, Mor had based the portrait of Philip on the full-length likeness of Charles V in armour, painted by Titian in 1548, the year of the emperor's decisive victory against the Protestant German princes of the Schmalkaldic League.[25] The work by Titian is now lost, but survives through a number of copies that show the emperor in armour and tall riding boots, holding a baton of command and standing beside a low table, where his helmet rests in front of a window. Mor's portraits of Philip in armour portray the king at the Battle of

Saint Quentin (1557), in northern France, where he scored a decisive victory over the French troops of Henry II. It was one of Philip's first major triumphs after inheriting the Spanish throne, a success that proved his martial competency and legitimized his authority. It was in the aftermath of this battle that arduous negotiations for peace had resulted in the Treaty of Cateau-Cambrésis, which forced France to withdraw from Italy, giving Spain political dominance in the area. Although Philip had not actually arrived at the battlefield until after the fighting, Mor portrays him as a ready and able knight, in his armour and long riding boots and spurs with his left hand resting on the pommel of his sword. The king's rank is further denoted through the baton of command grasped in his right hand, the symbol of the order of the Golden Fleece hanging from a simple crimson ribbon around his neck and the crimson scarves of a general knotted on his upper arms. The background seems dark and nondescript, but the battlefield is alluded to through the outdoor setting shown beneath the king's feet. This was Philip's testing ground, upon which he proved himself capable of defending, ruling, and succeeding in his father's place.

The Treaty of Cateau-Cambrésis included the agreement in which the Farnese claims to the duchies of Parma and Piacenza were publically formalized and recognized, including the stipulation regarding Alessandro's education in Philip's court. This makes the choice of Philip's Saint Quentin portrait particularly suitable as a model for Mor's depiction of Alessandro. In comparison to the king's appearance, however, Alessandro is shown markedly bereft of any sign of merit, command or membership in a knightly order. The young Farnese prince appears handsomely equipped with gold-trimmed armour, sword and dagger, but the image still represents only the future potential of the great deeds or acclaim he has yet to accomplish. The background is utterly nondescript, black with vague, smooth dark brown flooring along the bottom to suggest an interior setting. In neat gold letters to the left of his head, a simple inscription reads: ANNO AETATIS SVE. XVI. 1561 ('At age 16. 1561'). Alessandro's stated youthfulness is the primary context for this portrait, with a blank background and lack of titles or distinction, so much remains unfulfilled. He has yet to ascend to the head of a noble condottiere papal family or the titles of Duke of Parma and Piacenza. Even his place within the Habsburg court remained ill-defined beyond his blood relation as Philip's nephew. Alessandro held no official post or formal position and, on occasion, was stigmatized for being the son of a merely illegitimate daughter of the emperor. His force of character and nobility was conveyed, to a large degree, through his resemblance to the king's likeness.

Coello completed at least two copies of Mor's portrait of Alessandro in armour, a full-length duplicate and a three-quarter-length version.[26] These duplicates suggest that this image was a significant update of the prince's likeness, and the marked changes in the prince's appearance indicate a distinctly later phase of adolescence. Compared to his previous portraits, Alessandro appears notably taller and leaner, his face has lost much of its childish roundness and faint wisps of facial hair dust the tip of his chin and above his lips. Scholars observe a conspicuous rise in the display of facial hair as a necessary male adult attribute in early modern Europe, beginning in the first few decades of the sixteenth century.[27] Douglas Biouw tracks the conscientious progress of Cosimo de' Medici's struggle to grow a full beard in his portraits from the 1530s and 1540s.[28] The early beginnings of a beard and mustache would have been of some note in Alessandro's portrait. Moreover, his more mature physical stature separates him from the more distant fantasy of military accomplishment, as shown in Bedoli's allegorical representation from six years prior. Both portraits represent a liminal state of youthful promise, but Mor's later portrait depicts a confident young man closer to the brink of adulthood, upon the completion of his training and education and awaiting an official assignment of duties or titles.

Adapting an Adolescent Model for Portraits of Don Carlos and Don John

While Alessandro's portraits emulated those of the king, Mor's painting of the young prince from 1557 seems to have served as a model for Coello's later depictions of Don Carlos and Don John. However, Coello approached the two works very differently. Don John's portrait from 1560 is more embellished with a sumptuous display of ornamentation and a more complex twisting pose (Fig. 8.3). Then, the artist reverted back to Mor's composition, following it quite closely for Don Carlos's portrait in 1564 (Fig. 8.4). It is possible that, after some artistic experimentation, a more standardized format took hold.

Figure 8.3: Alonso Sánchez Coello, *Don John* (1560). Museo Soumaya, Fundación Carlos Slim, Mexico City.

Figure 8.4: Alonso Sánchez Coello, *Don Carlos* (1564). Kunsthistorisches Museum, Vienna. Gemäldegalerie.

On 22 February 1560, in Toledo, Philip II arranged a lavish swearing in ceremony, in which he officially recognized Don Carlos as his heir apparent and a grand procession of elite members of the court swore their allegiance to the prince. Don John stood beside Don Carlos and was formally recognized for the first time, as a royal prince, the natural born son of an emperor and half-brother to the king. Alessandro took part in the processional retinue, who were all reportedly adorned in a vast quantity of gold thread. At about this time, perhaps to commemorate the momentous occasion, Coello painted a full-length copy of Anguissola's portrait of Alessandro and the first formal, full-length portrait of Don John (Fig. 8.3).[29] Coello maintains the basic form of Mor's model, the three-quarter turn of the body to the right and direct gaze towards viewers. His changes might have been intended to give the impression of a more commanding figure, dispensing with any cape or coat that would obscure the bodily form, Don John's left wrist casually resting against the hilt of his sword, his left hand held before him and grasping gloves and his right hand firmly placed on his hip with his elbow projecting outward. Possibly, in an attempt to liven the pose, Coello depicts the prince with his hips swiveled, crossing his right leg in front of his left. His garments are also more sumptuous with gold buttons, intricate silver patterns woven into the gold cloth and a heavy gold chain around his neck. The lavish quality of the costume and overt courtly manner of Don John's portrait was possibly meant to demonstrate his superior status as the king's half-brother, while Alessandro was merely the king's nephew.

Also in about 1560, Jorge de la Rúa painted a more modest three-quarter length portrait of Don John. The work was commissioned at the bequest of Joanna of Portugal, who had begun to build a family portrait gallery in the convent of the Descalzas Reales in Madrid.[30] Between 1554 and 1559, Joanna had served as Regent of Spain on behalf of her brother, Philip II, and biographers often note the mutual affection that she held for the three princes. Kusche points out that Don John's portrait is reminiscent of both Mor's 1554 depiction of Alessandro and his similar half-length depiction of Joanna's late husband, Don João of Portugal (1537–54). The latter was painted in 1552, and compared to the image of Alessandro, differs in length, his arms fitted into the sleeves of his jacket, the rosy red of his doublet and a greater sense of presence as his broader shoulders fill the canvas. It would seem that while Coello aggrandized the model provided by Mor, Jorge de la Rúa simplified the three-quarter length figure of Don John, eliminating the gallant coat and jaunty hat. There is an understated assertiveness in the brilliant crimson of the entire costume, the hose, the sleeves, the slashed breeches and leather doublet overlaid with silver. He also stands with both legs straight, his right hand on his hip and right elbow confidently held out from his body.[31]

Four years later, in 1564, Coello closely replicated Mor's portrait of Alessandro to portray Don Carlos (Fig. 8.4).[32] The painting was to be sent to the

Habsburg court in Vienna, accompanied by a written assessment of the prince's marital potential and health. The matter was under close scrutiny after the prince had only narrowly recovered from a severe head injury in 1562.[33] The fact that Alessandro had been twelve in Mor's portrait, and that it was still seen as a suitable model for Don Carlos's portrait at the age of nineteen, perhaps indicates the broad age group associated with adolescence. Similar to Alessandro's portrait, Don Carlos appears in cream coloured attire with a dark coat thrown over his shoulders and a feathered cap atop his head. He stands with his body turned three-quarters to the right, one leg extended before him and looks outward towards viewers. The artist tries to minimize the uneven slant of the prince's shoulders and the awkward stretch of the shorter right leg. The placement of his hands is more commanding, his right resting on his hip and his left on the pommel of his sword, more closely resembling Coello's depiction of Don John. The Collar of the Golden Fleece proudly hangs on his chest and, compared to the other portraits, his codpiece stands out more prominently, emphasized by its overlap with his sword belt. Considering the function of the painting within the context of marriage negotiations, the size of the prince's codpiece might have been a subtle indication of the prince's virility in compensation for his lack of maturity or facial hair. In addition to his birth defects, visitors to court often observed that Don Carlos's growth seemed somewhat stunted, which may have been especially noticeable alongside the other two princes. It is perhaps for this reason that Don Carlos's portrait was modelled so closely after Mor's depiction of Alessandro. While the former was known for his violent and intemperate outbursts and cruelty towards animals, Alessandro and Don John were admired for their seemingly inherent nobility and grace. It is the character of the latter two princes that perhaps the artist was hoping to project onto the image of the crown prince. However, in the letter that accompanied the painting to Vienna, the Imperial Ambassador Adam von Dietrichstein (1527–90) criticizes Coello for glossing over the prince's physical defects, his pale and sickly complexion, his inattentive and perpetually slack-jawed facial expression, his uneven shoulders, sunken chest, hump on his back and the uneven length of his legs.[34] It would seem that the artifice of portraiture, its associative properties and perceived influence had reached its limits.

The almost standardized adoption of Mor's full-length and Jorge de la Rúa's three-quarter-length adolescent portrait formats in relatively neutral dress becomes more evident in the representations of the four Habsburg princes educated in Philip's court in the following decade.

Expanding the Early and Late Adolescent Models and Building Continuity

In 1564, accompanied by Adam von Dietrichstein, Archdukes Rudolf (1552–1612) and Ernst (1553–95) from the Austrian Habsburg branch arrived in Madrid, to be educated in the Spanish Habsburg court of Philip II. When Charles V had abdicated, he had bequeathed the title of Holy Roman Emperor to his brother, Ferdinand I (1503–64), whose son Maximilian II (1527–76) was married to María of Spain (1528–1603), the daughter of Charles V, and sister of Philip II. Their union produced sixteen children, of whom Rudolf and Ernst were the two eldest sons to survive past infancy. After Don Carlos's accident in 1562, Philip became concerned about his line of succession, which would have fallen to his Imperial relations. Bearing in mind that one of his sister's sons might one day take up the Spanish crown, Philip proposed that Rudolf and Ernst, who were respectively twelve and eleven years of age, complete their adolescent education in Spain, much in the same manner as Don Carlos, Don John and Alessandro.[35] María was eager to have her sons raised in a more Catholic environment and convinced her husband to comply. When Rudolf and Ernst returned to Vienna after eight years of their formative youth under Philip's guidance, they bore the aloof ceremonial mannerisms of the Spanish court, much to the consternation of their father and delight of their mother. Some of this courtly bearing is perhaps evident in their early portraits by Coello in 1567 (Fig. 8.5).

Figure 8.5: Alonso Sánchez Coello, *Emperor Rudolf II* (1567). Hampton Court. Royal Collection Trust / © Her Majesty Queen Elizabeth II (2014).

Coello's three-quarter-length portraits of Rudolf and Ernst were commissioned as a pendant pair, almost mirroring one another. The two compositions follow the format of Jorge de la Rúa's depiction of Don Juan in about 1560.[36] The colours of the archdukes' dress are more understated, simple black doublets with gold trim and buttons over pale gray sleeves, breeches and hoses. Rudolf stands with his body turned three quarters to the right, while looking out towards viewers from the corners of his eyes. His right elbow projects outward as he rests his right hand against his hip. Instead of grasping the hilt of his sword, he holds a pair of gloves in his left hand, which allows his brother to compliment the action more gracefully in his pendant portrait. Ernst turns three-quarters to the left, rests his left hand on the hilt of his sword that hangs on his hip and holds a pair of gloves in his right hand. Another subtle adjustment refers back to Mor's full-length model, as the boys appear to rest their weight on one leg and stretch the other out before them, giving the three-quarter length portraits a greater sense of energy. Each of these gestures, stepping forward, holding their gloves slightly away from their body and angling their elbows, contributes to their command of the space around them. And yet, they are presented in a fairly neutral manner, without symbols of rank or title, but as youthful adolescents readying themselves for their future positions. That forthcoming potential is suggested through another pair of portraits, of Don Carlos and Don John, which may have hung beside the original paintings of Rudolf and Ernst in Philip II's portrait gallery.

The portraits of Rudolf and Ernst had been probably commissioned for king's portrait gallery in El Pardo, Philip's idyllic country palace north-west of Madrid. Completed sometime in the 1560s, the entire collection was lost in a fire in 1604. There are two almost identical extant copies of the pair, one now in Hampton Court in London and the other in the Museum Enrique Larreta in Buenos Aries. Joanna Woodall posits that the gallery served to reinforce both Philip's genealogy and his identity as it was constituted through his subjects.[37] Through the written descriptions and the extant copies of the portraits, Kusche visually attempts to reconstruct the gallery, which would have occupied a long hall.[38] At one end of the hall, hung the king's portrait, with those of his parents to his right and two of his sisters to his left. At the other end of the hall, hung a portrait of the queen, with the two Austrian Habsburg princes on one side and Don Carlos and Don Juan on the other. Woodall argues that the genealogical theme may have been intended as a reminder to the royal couple of their duty to procreate, as the queen was flanked by portraits of Philip's heir apparent and potentially three presumptive heirs.[39] However, from the perspective of the princes, when considering the juxtaposition of the two pairs of portraits, two distinctive stages of early and late adolescent development becomes apparent.

In contrast to the sparse form of Rudolf and Ernst in Coello's paintings, the images of Don Carlos and Don John, who were five to seven years older, were laden with symbols of duties, titles and official courtly positions. The portrait of Don Carlos chosen to hang in Philip's El Pardo portrait gallery was probably a heavily idealized three-quarter-length likeness devised by Anguissola in 1567, now known through copies by Coello and his workshop.[40] In the paintings, the prince appears quite regal, wearing silvery white brocade trimmed with gold, a thick white fur coat and the full gold collar of the Order of the Golden Fleece. It is the only likeness of Don Carlos, at the age of twenty-two, to have just the slightest hint of a growing mustache above his lips. Also in about 1567, Coello painted two portraits of Don Juan, one for Philip's gallery in El Pardo and the other for Joanna of Portugal's gallery in the Descalzas Reales, where the painting still remains.[41] The painting displays the twenty-year-old Don John on the eve of his first official assignment to Naples. He wears gold-embossed armour, a red officer's sash bound across his chest and the collar of the Order of the Golden Fleece around the base of his neck. He grasps the hilt of his sword in his left hand and a baton of command in his right. Similar to Don Carlos, he appears much more mature, with broader shoulders, more defined facial features and the faint beginnings of a mustache.

Woodall theorized that the portrait gallery in El Pardo, with its representations of royalty and prominent individuals in Philip's court, might be understood as a visual embodiment of the literary genre of the mirrors of princes.[42] These were instructional treatises that were meant to direct young rulers, much like Erasmus's *On the Education of the Christian Prince* mentioned above. While the monarch served as the ideal embodiment of virtue and personality, this did not preclude the contribution or perpetuation of the ruler's image through his relations and his own courtiers. Thus, the young Rudolf and Ernst might gaze upon the late adolescent forms of Don Carlos and Don John as their immediate counterparts, into which they will grow.

Conclusion

In 1570, before the Archdukes Rudolf and Ernst returned to Vienna the following year, they were joined by two of their younger brothers, Albert (1559–1621) and Wenceslas (1561–78). The younger brothers arrived in Spain with their eldest sister, Anna of Austria (1549–80), who was to become Philip's fourth wife. The young princes were also there to take their elder brothers places, to be educated in their uncle's court.[43] In 1574, when Albert and Wenceslas were fifteen and fourteen years of age, Coello painted their portraits (Fig. 8.6). The process seemed almost familiar, at that point. Three sets were made, a pair sent to Vienna, another to El Pardo, though they were not displayed as a part of Philip's official gallery and another to Joanna's galleries in the Descalzas Reales.[44] In full-length portraits that loosely mirrored one another, the young boys stood at a three-quarter angle, one leg extended in front of them, one hand resting on the hilt of their sword or a window sill and the other hand, either petting a dog or holding a falcon, which adds a playful and informal element. They are dressed in fine white and gray outfits, but wear no titles or offices, which they have yet to obtain. Then, in 1577, Albert became a cardinal at the age of eighteen and Wenceslas became the Grand Prior of the Order of Malta in Castile. Coello was once again called upon to commemorate the princes's passages into early adulthood. He depicts them in full-length portraits, Albert in red cardinal robes and Wenceslas in the dark cloak and white eight pointed star of the Order of Malta. Their smooth faces and thin gangly bodies belies the official positions they are expected to fulfill.

Figure 8.6: Copy after Alonso Sánchez Coello, *Archduke Albert with a Hound* (1574). Kunsthistorisches Museum, Vienna. Gemäldegalerie.

9 TITIAN'S *CLARISSA STROZZI*: THE INFANT AS IDEAL BRIDE

Brian D. Steele

Titian's painting of the two-year-old Clarissa Strozzi (Fig. 9.1) embodies characteristics of childhood esteemed during the sixteenth century.[1] She stands within an interior on the painting's central axis and embraces a lapdog seated upon a table inscribed TITIANUS F, below which rests a relief carved with putti. The diagonal of the left putto's rear arm recurs in the crease of red velvet; above, drapery reiterates that diagonal in folds crumpled upon a window-ledge opening to landscape. Paralleled folds formally link putti with two diminutive swans discernable in the distance. At upper left, a tablet declares Clarissa's age and dates the image 1542.[2] Luba Freedman identified the interior with figure-at-window as a formula of state portraits, as for example Titian's depiction of Eleonora Gonzaga, *c.*1536–8 (Fig. 9.2), and directed attention to figural proportions true to infancy, leading Freedman to characterize the image as the state portrait of a child as child.[3] Since the emotional focus constitutes child embracing dog, elements that Pietro Aretino had praised for living naturalism in his letter dated 6 July 1542,[4] Freedman identified the motif as manifestation of the artist's *concetto*, 'Clarissa's childlike essence'. 'Child-like', for Freedman, comprised emotive characteristics of modern childhood, prompting elucidation of swans as purity, landscape as threat, dog as protector and putti as *innocenti*. Challenging the notion of a childlike child according to modern norms, Lauren Reed analyzed bodily axes that articulate a slightly unbalanced posture, which she attributed to inexpert execution of a *figura serpentinata*: lacking *sprezzatura*, the child's attempts embody adult-in-making.[5] This essay examines the painting as product of a dialogue among patron, artist and societal expectations which thus evokes characteristics of childhood, Clarissa's anticipated role as wife and affective and patrilineal issues; ultimately, it facilitates understanding how the portrait generates meaning by combining elements that intimate development toward her adult role. Doing so requires consideration of sixteenth-century expectations of portraiture, notions about childhood and familial issues that shaped expectations of Clarissa herself.

Figure 9.1: Titian, *Portrait of Clarissa Strozzi at the Age of Two Years* (1542).
Photo Credit: bpk, Berlin / Gemäldegalerie, SMB / Jörg P. Anders / Art Resource, NY.

Figure 9.2: Titian, *Eleonora Gonzaga della Rovere, Duchess of Urbino* (c.1536–38).
Photo Credit: Scala / Art Resource, NY.

Rather than simply presenting likeness, early modern portraiture in Italy assumes the status of representation. This could hardly be other since portraits present the essential rather than the momentary and they functioned within a display culture, in which appearance marked social standing, external beauty signaled inner virtue and ability to evoke qualities of the soul challenged artists in the *paragone* between painting and poetry.[6] In fact, Pomponius Gauricus praised physiognomy in 1504 as 'a way of observing by which we deduce the qualities of souls from the features of bodies'; however, equation of appearance with social standing also situated portraiture as cultural document to be examined in the context of societal expectations.[7] In the case of children lacking agency, portraiture modulated likeness with ideas about children that parents and patrons desired to project, whether to promote dynastic continuity, preserve perceptions of patrilineal values or trace bonds of affection. Moreover, Sally Hickson has shown that Isabella d'Este completed and corrected the visual image with oral testimonials to the sitter's character: thanking the Countess of Acerra for her portrait gifted in 1493, Isabella proposed to 'often look at [the portrait of the Countess] correcting the defects of the artist with the help of the information from Jacopo and others who have seen you, so that we may not be deceived in our concept of you'.[8] Thus, conjoining verbal discourse and visual representation demonstrates the probable means by which patron and painter created Clarissa's portrait, others could delight in 'correcting' qualities discerned therein and the portrait could be presented as a moral mirror for Clarissa's own development in a process of generating meanings evoked by the image, as circumstances of viewing altered.

Scale and imagery suggest transitory time and change. Titian's portrait of Pietro Aretino, *c.* 1545 (Fig. 9.3),[9] whose bulk oppresses the frame, is nearly the same size (1.08 x 0.76 m) as is that of Clarissa Strozzi (1.15 x 0.98 m). As a result, she seems childlike in figural proportions *and* in proportional relationship to the pictorial field. However, its bifurcation engenders notable affects: concentrating on the left portion situates the infant in a shadowed setting that emphasizes her fragility vis-à-vis the frame; when continuing scansion toward the right, Clarissa seems subtly more assured. A stable stance, implied by arm cradling puppy, contributes to this effect; more important, to judge from hip and waist, she would be able to sit at the low table just as Eleonora Gonzaga does at adult-scaled furniture (Fig. 9.2). Eleonora's window has a sill situated at a standing adult's waist-level, while Titian lowered Clarissa's window-ledge to the waist of a two-year-old, thereby permitting her head's silhouette to dominate the horizon, just as that of a *seated* adult, like Eleonora, could do were her chair situated in front of the window. In the right half of Clarissa's portrait, effects drawn from the portrait-repertoire for adults 'age' and dignify the child by implication; moreover, pictorial weighting of picture in this direction with interrelated objects, bracketed by Clarissa's slipper and a rhyming slipper-like drapery fold at the right, intimates that this portion concerns her. Scansion concludes in convoluted drapery: its folds rhyme with slipper, reveal putti to view and spread over sill as gesture toward landscape. Fabric closes the pictorial narrative with a nexus of objects and allusions. The totality of narrative scansion thus moves from fragile child to implications of adult dignity and to an unspecified, more portentous state: these factors intimate a transitive process of becoming, what I discuss as schooling the infant's demeanor into her potential as Petrarchan beauty and ideal wife.

Figure 9.3: Titian, *Portrait of Pietro Aretino* (*c*.1545). Photo Credit: Scala / Art Resource, NY.

Current scholarship complicates received ideas about Early Modern childhood. The Paduan physician Michele Savonarola's publication of his treatise covering pediatric illnesses up to the age of seven, most likely composed between 1450 and 1460, indexes concern for childhood; with regard to emotional investment, parents mourned children's deaths, valued children in and for themselves, delighted in their play and could view them as either angelic innocents or, as a result of their unrestrained antics, as imps or sprites.[10] Notwithstanding interest in childhood, adult roles coloured the perception of children, particularly in the case of girls: their normative trajectory led from child and daughter to adult and mother and, as recommended by theorists including Giovanni Dominici and Desiderius Erasmus, training commenced early while the child, still 'untainted', could be shaped like wax. The age of two demarcated a significant stage that signaled weaning, closure of greatest susceptibility to childhood disease, first steps and onset of teeth and speech; so, well before the age of seven marking reasoned behavior, children were 'bent' to conform to expectations for adulthood: Erasmus disparaged a mother drilling her five-year-old daughter in courtly social forms while driving the child to tears in the process.[11] A principal goal of girls' education was producing a moral life that expressed virtues including faith, charity, reason and moderation; secondary aims comprised development of abilities and intellect. Differing in prescriptive details, authors including Erasmus, Ludovico Dolce and Juan Luis Vives considered females' education to promote virtues of modesty, obedience and chastity if confined to moral precepts of classical authors, religious studies and readings from the church fathers; an essential foundation since, as Erasmus wrote, 'A woman's spirit is necessary to hold a family together, to form and fashion the habits of children which of all things is most satisfying to a husband'.[12] Schooled in virtues, a girl prepared to model behavior for and to instill virtues in future progeny.

Virtues notwithstanding, genealogy, familial networks and circumstances determined what Clarissa's horizons of expectation might portend. Scion of noble Florentine and Roman families, the infant was daughter of Roberto Strozzi and Maddalena di Pierfrancesco de' Medici.[13] Roberto was son of Filippo Strozzi the Younger, who had married Clarice di Piero de' Medici, daughter of Piero II and Alfonsina Orsini, herself granddaughter of Lorenzo il Magnifico and Clarice Orsini. Having prospered in banking, Filippo moved to Venice by 1536 where he constituted a leader of the Florentine Republican faction until his death in 1537/38. Owing to precipitous actions of Roberto's brother Piero, the Strozzi family was expelled from Venetian territories in 1542 but, with exception of the latter, was readmitted in 1544, although Roberto moved his own family to Rome by 1546. Despite turmoil incurred by patrilineal politics, Clarissa had inherited an illustrious ancestry of powerful females. Through Filippo the Elder, Clarissa was great-great-granddaughter to Alessandra Macinghi Strozzi who competently managed familial interests and, through the Medici line, Clarissa was great-great-granddaughter of Clarice Orsini de' Medici, wife of Lorenzo il Magnifico. She, like other Medici women, noted for acts of intercession and charity, was addressed in Marian terms, emphasizing her role as benefactor of the poor who intervened when clients needed charity or mercy.[14] Clarissa's grandmother and namesake, Clarice de' Medici Strozzi, similarly acted in matters of charity and liberality: she mediated on behalf of her spouse to reduce his exile's duration, obtained benefits for her sons and instructed male associates to ignore debts as a matter of charity. Charity, liberality, capable management and ability to negotiate positions of power within the patriline constituted the 'dowry of virtue' bequeathed to the infant.

Clarissa's image and its interpretation, as we shall see, was likely inflected by its commission from a household known for patronage of music. Roberto Strozzi inherited his father, Filippo's, interests and continued his own patronage of madrigalists including Jacques Arcadelt and Adriaen Willaert. Known for musical entertainments, Roberto garnered Silvestro Ganassi's praise (1542), 'you are more adorned with harmony of the soul, harmony of the body, and vocal and instrumental harmony within your magnificent house, and delight in it more than do others'.[15] Whatever Roberto's motivations for the commission may have been, Clarissa was the only of seven children to be commemorated in infancy. He implicitly requested full length presentation when ordering a portrait of this size for a child's representation, while Titian, himself father of a daughter, probably projected hopes for a girl's development into comely wife: indeed, at the age of fifteen Clarissa married the Roman noble Cristoforo di Antonio Savelli.[16] The full-length portrayal that Titian provides, projects continued prestige, culture and wealth of the Strozzi through the image of a child expected to embody the virtues of Medici/Strozzi/Orsini women.

The unusual affective centrality of child embracing dog commands attention.[17] Physical proximity and similarity in brown and light colouration invite comparisons between the faces of infant and beast that recall Titian's interest in paralleling a puppy with childhood by physiognomic likeness. A treatise on physiognomy (1544) by the Venetian physician Michelangelo Biondo explicates qualities discernable in Clarissa's visage. Particularly important in assessing females is the quality of lips and smile: rosy lips index humoral balance indicating 'good constitution and purest blood'; smiling moderately 'reveals interior joyousness'; a 'precious quality of spirit', the smile 'indicates a sweet and affable soul'.[18] Eyes that in form are 'seemly, agreeable, and amiable exhibit kindness (bontà)', while 'sparkling eyes manifest a spirited nature'.[19] Affability, kindness and high spirits constitute admirable qualities to be shaped by education, as the puppy's very presence suggests. The association of dogs with education finds its *locus classicus* in Plutarch's parable of Lycurgus of Sparta, who demonstrated that dogs of the same stock could be habituated to differing actions, thus showing that training disciplines nature. The concepts recur in Giovanni Dominici's *On the Education of Children*, c.1401–3:

> A child is established in the habits of life ... when he begins to learn the use and direction of his own will ... And therefore, that which you wish him to be when he grows up accustom him to as a child. A dog used to the butcher shop does not become a good hunter, and a greyhound nourished on domestic food does not catch hares ... You will give the initiative, nature the increase, and the child himself when he is grown will attain the end.[20]

Owing to their perseverance, sagacity, reasoning and foresight, dogs assumed symbolic valence in fifteenth- and early sixteenth-century images of the scholar's study, and Andreas Alciatus included a dog with Diomedes as symbol of intelligence that conjoins with Ulysses's strength in Emblem 41, '*Unum nihil, duos plurimum posse*', in the authorized edition of *Andreae Alciati Emblematum Libellus* (Paris: Wechel, 1534).[21] Thus, sixteenth-century viewers could parallel intelligence and training evoked by the puppy with shaping Clarissa's amiable spirit into desirable manifestations, an idea that her clothing enhances.

Within Early Modern cultures, clothing as one's 'habit' implied a cultural way of life, externals materialized status and things-as-gifts assumed a life of their own, so appearance competed with implication of a sitter's inner life. Mary Rogers has shown how Paolo Veronese's representation of Giustiniana Giustiniani (Fig. 9.4) in the Villa Barbaro at Maser embodies virtues of the ideal wife, including sartorial display modest relative to familial prestige, gems as gifts appropriate to the husband's wealth and movements both controlled and graceful.[22] The roses she holds symbolize sensual love, while Divine Wisdom in the ceiling above the portion illustrated here gestures toward her to evoke spiritual conjoined with physical love that produces a shining exemplar, an idealizing tendency ascribed to Venetian authors' neoplatonizing exaltation of divine beauty. With regard to Clarissa's dress, in Florence white or silver satin constituted a fabric for special festivities, which has been fashioned into a gown with puffed sleeves that, paired with matching slippers, constituted standard at-home attire.[23] Since even infants were dressed to indicate station, the lightly constrained volume of Clarissa's torso, in tandem with the slight break of fabric over her advancing thigh, suggests that she trains her body in the upright posture expected of chaste wives by means of a corset. The vasquine or tight-fitting bodice of an undergarment, lacking hard stays, rounded over the stomach and sometimes exhibiting stitching with which to attach a short underskirt, was introduced to Italy during the first half of the sixteenth century as precursor to the corset per se; often termed stays, the vasquine's interlined velvet facilitated the softened contours exhibited in portraits of Italian females. More restrictive binding, which stiffened the bodice of the petticoat to form a carapace-like structure, originated during the 1540s: in 1547, the Venetian senate forbade wearing 'A new type of bodice which being very high and going very low over the stomach – these harmful and pernicious styles produce trouble, inconveniences and ruin'.[24] More than mere fashion, corseting constituted a cultural reference to standards of civility, advocated in Baldassare Castiglione's *Book of the Courtier*, as manifested in bodily control and disciplined self-presentation. Already by 1536, a French treatise on childbirth recommended corseting because, 'A young tree, if it is kept straight and bent, keeps the same shape as it grows. The same happens with children, who, if they are bound sideways and crookedly, they will remain the same way as they grow'.[25] Clarissa's body, modestly garbed relative to Strozzi prestige, and her high spirits, then, could be seen to be gently disciplined into societal expectations of controlled behavior that match the status implied by sumptuous fabric and jewels.

Figure 9.4: Paolo Veronese, *Giustiniana Barbaro and the Wetnurse with the Dog Standing at a Balcony* (Villa Barbaro, Maser) (c.1560). Photo Credit: Scala / Art Resource, NY.

Clarissa's gems and pearls at throat and wrist, modest in size only if adorning an adult, intimate multiple references the relevance of which changed as she aged. Pearls, sapphires and rubies with settings of gold in proximity to the face and hand evoke Petrarchan metaphors that complimented beauties whose hair is gold, eyes are sapphires, lips are rubies, teeth or fingernails are oriental pearls and so on, compliments that might honour a betrothed bride.[26] In reciprocal fashion, jewels heighten desirable features such as the pearly flesh; small mouth, lips smiling but revealing no teeth; and averted eyes that hint at Clarissa's self-possession and incipient power to entrance the lover with sympathetic response. Unbound curls befit her age, but jewelry already metaphorizes the lover's touch: a girdle tenderly clasps waist, a bracelet indents rosy skin and, pressing gently, her necklace culminates in pendant weighing at breast with the gold setting warmed by flesh. Although natural beauty was more esteemed than outward display, its artifice could nonetheless evoke virtues of character. Abundant gemstones betoken a foreign family's wealth and rank since they exceed display permitted by Venetian sumptuary law only to women newly wed and, in the form of clustered gems and pearls, sometimes termed a 'wifehood pendant' (*pendetta di mogliazna*), they signify Clarissa's honour and imply the dowry or counter dowry that might be expected of father and spouse upon her marriage.[27] Smaller jewels embellish her girdle, which constituted a principal ornament for women, symbolizing wealth, love and marriage, that Venetian sumptuary legislation attempted to regulate: even late in the century Cesare Vecellio indicated that unmarried brides 'wear a jeweled, floor-length belt ... '.[28] Evoking a love token and suggesting bridal finery, Clarissa's girdle, interwoven with gems comprising rubies, pearls, emeralds, and perhaps enameled blossoms intimated the infant evolving into adult. Its pendant terminal, a *Muskapfel* (apple for musk), enhanced evocations of wealth, health and love. Like a pomander, the smaller *Muskapfel* might be gifted by lovers and encased musk the strong smell of which was thought to inhibit disease. Occasionally jeweled and sometimes confused with a paternoster bead, a *Muskapfel* was divided into halves united by central screw or hinges on rims, as depicted in the portrait.[29] Either of these scented forms appropriately ornamented the girdle of infant heiress, bride or any beloved adult Venetian woman respectably garbed, given connotations comprising health and potential matrimony. The latter is augmented in Clarissa's portrait since pearls, sapphires, rubies and emeralds were often featured in marital gifts. Traditionally, pearls symbolized purity, sapphires promoted concord, diligence in prayer and chastity and emeralds embodied chastity in accordance with the idea that they shattered when a virgin is violated.³⁰ Jewels thus refer to moral virtues valued in wives, but their representation also intimated *social* virtues: Clarissa's motion is as delicate as that of the still-swaying girdle and, already controlled, will, when schooled, manifest a *figura serpentinata* enacted with *sprezzatura*. Education in social *and* moral virtues produced the ideal wife.

References to marital virtue prompt reevaluation of discursive aspects of dress and the puppy, the focus of Titian's portrait. White satin, according to Cesare Vecellio, constituted fabrics worn by unmarried brides 'to signal their fidelity and chastity', and the dog symbolized both faithfulness and fidelity, as indicated in Alciatus's emblem *In fidem Uxoriam*, reading in part, 'See the girl, who is joined to her husband (*vir*) with her right hand; see how she sits, how the puppy plays at her feet ... '³¹ Clarissa's gestures, as she embraces and perhaps feeds the dog, connoted the primary uxorial role articulated in handbooks, the nourishing procreator of offspring. At Maser (Fig. 9.4), the nursemaid, positioned beneath a grisaille representing Fecundity, protects her mistress's lapdog to complete a dyad of mistress-as-beloved and nurturer-of-family; thus, Clarissa's actions would have been construed to imply responsibilities for charitable actions toward dependents that characterized Medici and Strozzi ancestresses. The item she holds is a type of ring-breads variously termed *ciambelle*, *bracciatelle*, *brusolai*, etc., which were produced in hard forms, sometimes par-boiled and in a variety of short-lived forms rich with eggs, shortening and sugar. Costanzo Felici wrote during the 1560s of *ciambelle* ' ... made to titillate the industrious palate with many varieties ... made with flour mixed and kneaded with eggs ... some of these are light and very spongy, some covered with powdered sugar, some smoother, some harder, some low and flattened, large or small in shape ... '³² Nuns are known to have sold more delicate forms to support their convents, a religious connection perhaps commemorated in the *ciambellette di monache* which constituted a staple of the cold credenziere courses at banquets in the Este and Papal courts.³³ *Ciambelle* and other ring-breads carried Lenten associations: Bartolommeo Scappi's *Il Scalco* (1570) provides a recipe for a rich form, the *crostolo*, that is fried in oil 'for a Lenten day' and, even now, a 'version from the Veneto, *brasadèle broè*, is an Easter speciality of Pazzon di Caprino on the slopes of mount Baldus'.³⁴ The *ciambella's* role as nourishment provided by Clarissa to her puppy intimated relationship with a season of piety.

Ciambelle constitute naturalistic signs of childhood that gradually expressed more overt symbolic content. Titian's centring of the boy teasing the dog with *ciambella* in his *Presentation of the Virgin*, 1534–38 (Figs. 9.5 and 9.6),[35] evokes symbolic comment, spaced equidistant from the member of the Confraternity della Carità, dispensing alms to a woman at left, and the ancient egg seller representing the Old Testament, displaced in front of the stairway at right; above her, but behind the stair, a confraternal member restrains the crowd; above the boy and dog, another member engages the viewer with a portentous gaze. Whether the boy's action is interpreted as charity or denial, its presence in significant location comments on the principal action in genre-like form, just as the egg seller's genre-activity masks content. By the early seventeenth century, the *ciambella* was associated with charity, nurture and Christian education and, in 1634, the Florentine Cesare Dandini combined infant holding half-consumed *ciambella* with the allegorical figure of *Carità (Charity)*:[36] the later work affirms relationships among infants, breads and a 'natural' type of charity that corresponded to the virtue of liberality or generosity, consisting ' ... in giving one's belongings within reason to deserving and needy people ... ' inculcated in children, by such tracts as the *Fior di Virtu*.[37] The exemplar of homely charity provides another conceit by which Clarissa's image would have been 'corrected' to convey psychological and moral characteristics that animated outward appearance.

Figure 9.5: Titian, *Presentation of the Virgin in the Temple* (1534–8). Photo Credit: Scala / Art Resource, NY.

Figure 9.6: Titian, *Presentation of the Virgin in the Temple*, det. (1534–8). Photo Credit: Scala / Art Resource, NY.

The fictive stone relief, rarely incorporated in Titian's portraiture, suggests varied concepts applicable to family and the individual. Alluding to wealth, status and eternity, stone monuments were commissioned by Venetian patricians, so the inclusion of marmoreal relief implied the nobility and longevity of the Strozzi lineage, despite its current dispersion in exile.[38] However, since Clarissa's slipper and rhyming drapery bracket the relief and the right putto's features resemble her own, the putti implicitly refer to her own characteristics. Dancing ecstatically, fictive putti, as in Titian's *Offering to Venus*, 1518–19 (Fig. 9.7), incarnate infantile erotic vitality in service of Venus and were understood as *spiritelli*, rarified animal spirits that manifested as random impulses such as 'unwilled reactions beyond rational control produced by gazing into the lover's eyes'.[39] These animating sprites actively engendered all bodily functions, so living children, too, sometimes were termed *spiritelli* in acknowledgement of impish behavior. The vital spirits of painted putti, displaced from living *spiritella*, foreshadowed Clarissa's future as Petrarchan beauty gazing outward toward a viewer in whom a turbulence of spirit would give rise, in poetry, to the lover's sigh. In contrast to their vigorous motion, though, Clarissa's governed steps, foot skimming floor as she turns and halts, evoked the beauty moving with *leggiadria*, that demonstrated grace, modesty, nobility, charm and chastity in movements, the lightness, agility and fluid uprightness of which were appropriate for youth and nymph, i.e. the Petrarchan beloved.[40] For Pietro Bembo, in *Gli Asolani* (1505), the lady ' ... singing and dancing in a circle, moving her honest and upright and collected form to the sound of the instruments, now with slow steps showing herself worthy of the greatest reverence, now with exquisite turns, or, pausing to bow, filling, *leggiadrissima*, with beauty, the entire circle, and when with swifter steps across she is almost like a passing sun, which strikes the eyes of the beholders'.[41] Gliding forward, Clarissa's upright form implies virtues that conjoin with chastity in Matteo Bandello's *Canzoniere*: 'That celestial movement, / Her foot barely touching the ground, / The beautiful turn of that golden head, / Pausing a while so that beauty / And chastity fall all around: / Her bearing full of *leggiadria* ... , / Her noble greetings, her sweet and modest speech'.[42] Clarissa pauses, foot lightly meeting floor, for admiration of her divine beauty, modesty and chastity. *Spiritelli* on fictive relief, then, instigated multiple allusions to Clarissa's future as a Petrarchan beauty worthy of espousal.

Figure 9.7: Titian, *Offering to Venus* (1518–19). Photo Credit: Erich Lessing / Art Resource, NY.

The right portion of the painting concentrates a dense webwork of allusions and iconographic suggestiveness. Puppy and painterly materiality from which images evolve suggest the process of becoming within the flux of time;[43] airily painted *spiritelli* solidify into stone or evaporate from it as volatile spirits; velvet conceals a portion of the putto resembling Clarissa even while its convolutions suggest complete disclosure of its form; repeated rectangles of table, window and picture plane collapse background onto surface; and drapery cast over sill ruptures the window plane to unite interior scene with distant swans. When considering the passage from child to spouse, paired putti, dancing with right hands clasped in marriage, evoked the bridal state and hopes for fertility since they often adorned marital jewelry and *deschi da parto* (birth salvers); these references multiply in paired swans which recurred also on pendants or hairpieces associated with the marital state.[44] Swans underscored implications of love, grace and poetic song since they were known as creatures of Apollo, the Muse Erato inspiring lyric poetry and Venus, as for example, those swimming in the background of Titian's *Venus with Lute Player*, 1565–70 (Fig. 9.8), where they evoke both Venus and, situated in distance below the lute's neck and pegbox, lyrics sung to honour her.[45] At a wedding banquet in 1475, a swan introduced the Muse Erato and the course dedicated to Venus; according to the allegorical legend, 'the swan, because of its beauty, was an attribute of Venus, and was believed to love music and to sing most beautifully just before it died'; and, hence, 'Sacred Venus sent Erato, the Muse entrusted with marital harmony'.[46] The thematic of Venus guiding marriage is augmented by red drapery that visually connects Clarissa, *spiritelli*, and united swans. Given Strozzi interest in madrigals, the doubled swans surely recalled the erotic innuendo of Jacques Arcadelt's 'Sweet White Swan' of 1538, with its plea for 'That death, which is not to die but to fill me with all joy and desire: if in dying thus I will not feel sorrow, I will be pleased to die a thousand times each day'.[47] The paired swans' sweet music and paired *spiritelli* united in marital dance thus presaged Clarissa's spousal future, with *spiritelli* evoking as well transition from infant amatory verve to its nuptial equivalent as the surge of sensual arousal.

Figure 9.8: Titian and Workshop, *Venus and the Lute Player* (c.1565–70). The Metropolitan Museum of Art, Munsey Fund (1936) (36.29). Photo Credit: ©The Metropolitan Museum of Art.

Titian's portrait of Clarissa Strozzi unites likeness, living naturalism, suggestions of spiritual interiority and external signifiers that constructed her image as representation. Forms, imagery and painterly materiality hint at a transitive process of becoming: that of schooling the infant into Petrarchan beauty and, potentially, the ideal wife as delineated by ancestry, familial circumstances and societal expectations. Physiognomic likeness portends joyous and affable soul, kindness and spirited nature, qualities which are shaped socially by means of dress and bodily training and morally by means of intelligence disciplined by education as intimated by puppy. Gems and girdle evoke the Petrarchan beauty and underscore the symbolism of wealth, health, love and marriage with virtues comprising purity, concord and chastity; these allusions to marital virtues the puppy completes with fidelity and faithfulness, while the infant's own actions in feeding it connote familial nurture, liberality and charity. The pictorial evocations would have stimulated conversational exploration in order to complete the image in the process of discourse; allusions to virtues could have strengthened young Clarissa's impulse toward moral development by presenting the 'completed' portrait as a model for reciprocal imitation; when a bride, her portrait would have been held to reveal prescient intimations of virtues ascribed to her in marital state. Clarissa's active and emotive presence suggests character traits that would allow her to negotiate positions of power and influence as had so many of her Medici and Strozzi ancestresses. For all that, however, she remained the ideal wife of Early Modern Italy: aside from portrait and notices of birth, marriage and death, Clarissa di Roberto Strozzi seems to have vanished quietly into the mists of history.

10 UNCLE URBAN RAISES THE BARBERINI NEPHEWS: THE EDUCATION AND EXPECTATIONS OF PAPAL *NIPOTE*

Matthew Knox Averett

This essay examines Pope Urban VIII Barberini and his three nephews, to explore the role children played in the dynastic ambitions of papal families, the functioning of nepotism in papal government and the phenomenon of surrogacy (specifically in terms of education) in early modern Italy. Urban VIII (r. 1623–44) (Fig. 10.1) and his family, the Barberini, were one of the most important clans in early modern Rome. Volumes have been written on the Barberini and their heraldic bees swarm over Rome.[1] Urban reigned for twenty-one years and, during this extended period, he guided the papacy through significant events as diverse as the Thirty Years' War and the Galileo affair. The Barberini systematically patronized the sciences, theater, music and poetry, and established one of Rome's greatest libraries.[2] Under the family's watch, the visual arts in Rome experienced the glittering High Baroque, boasting the masterpieces of Gian Lorenzo Bernini, Pietro da Cortona and Francesco Borromini. The Barberini nephews (Fig. 10.2), Francesco (1597–1679), Taddeo (1603–47) and Antonio (1608–71), were elevated to some of the most important political positions in Rome and ecclesiastical positions in the Catholic Church. Altogether, these moves were undertaken to ensure that the Barberini dynasty enjoyed long-term political and financial power. Ultimately, Urban and his three powerful nephews ushered in a period of fantastic artistic patronage, outrageous nepotism and shocking political excesses.

Figure 10.1: *Pope Urban VIII Barberini* after Peter Paul Rubens (1630s). Photo Credit: National Portrait Gallery, London.

Figure 10.2: *Portraits of the Barberini Nephews* by Johann Friedrich Greuter after Andrea Camassei, in the *Aedes Barberinae* (1642). a. Cardinal Francesco, b. Don Taddeo, c. Cardinal Antonio. Photo Credit: Matthew Knox Averett, author.

Nepotism: Children, Dynasties and the Papal Government

Children played an essential role in both the ecclesiastical and secular arms of government in early modern Rome. The participation of children in government was a common, and indeed essential, phenomenon across early modern Europe. Most monarchies, however, claimed a continuous lineage and there were prescribed rules for heredity inheritance of titles and wealth. This was not the case in papal Rome where popes were elected. Moreover, popes were required to be celibate (in theory at least) since Pope Gregory VII attempted to enforce this requirement with vigor at the end of the eleventh century. In practice, concubinage continued through the Renaissance: by one calculation, of the fifteen men who sat on the Throne of St Peter between 1471 and 1585, at least seven had children.[3] Still, the offspring of popes did not inherit the papal throne. After the Council of Trent, celibacy was strictly practiced. Since the papacy could not descend through the male heirs of a family, the office was passed among noble Italian families. Papal dynastic ambitions therefore could only be satisfied by placing a male member of the family in the College of Cardinals, the body from which future popes were mostly selected. Marriage still played an important role, though, as the offspring of the union of two noble families was a strong candidate for the papacy once he was made a Cardinal. The first necessary step was always to become a Cardinal and, so, among the first acts of any pope was to start elevating family members, often nephews, to the purple. This is largely the basis for papal nepotism, which was officially approved by the Fifth Lateran Council in 1514.

The general pattern was for a pope to elevate a single nephew to the Cardinalate, although there were some extreme outliers, including Sixtus IV who made cardinals of six nephews. Often, future Cardinals began their ecclesiastical career under an older relative who worked in the Curia.[4] Popes did not merely elevate nephews, normally one would be made the *cardinale nipote* and he would usually be the Superintendent of the Ecclesiastical State, one of the most powerful positions in the papal government. Nepotism did not end with making nephews Cardinals: brothers and male in-laws (and in at least one case, Alexander VI, a son) could be also elevated. Once a man was elevated he was eligible to hold any number of titular titles and other government positions, as well as to receive the substantial income from these holdings. Nepotism was also viewed as a means of protecting the pope: the elevation of a nephew, for example, was not merely a dynastic consideration, as the typically short reigns of popes meant each new pope needed a near relative in the Sacred College for support.[5] Nepotism also influenced the course of future papal elections: such affairs were normally tightly contested, and the election of a new pope largely came down to who held the largest faction of Cardinals, as Cardinals tended to vote with the nephew of the pope who created them.[6] This demonstrates that the power of the papal nephew (and therefore the long-term influence of nepotism) outlasted the reign of a given pope.

There were secular benefits outside the Cardinalate, and nephews and other family members were showered in wealth, territories, titles and government positions.[7] This could give them direct roles in wider European politics, those of Italy, or even within the city or Rome. Don Taddeo, for example, ultimately could act both as Prince of Palestrina, as well as Prefect of Rome. As important as the College of Cardinals was, Rome was an international capital, and political power there was exercised, not just by the papal government, but also Catholic kings and Italian states represented by ambassadors, various religious orders, as well as the Roman aristocracy.[8]

The general concensus on papal nepotism is that it served as a stabilizing element for papal government.[9] Moreover, in the early modern period, it was viewed as a desirable, if not necessary institution: Paul III is reported to have argued that it was his duty to favour his family.[10] Still, the value of governmental nepotism was rapidly outstripped by its abuse, with millions of scudi flowing from the Apostolic Camera to papal families.[11] Ultimately, the nepotistic excesses of the seventeenth centuries prompted Innocent XII in 1692 to issue the *Romanum decet pontificem*, a papal bull, which, among other things, abolished the *cardinale nipote* and limited the number of nephews that a pope could make a Cardinal to one.[12]

Urban and the Barberini Nephews

The basic goal for elite families in early modern Italy were to acquire wealth and power, embodied by land, houses, offices and territorial titles. Additionally, elite families sought to improve and strengthen their social position by marriage into feudal aristocracy and establish a patrician family of one's own. Ultimately, dynastic ambitions called for the family to demonstrate its wealth and nobility through conspicuous consumption, including magnificent patronage of art and learning. The Barberini family was no exception, and in the seventeenth century they succeeded spectacularly in this regard. After the death of his father in 1571, the three-year-old Maffeo Barberini was sent to Rome as the protégé of his uncle Francesco (then an apostolic protonotary), establishing a tradition of surrogate parenting between uncle and nephew to advance the family. In 1606 Maffeo was made Cardinal, and in 1623 he ascended to the Throne of St. Peter as Pope Urban VIII. Maffeo's brother, Carlo, had also come to Rome and prospered. Critically, he had three sons: Francesco, who later became a cardinal; Taddeo, later Prince of Palestrina; and Antonio, also a cardinal. As their uncle, Maffeo would largely assume the responsibilities of grooming his nephews as heirs to the family's prosperity in Rome and in the Papal government. He would be pope for twenty-one years, and in that time he would guide his three young nephews to great success.

On 2 October 1623, Urban raised Francesco to the Cardinalate and was *cardinal nipote*, a semi-official position that highlighted his familial relationship to the pope and suggested a role as confidant and agent.[13] At the same time, Francesco was made *Sopraintendente dello Stato Ecclesiastico* (essentially the secretary of state), a position commonly referred to as the *Cardinale padrone*.[14] In addition to his significant political power, Francesco held a number of titular churches in succession and derived large incomes from them. Francesco was groomed for international politics and even spent some time in France on a diplomatic mission.[15] Upon Francesco's return to Rome he became head librarian of the Biblioteca Vaticana, a position he held for several years. While Francesco headed up the ecclesiastical branch of the family, his brother Taddeo led the secular branch of the Barberini clan. Also in 1623, Urban made Taddeo Gonfaloniere of the Church, a powerful military position in the Papal States. A few years later in 1627, Taddeo wed Anna Colonna, thus uniting the Barberini family with one of the greatest Roman baronial clans. In 1630, he succeeded his father as duke of Monterotondo and Prince of Palestine. The next year, with the death of the last male Della Rovere, the position of Prefect of Rome reverted to the pope, and Urban immediately conferred it on Taddeo in a grand ceremony held on 6 August, the eighth anniversary of Urban's election. This powerful position, which had been held exclusively by the Della Rovere family since the fifteenth century, was perhaps the most prestigious of the many powerful positions Taddeo held. With the two older Barberini nephews, it was originally thought that Francesco would lead the secular branch and Taddeo the ecclesiastical. They switched, but no position was settled on for the youngest brother, Antonio, until after Francesco had been made Cardinal and Taddeo had been married and produced viable male offspring. Finally, Antonio was elevated to the purple on 30 August 1627.[16] The unusual step of making two nephews Cardinals broke a long-standing, but unwritten rule limiting papal nepotism. But if this was excess, it was just the beginning. In short order, Antonio held numerous titular titles and official Church positions included secretary of *breves* (1632–44), prefect of the Congregation of the Propaganda Fide (1632–44) and protector of the Capella Sistina (1638).[17] The elevation of Antonio to the Cardinalate facilitated the process of concentrating secular political power in Taddeo's hands, expanded Barberini power in the Church and doubled the potential candidates for another Barberini pope.

The Education and Expectations of the Barberini Nephews

Though the Barberini nephews received their positions due to institutional nepotism, this does not mean that they were necessarily unqualified to hold these positions. Indeed, they had been groomed and educated from birth to assume positions in the Church and government. Francesco received a Jesuit education at the *Collegio Romano*, matriculating perhaps as young as seven years old.[18] Francesco excelled at Greek and Latin, while also studying rhetoric, history and physics. In 1623 he received degrees in both canon and civil law from the University of Pisa, where he had been tutored by Galileo.[19] Francesco's youngest brother, Antonio, was educated at home, as by now the Barberini were a papal family and members of the Roman aristocracy, and this type of education was more typical for families of this rank. In the Barberini family palace, the Casa Grande, Jesuit tutors from the *Collegio Romano* taught young Antonio poetry, theology and mathematics, and he composed music and excelled in Latin and French.[20]

Taddeo studied with the Jesuits at the *Collegio Romano*, but by the age of sixteen he was living with his uncle (then still Cardinal Maffeo Barberini).[21] An account of Taddeo's life, written by his brother Francesco, between 1653 and 1666 indicates that during his time with his uncle Taddeo was groomed for the Cardinalate.[22] Once the Barberini decided to place Francesco in an ecclesiastical career, Taddeo settled into the life of a secular prince. Aristocrats needed literary educations in order to participate in business and government.[23] Contemporary elite education, however, also retained elements of the older Medieval education. Thus, Taddeo additionally took dance lessons, learned to play the guitar, rode horses, participated in sports and was trained to handle weapons and received general military training.[24] Since the Middle Ages, a good bit of elite male education focused on chivalric and martial arts.[25] Yet, by the Renaissance, governments began to rely on hired mercenaries for combat, and armoured knights waned in military significance. Still, the idea of the knight persisted as a symbol of nobility and the use of coats of arms and armoured portraits survived into the Renaissance. A ceremonialized version of Medieval martial arts and chivalric games remained a cornerstone in the education of elite males, with young aristocrats learning riding, fencing and falconing. During one exchange in Baldassare Castiglione's *Il Cortegiano*, Count Ludovico da Canossa's asserted that the courtier would be a hunter, noting that it bore a 'certain resemblance to war'.[26] Indeed, didactic literature for Italian elite, such as Castiglione's book, abounded in the Renaissance.[27]

The education of the Barberini nephews was also, however, profoundly impacted by Jesuit pedagogy. As the shopworn tale goes, the Jesuits were not founded as a teaching order, but soon became one. In the sixteen years between the founding of the order in 1540 and the death of its founder, Ignatius of Loyola, in 1556, the Jesuits opened seventy-four colleges in Europe. By 1600, the order had founded 245 schools around the world and would add nearly 500 more over the course of the seventeenth century.[28] As the *Constitutions* of the order makes clear, Aristotle stood at the centre of the formation of a Jesuit: 'In logic, natural and moral, philosophy, and metaphysics, the doctrine of Aristotle should be followed, as also in the other liberal arts'.[29] Once Diego Laníez, Ignatius's successor as second Superior General of the Society of Jesus, made the decision for the order to focus on education, the primacy of Aristotle in the formation of a Jesuit was extended into Jesuit education. Aristotle was not, however, to be taught for the sake of philosophy; rather, philosophy was to be taught as a support for theology, giving theologians the final authority.[30] The subsequent *Ratio Studiorum* (or the 'Official Plan for Jesuit Education') of 1599, while confirming the primacy of Aristotle, gave final authority to the Church in matters where Aristotle was silent or contradicted official teachings. The deferential position into which Aristotle was forced demonstrates the primacy of Church teachings in the intellectual life of seventeenth-century Rome. The Jesuits emphasized learning languages (with an emphasis on Latin and Greek), mathematics, sciences, classical literature and poetry and the basics of Renaissance humanism, housed within Catholic Scholasticism.[31] In the seventeenth century, at Jesuit boarding schools, a number of traditional subjects of elite education, advocated by the likes of Castiglione, were added to the curriculum of the *Ratio*, including 'riding, singing, dancing, playing musical instruments, fencing, designing fortifications, and learning vernacular languages'.[32] The subsequent attitudes towards history, science and the arts, displayed by Urban and his nephews, demonstrate how profoundly Jesuits education shaped their thought.

The Barberini nephews also benefitted from informal education. For the nephews, as for all elite children, it was an essential matter honour to act in accordance with proper court manners. Dissimulation and proper etiquette were vital to success in Baroque Rome.[33] Precedence, a regulating behavior in court manners, could even be a matter of life and death.[34] An essential subject to be educated in was the *Ceremoniale Romanum*, the apparently superficial code of manners that were reflections of very real political battles.[35] Often, these lessons were communicated in letters, but could be reinforced in art. A prime example is Botticelli's famous *Primavera* (*c.*1482), which is known to have been in the house of Lorenzo di Pierfrancesco de Medici by 1498.[36] Around 1478, Marsilio Ficino wrote to Lorenzo, then only fourteen years old, and extolled to the youth the virtues of Venus. Ficino wrote this letter to help Lorenzo find the right Florentine maiden to wed, which presumably he did with his marriage to Semiramide d'Appiano, and likely occasioned the Botticelli painting. The existence of didactic letters from parents to children as they entered the world of adults are common, and they offer the kind of advice Polonius gave to Laertes in *Hamlet*. Uncles, too, could give advice to nephews: for example, Peter Abelard dedicated Treatise II of *Dialectica* to his nephews. Advice like this was often communicated in physical form such as letters or paintings when the youth was going to be absent from a parent. This was a common occurrence for early modern children of elite families. An illustrative parallel is child hostageship, which has a long political history. Romans used hostages as a means of religious communication and potentially religious conversion.[37] By the Middle Ages, hostageship was firmly embedded in politics, often forming the basis of alliances. As the Middle Ages progressed, territorial sureties tended to replace hostages in the process of reaching agreements.[38] Thus, in the Renaissance, hostageship evolved as a phenomenon that facilitated communication between parties, and potentially fostered the education of the hostage, improving his performance as an ambassador. The role of the hostage as ambassadors in training is illustrated by didactic letters and texts written by parents for their children, while they were captive. In the middle of the ninth century, for example, a Frankish duchess, Dhuoda, wrote a handbook of advice for her son, William, while he was a hostage.[39] It was therefore not always negative, but comparable to processes such as child oblation, commendation, fosterage or even sponsorship.[40] Hostageship was not the only way children could be placed outside the home for political reasons. Sometimes children were placed with relatives to strengthened kinship. Better yet, children could be placed in the court of a noble of higher rank (such as Michelangelo in the Medici household), possibly even a royal court. Such placements gave children *entrée* into a broader political world, refined manners, and an education from erudite masters. Indeed, surrogacy was common in early modern dynastic families. With his three nephews, Urban sought to create *papabile* cardinals and long-term secular figures. Directing their lives in this way necessitated Urban assuming an authority over the boys that today might seem the normal domain of fathers. As we shall see, Urban often communicated lessons to his nephews via didactic poetry.

Francesco Remembers His Lessons

In many ways, Urban was remembered as the primary male role model for the Barberini nephews. Urban died on 29 July 1644 after twenty-one years as pope. With his death, a tide of anti-Barberini sentiment washed over Rome, and the Barberini nephews fled Rome for Paris, but returned from exile in 1646 (except for Taddeo who died in Paris that year). The family was reconciled to Pope Innocent X of the Pamphilj clan (great rivals to the Barberini) by way of marriage between Taddeo's son, Maffeo, and Innocent's grand-niece, Olimpia Giustiniani. The Barberini would prosper for the next few centuries. Already in 1627 Taddeo had married Anna Colonna (of the venerable Colonna clan, one of the most important families in Rome), and as a result of this marriage, Taddeo became Prince of Palestrina. Through Anna, this marriage tied the Barberini to the Colonna, Orsini, Farnese and Sforza, each among the most important families in Italy.[41] The couple had five children. One, Camilia, died in infancy; of the others, Maffeo Barberini married Olimpia Giustiniani (of Pamphilij and Ciustiniani families) and followed his father as Gonfaloniere of the Church and Prefect of Rome, and added other territories and honours as well. Maffeo's brothers, Carlo and Niccolò, became cardinals, while their sister, Lucrezia, married into the important d'Este family. The family's fortunes continued through the nineteenth century.[42]

As good as things were for the Barberini, in one important area they failed to achieve their goal: there was never another Barberini pope after Urban. This was not from a lack of effort. Almost immediately upon the return of the Barberini from exile, the family initiated a massive program to repair the legacy of Urban and the honour of the family. This included commissioning panegyrics, biographies, histories, music, and art that praised Urban and the Barberini. Francesco led the charge. For example, he compiled one of the truly great libraries in Europe: the Barberini collection, which is a major element of the Vatican collection.[43] He also established an important tapestry workshop, a chief product of which was a series of tapestries called *The Life of Urban VIII*, commissioned by Francesco between 1663 and 1679.[44] The tapestries were hung in the Grand Salon of the Palazzo Barberini beneath Pietro da Cortona's famed *Triumph of the Barberini* (1633–9) ceiling fresco. They were intended to revitalize Urban's legacy, but also to enhance the family's reputation, especially in these years when Francesco was most *papabile*.

The Palazzo Barberini, built between 1627 and 1633, emerged as the centre of the Barberini presence in Rome. The palazzo was a double palace for Cardinal Francesco and Don Taddeo, and was located on the Quirinale. The eastern hills of Rome were dominated by the elite of Roman society in the seventeenth century and were covered with sumptuous villas with expansive gardens, fountains and ancient art collections. The construction of the Palazzo Barberini announced the arrival of the family into the Roman aristocracy and augured long-term familial prosperity. This was true of the ecclesiastical line too. As Patricia Waddy puts it, a Cardinal needed 'something that was prestigious enough in its appearance and quality and location to complement his high rank in society'.[45] In 1642, Girolamo Teti completed the *Aedes Barberinae*, a panegyric that not only commemorated the completion of the Palazzo Barberini, but more importantly used the building and its decoration as a symbol of the majesty of the Barberini. Indeed, the palazzo with its immense proportions, sumptuous decorations, vast grounds, and strategic location was a physical manifestation of a successful Barberini dynastic strategy initiated by Urban and continued by his nephews and grand-nephews. The calculated strategy of dynastic succession from uncles to nephews is underscored by an illustration in the *Aedes Barberinae*, which shows the Barberini grand-nephews presenting Urban with a copy of Teti's panegyric (Fig. 10.3). The young boys represent the future of the clan and acknowledge this role by offering, almost as a votive, a copy of the *Aedes Barberinae* to the family patriarch.

Figure 10.3: *Urban VIII Receiving from His Great-Nephews a Copy of the Aedes Barberinae by Girolamo Teti,* by Johann Friedrich Greuter after Andrea Camassei, in the *Aedes Barberinae* (1642). Photo Credit: The Metropolitan Museum of Art, New York.

Francesco's final contribution to the iconographic program of the Palazzo Barberini was a series of frescoes commissioned for his suites, and completed just a year before his death on 10 December 1679. The frescoes depict various mythological heroes and their adventures: *Theseus and Ariadne* by Urbano Romanelli, *Ulysses and the Sirens* by Giacinto Camassei, and *Bellerophon Overcoming the Chimera* and *Jason Returning from Colchis with the Golden Fleece* both by Giuseppe Passeri. These frescoes elaborate on themes alluded to in a lost fresco in the Palazzo Barberini that depicted the same heroes. Though lost, the fresco is known from an engraving in Girolamo Teti's *Aedes Barberinae* (Fig. 10.4). The fresco, *Apollo in Parnassus*, shows Apollo surrounded by the Muses and playing the lyre. The god's music charms the Fates, lulling them to sleep at the entrance to the underworld at Taenarum. Thus incapacitated, they are unable to cut the thread of life of each of the four heroes, Theseus, Ulysses, Jason and Bellerophon, who instead approach the Temple of Virtue. The decoration of Franceso's suites with monumental frescoes depicting four heroes who are not otherwise connected to each other, nor linked to Parnassus, compels us to search for their significance to Francesco.

These classical heroes feature in a poem Urban dedicated to Francesco titled *Exhortatio ad Virtutem* (*Exhortation to Virtue*) that was included in Urban's *Poemeta*, a collection of poems published decades earlier in 1620, while Urban was still a cardinal. The *Exhortation to Virtue* appeared when Francesco was just twenty-two years of age, but like most of the poems in *Poemata*, it was composed a number of years before publication. Urban was a poet of some note, excelling in Latin and Greek verse, and Giovanni Battista Marino, the important seventeenth-century poet, declared Urban *virtuosissimo*.[46] Most of Urban's *Poemata* celebrates Christian heroes, with verses dedicated to various figures including Jesus of Nazareth, St John the Baptist and St Lawrence, as well as Urban's contemporaries, including Pope Clement VIII, Cardinal Alessandro Farnese and Urban's brothers, Carlo and Antonio. There is also the poem dedicated to his nephew, Francesco. In this poem Urban mentions a number of figures from classical mythology, including Apollo, Theseus, Ulysses and Bellerophon, while alluding to Jason. Later in the poem, Urban describes the Choice of Hercules, which was painted in another room near to Francesco's suites.[47] Urban generally condemned poetry that made celebratory use of pagan gods, contending that such poetry can lead the reader into grave spiritual error.[48] Urban explains his conception of his poetry:

> Why do we sing of Orpheus descending into the nether world instead of the Saviour ascending into heaven, with the victorious emblem of the cross in his hand? May it be granted to me, like the ancient Fathers, to spread useful thoughts by means of my poems! May Moses be my guide who led the people through the Red Sea.[49]

Figure 10.4: *Apollo in Parnassus* by Johann Friedrich Greuter after Andrea Camassei, in the *Aedes Barberinae* (1642). Photo Credit: Matthew Knox Averett, author.

Urban used poetry to educate, and tolerated pagan imagery only if it were put to 'positive Christian ends'.[50] When using pagan imagery, Urban invariably adapted it to express an appropriate Christian message, forging what Peter Rietbergen describes as a 'synthesis between the *eloquentia profana* and the *eloquentia sacra*'.[51]

This use of pagan imagery to express positive Christian values is exactly what Urban does in this poem for Francesco. At the beginning, Urban acknowledges that Francesco has now become an adult, but danger is ever-present and so he is worried for his nephew. Urban notes that Francesco takes after his father, Urban's brother Carlo, and that although this is good, life is fraught with great perils. Therefore, Francesco is urged to stay with Urban and let him continue to be his guide. If Francesco will do so, Urban promises this life will be good: he will hear Apollo's music and the melody of the Muses, which save virtuous heroes from the Underworld. Urban urges Francesco to be wise and prudent like Theseus, who was not fooled by the deceitful craftsmanship of the maze. Francesco should also be like Ulysses, who travelled over perilous seas but, in his temperance, was not seduced by the Sirens nor poisoned by Circe. Urban implores Francesco to persevere in his pursuits against all challenges, like Jason who, to win the Golden Fleece, yoked the fierce Khalkotauroi (fire-breathing bulls with bronze hooves and mouths), used them to plough the field in which were then sown Drakon's teeth and finally outwit the ferocious Spartoi who sprung from the teeth. Urban then cautions Francesco to be wary of intrigues against him, like Bellerophon, whom Proteus and Iobates attempted to send to his death and instead defeat his enemies as Bellerophon did the Chimera. All this was good advice considering the treachery of Baroque politics in Rome, yet it would be difficult to heed such advice throughout one's life. Urban acknowledges the sacrifices he is asking of Francesco, but reminds him that the 'honey of Helicon' is not for man. Instead, man must pursue virtue, taking pleasure only in overcoming monsters, for which Apollo crowns victors with laurels. In all, then, the frescoes in Francesco's suites in the Palazzo Barberini, his last statement in defense of his uncle and promotion of his family, are visual representations of the didactic poem Urban composed for his nephew decades earlier. Francesco loved Urban, and here at the end of his life Francesco recalled the lessons he had learned from his uncle. By depicting these images in his suites, Francesco confirmed his fealty to his Urban and the values by which his uncle had raised him and that had guided him through his life.

NOTES

Averett, 'Introduction: The Early Modern Child in Art and History'

1. E. Welch, 'Art on the Edge: Hair and Hands in Renaissance Italy', *Renaissance Studies*, 23:3 (June 2009), pp. 241–68, on p. 242.
2. T. Standring, *600 Years of British Painting: The Berger Collection at the Denver Art Museum* (Denver, CO: The Denver Art Museum, 1998), p. 65. The could also indicate an early betrothal.
3. T. Hill and R. Mabey, *The Gardener's Labyrinth* (Oxford: Oxford University Press, 1987) pp. 139–40.
4. Denver Art Museum 'Three Young Girls', at http://creativity.denverartmuseum.org/tl_18018 [accessed 11 December 2014].
5. S. Miller, 'Parenting in the Palazzo: Images and Artifacts of Children in the Italian Renaissance Home', in E. Campbell, S. Miller and E. Consavari (eds), *The Early Modern Italian Domestic Interior, 1400–1700: Objects, Spaces, Domesticities* (Burlington, VT: Ashgate, 2013), pp. 67–88, on p. 76.
6. E. Currie, *Inside the Renaissance House* (London: Victoria and Albert Museum, 2006), p. 61; and J. M. Musacchio, *Art, Marriage, & Family in the Florentine Renaissance Palace* (New Haven, CT: Yale University Press, 2008), p. 202.
7. Miller, 'Parenting in the Palazzo', p. 67.
8. Translated and published in English as *Centuries of Childhood*.
9. A. Classen, 'Pilippe Ariès and the Consequences: History of Childhood, Family Relations, and Personal Emotions. Where Do We Stand Today?', in A. Classen (ed.), *Childhood in the Middle Ages and the Renaissance: The Results of a Paradigm Shift in the History of Mentality* (Berlin: Walter de Gruyter, 2005), pp. 2–65, on p. 46.
10. For an overview of the impact of Ariès's work, see P. Hutton, *Philippe Ariès and the Politics of French Cultural History* (Amherst, MA: University of Massachusetts Press, 2004), pp. 92–112. See also, Classen, 'Pilippe Ariès and the Consequences', pp. 2–65. For a historiography of the child in history, see H. Cunningham, *Children and Childhood in Western Society since 1500* (London: Longman, 1995), pp. 4–18.
11. Marilyn Brown (ed.), *Picturing Children: Constructions of Childhood between Rousseau and Freud* (Aldershot: Ashgate, 2002), p. 2.
12. N. Terpstra, *Abandoned Children of the Italian Renaissance: Orphan Care in Florence and Bologna* (Baltimore, MD: Johns Hopkins University Press, 2005), p. 1. See also C. Klapisch-Zuber, *Women, Family, and Ritual in Renaissance Italy* (Chicago, IL: University of Chicago Press, 1985), p. 98.

13. H. Kamen, *Early Modern European Society* (New York: Routledge, 2000), p. 26.
14. P. Ariès, *Centuries of Childhood: A Social History of Family Life* (New York: Alfred A. Knopf, 1962), p. 33.
15. Ariès, *Centuries of Childhood*, p. 33.
16. Ariès, *Centuries of Childhood*, p. 34.
17. Ariès, *Centuries of Childhood*, p. 329.
18. Ariès, *Centuries of Childhood*, p. 51.
19. Ariès, *Centuries of Childhood*, p. 67.
20. Ariès, *Centuries of Childhood*, p. 100.
21. Ariès, *Centuries of Childhood*, p. 105.
22. Ariès, *Centuries of Childhood*, p. 38.
23. M. Montaigne, *Essays: A Selection* (New York: Penguin, 1987), p. 149. Montaigne goes on to talk about how a father should love his children and treat them well, though death (either the child's or the father's) should be dealt with stoically.
24. N. J. Miller and N. Yavneh (eds), *Gender and Early Modern Constructions of Childhood* (Burlington, VT: Ashgate, 2011), pp. 157–80, on p. 2; and Cunningham, *Children and Childhood*, p. 91.
25. Cunningham, *Children and Childhood*, p. 90.
26. Miller, 'Parenting in the Palazzo', p. 77.
27. C. Heywood, *A History of Childhood: Children and Childhood in the West from Medieval to Modern Times* (Cambridge: Polity Press, 2001), p. 151.
28. J. Boswell, *Kindness of Strangers: The Abandonment of Children in Western Europe from Late Antiquity to the Renaissance* (New York: Vintage Books, 1988).
29. F. Gies and J. Gies, *Marriage and the Family in the Middle Ages* (New York: Harper & Row, 1987), pp. 34–5.
30. Cunningham, *Children and Childhood*, p. 93.
31. C. Panter-Brick and M. Smith (eds), *Abandoned Children* (Cambridge: Cambridge University Press, 2000); J. F. Harrington, *The Unwanted Child: The Fate of Foundlings, Orphans, and Juvenile Criminals in Early Modern Germany* (Chicago, IL: University of Chicago Press, 2009); and A. Bideau, B. Desjardins and H. P. Brignoli (eds), *Infant and Child Mortality in the Past* (Oxford: Clarendon Press, 1997).
32. Terpstra, *Abandoned Children*; P. Gavitt, *Gender, Honor, and Charity in Late Renaissance Florence* (New York: Cambridge University Press, 2011); D. B. Presciutti 'Dead Infants, Cruel Mothers, and Heroic Popes: The Visual Rhetoric of Foundling Care at the Hospital of Santo Spirito, Rome', *Renaissance Quarterly*, 64:3 (Fall 2011), pp. 752–99; and Presciutti, '*Carità e potere*: Representing the Medici Grand Dukes as "Fathers of the *Innocenti*"', *Renaissance Studies*, 24:2 (April 2010), pp. 234–59.
33. Klapisch-Zuber, *Women, Family, and Ritual*, p. 104.
34. Cunningham, *Children and Childhood*, p. 94. See also D. I. Kertzer, *Sacrificed for Honor: Italian Infant Abandonment and the Politics of Reproductive Control* (Boston, MA: Beacon Press, 1993).
35. P. Gavitt, *Charity and Children in Renaissance Florence: The Ospedale degli Innocenti, 1410–1536* (Ann Arbor, MI: University of Michigan Press, 1990), pp. 190–97.
36. N. Terpstra, *Lost Girls: Sex and Death in Renaissance Florence* (Baltimore, MD: John Hopkins University Press), pp. 29–37; amd Harrington, *The Unwanted Child*, pp. 195–214.
37. Cunningham, *Children and Childhood*, p. 79.
38. L. DeMause (ed.), *The History of Childhood* (New York: The Psychohistory Press,

1974), p. 1.
39. E. Shorter, *The Making of the Modern Family* (London: Basic Books, 1976), p.168.
40. L. Stone, *The Family, Sex and Marriage in England, 1500–1800* (New York: Harper & Row, 1979).
41. E. Badinter, *The Myth of Motherhood: An Historial View of the Maternal Instinct* (London: Souvenir Press, 1981).
42. S. Schama, *The Embarrassment of Riches: An Interpretation of Dutch Culture in the Golden Age* (London: Alfred A. Knopf, 1987), p. 521.
43. L. Pollock, *Forgotten Children: Parent-Child Relations from 1500–1900* (Cambridge: Cambridge University Press, 1983). See also Pollock, *A Lasting Relationship: Parents and Children over Three Centuries* (Hanover, NH: University of New England, 1987).
44. Boswell, *Kindness of Strangers*.
45. S. Shahar, *Childhood in the Middle Ages* (London: Routledge, 1990). See also Heywood, *A History of Childhood*, p. 11–18. For the child in antiquity, see Cunningham, *Children and Childhood*, p. 19–40.
46. S. Ozment, *Ancestors: The Loving Family in Old Europe* (Cambridge, MA: Harvard University Press, 2001). On being sick as a child, see Heywood, *A History of Childhood*, p. 123.
47. S. Ozment, *When Fathers Ruled: Family Life in Reformation Europe* (Cambridge, MA: Harvard University Press, 1983).
48. R. Woods, *Children Remembered: Responses to Untimely Death in the Past* (Liverpool: Liverpool University Press, 2006).
49. B. Hanawalt, *Growing Up in Medieval London* (Oxford: Oxford University Press, 1993), p. 61.
50. L. Haas, *The Renaissance Man and His Children: Childbirth and Early Childhood in Florence, 1300–1600* (New York: St Martin's Press, 1998); B. Roberts, *Through the Keyhole: Dutch Child-Rearing Practices in the 17th and 18th Centuries. Three Urban Elite Families* (Hilversum: Verloren, 1998); and Mulder-Bakker (ed.) *Sanctity and Motherhood: Essays on Holy Mothers in the Middle Ages* (New York: Garland, 1995).
51. Cunningham, *Children and Childhood*, p. 82.
52. Classen, 'Pilippe Ariès and the Consequences', p. 38.
53. K. Arnold, *Kind und Gesellschaft in Mittelalter und Renaissance: Beiträge und Texte zur Geschichte der Kindheit* (Paderborn: Schöningh, 1980), p. 69.
54. Classen, 'Pilippe Ariès and the Consequences', p. 39 (referencing Dorota Żołądź-Strzelczyk, *Dziecko w dawnej Polsce*. (Poznań: Wydawn, Poznańskie, 2002)).
55. K. Calvert, *Children in the House: The Material Culture of Early Childhood, 1600–1900* (Boston, MA: Northeastern University Press, 1992).
56. R. Ago, *Gusto for Things: A History of Objects in Seventeenth Century Rome*, trans. B. Bouley, C. Tazzara and P. Findlen (Chicago, IL: University of Chicago Press, 2013), pp. 73–5.
57. Klapisch-Zuber, *Women, Family, and Ritual*, pp. 310–30.
58. Plato and R. Allen, *The Republic* (New Haven, CT: Yale University Press, 2006) pp. 81-82.
59. R. Goldthwaite, *Wealth and the Demand for Art in Italy, 1300–1600* (Baltimore, MD: John Hopkins University Press, 1993), p. 66.
60. P. Tafur and M. Letts, *Travels and Adventures: 1435–1439* (New York: Harper & Bros, 1926), p. 200.
61. W. Brulez, *Cultuur en getal; Aspecten van de relatie economie-maatschappij-cultuur in*

Europa tussen 1400 en 1800 (Amsterdam: Nederlandse Vereniging tot beoefening van de Sociale Geschiedenis, 1986), pp. 64–5. See also M. J. Bok, 'Review: *Cultuur en getal: aspecten van de relatie economie-maatschappij-cultuur in Europa tussen 1400 en 1800* by W. Brulez, Michael Hoyle', *Simiolus: Netherlands Quarterly for the History of Art*, 18:1/2 (1988), pp. 63–8.

62. J. I. Israel, *The Dutch Republic: It's Rise, Greatness and Fall, 1477–1806* (Oxford: Clarendon Press, 1995), p. 555; M. Prak, 'Painters, Guilds, and the Art Market during the Dutch Golden Age', in S. R. Epstein and M. Prak (eds), *Guilds, Innovation and the European Economy, 1400–1800* (Cambridge: Cambridge University Press, 2008), pp. 143–71, on p. 147; and J. M. Montias, 'Socio-Economic Aspects of Netherlandish Art from the Fifteenth to the Seventeenth Century: A Survey', *The Art Bulletin*, 72:3 (September 1990), pp. 358–73.
63. Durantini, *The Child in Seventeenth-Century Dutch Painting* (Ann Arbor, MI: UMI Research Press, 1983).
64. Miller, 'Parenting in the Palazzo', p. 67.
65. J. M. Musacchio, 'Conception and Birth', in M. Ajmar-Wollheim and F. Dennis (eds), *At Home in the Renaissance* (London: Victoria & Albert Museum, 2006), pp. 124–35, on p. 135.
66. P. F. Brown, 'Children and Education', in M. Ajmar-Wollheim and F. Dennis (eds), *At Home in the Renaissance* (London: Victoria & Albert Museum, 2006), pp. 136–43, on p. 140.
67. Musacchio, 'Conception and Birth', p. 128; and Musacchio, *Art, Marriage, and Family*, p. 202.
68. Ariès, *Centuries of Childhood*, p. 34–35.
69. X. Brooke and P. Cherry, *Murillo: Scenes of Childhood* (London: Merrell, 2001).
70. G. M. Radke, 'Good, Better, Best', in G. M. Radke, G. Giacomelli, P. Macey, M. Tacconi and T. Verdon (eds), *Make A Joyful Noise: Renaissance Art and Music at Florence Cathedral* (Atlanta, GA and New Haven, CT: High Museum of Art and Yale University Press, 2014), p. 29.
71. R. L. Mode, 'Adolescent *Confratelli* and the *Cantoria* of Lucca della Robbia', *The Art Bulletin*, 68:1 (March 1986), pp. 67–71.
72. P. Macey, 'Singing in and Around Florence Cathedral: Oral and Written, Local and Imported Traditions', in Radke, Giacomelli, Macey, Tacconi and Verdon (eds) , *Make A Joyful Noise*, p. 63.
73. Miller, 'Parenting in the Palazzo', p. 81.
74. Klapisch-Zuber, *Women, Family, and Ritual*, p. 115.
75. Klapisch-Zuber, *Women, Family, and Ritual*, p. 115.
76. C. Franceschini, 'The Nudes in Limbo: Michelangelo's *Doni Tondo* Reconsidered', *The Journal of the Warburg and Courtauld Institutes*, 73 (2010), pp. 137–80, on pp. 154–163.
77. N. Marshall, *City of Gold and Mud: Painting Victorian London* (New Haven, CT: Yale University Press, 2012), pp. 145–178.
78. Ariès, *Centuries of Childhood*, p. 152.
79. Ariès, *Centuries of Childhood*, p. 335.
80. N. Orme, *From Childhood to Chivalry: The Education of the English Kings and Aristocracy, 1066–1530* (London: Methuen, 1984), p. 237.
81. P. F. Grendler, *Schooling in Renaissance Italy: Literacy and Learning, 1300–1600* (Baltimore, MD: John Hopkins University Press, 1989), p. 71.

82. B. Castiglione and C. S. Singleton, *The Book of the Courtier* (Garden City, NY: Anchor Books, 1959), pp. 77 and 211.
83. C. Woodrow, 'Revisiting Images of the Child in Early Childhood Education: Reflections and Considerations', *Australian Journal of Early Childhood*, 24:4 (December 1999), pp. 7–12.
84. A. Coudert, 'Educating Girls in Early Modern Europe and America', in A. Classen (ed.), *Childhood in the Middle Ages and the Renaissance: The Results of a Paradigm Shift in the History of Mentality* (Berlin: Walter de Gruyter, 2005), pp. 389–413, on p. 394.
85. J. Tracy, *Erasmus, the Growth of a Mind* (Geneva: Droz, 1972), p. 120.
86. Grendler, *Schooling in Renaissance Italy*, p. 35.
87. P. Jimack, *Rousseau: Émile* (London: Grant and Cutler Ltd, 1983), p. 33.
88. C. G. Nauert, *The Age of Renaissance and Reformation* (Washington, DC: University Press of America, 1981), p. 80.
89. Brown, 'Children and Education', p. 141.
90. Cunningham, *Children and Childhood*, p. 101.
91. Grendler, *Schooling in Renaissance Italy*, p. 101–2.
92. B. Whitehead (ed.), *Women's Education in Early Modern Europe. A History, 1500–1800* (New York: Garland Press, 1999).
93. Coudert, 'Educating Girls', p. 406. See also Grendler, *Schooling in Renaissance Italy*, pp. 87–9.
94. Roger Ascham, tutor to Lady (later Queen) Elizabeth, describes the uniqueness of his pupil by saying, 'the constitution of her mind is exempt from female weakness, and she is endued with a masculine power of application. No apprehension can be quicker than hers, no memory more retentive'. He goes on to relate her excellence in multiple languages, reading and music. See F. Mumby and Elizabeth I, Queen, *Girlhood of Queen Elizabeth: A Narrative in Contemporary Letters* (London: Constable, 1909), p. 70.
95. Coudert, 'Educating Girls', p. 404.
96. D. I. Kertzer and M. Barbagli, *The History of the European Family* (New Haven, CT: Yale University Press, 2001), p. 146.
97. Heywood, *A History of Childhood*, p. 162.
98. J. Dunn, *Elizabeth and Mary: Cousins, Rivals, Queens* (New York: Alfred A. Knopf, 2004), p. 96.
99. Heywood, *A History of Childhood*, p. 161.
100. Grendler, *Renaissance Education between Religion and Politics* (Aldershot: Ashgate, 2006), p. 256.
101. Cunningham, *Children and Childhood*, p. 101.
102. Cunningham, *Children and Childhood*, p. 102.
103. S. Ozment, *A Mighty Fortress* (New York: Harper Perennial, 2005), pp. 229–230.
104. Cunningham, *Children and Childhood*, p. 79.
105. Heywood, *A History of Childhood*, p. 155.
106. Ozment, *A Mighty Fortress*, p. 141.
107. J. Melton, *Absolutism and the Eighteenth-Century Origins of Compulsory Schooling in Prussia and Austria* (Cambridge: Cambridge University Press, 1988), p. xiv.
108. Heywood, *A History of Childhood*, p. 157.
109. Heywood, *A History of Childhood*, p. 123.
110. Grendler, *Schooling in Renaissance Italy*, p. 89.

1 Hadley, 'Cradle and Grave: Commemorating Individual Victims of Infant Mortality'

1. A complete, colour facsimile of Prestesaille's book is online. See the BnF website: http://gallica.bnf.fr/ark:/12148/btv1b8446945q/fl.image.r=latin%201179.langEN [accessed 6 January 2015]. All folio references in this essay without additional precision refer to BnF Lat. 1179; hereafter *Book of Remembrance*.
2. This master also worked collaboratively – sometimes on the same folio alongside other distinct Fouquet-circle hands, who are perhaps best classified as workshop assistants – in Rheims, Bibliothèque municipale, MS 235 and Tours, Bibliothèque municipale, MS 191. M. E. Hadley, 'The Yale Missal (Beinecke MS 425): Mendicant Spirituality and a Vernacular Mass Book from the Fouquet Circle' (PhD dissertation, Yale University, 2007), p. 275.
3. See Hadley, 'Yale Missal', pp. 26, 64 and 275–6, for selected bibliography on Prestesaille's volume. Note the catalogue in V. Leroquais, *Les Livres d'heures manuscrits de la Bibliothèque nationale*, 3 vols (Mâcon: Protat frères, 1927), vol. 1, pp. 119–21. See Reynaud's valuable commentary in F. Avril and N. Reynaud, *Les Manuscrits à peintures en France, 1440–1520* (Paris: Flammarion, 1993), pp. 154–5. A broad and profusely illustrated introduction to Fouquet can be found in F. Avril, *Jean Fouquet: Peintre et enlumineur du xve siècle* (Ghent: Hazan, 2003), where BnF Lat. 1179 is referenced on p. 386.
4. C. Couderc, *Album des portraits d'après les collections du département des Manuscrits* (Paris: Berthaud frères, 1908), p. 52.
5. Fols 3r–4r. Reinburg connected Macé's manuscript dedication to inscriptions on funerary sculpture and memorials the clergy read in commemoration ceremonies. V. Reinburg, *French Books of Hours: Making an Archive of Prayer, c. 1400–1600* (Cambridge: Cambridge University Press, 2012), p. 64. For the French version, see: Couderc, *Album*, pp. 52–3.
6. Fols 9v–14r. Couderc, *Album*, pp. 53–4.
7. J. M. Musacchio, *The Art and Ritual of Childbirth in Renaissance Italy* (New Haven, CT: Yale University Press, 1999), p. 27. This sentiment, contrary to Ariès's more indifferent approach to those who might 'disappear', was also expressed by Orme. P. Ariès, *Centuries of Childhood*, trans. R. Baldick (New York: Knopf, 1962), p. 128; and N. Orme, *From Childhood to Chivalry: The Education of the English Kings and Aristocracy, 1066–1530* (London: Methuen, 1984), p. 3. Ariès's work has already been properly critiqued in Averett's Introduction, pp. 3 and 5.
8. Fols 10v–11r, 12r and 13r.
9. Fol. 9v. Prestesaille's detailed records about his wife and her family contrast with the contemporary Quetier family history, which specifies a marriage date without including the wife's name. Lat. 1389, MS Paris, BnF, fol. 112v: 'Le [14 January 1459] ... je espouse ma femme'.
10. Fols 13v–14r.
11. '... en l'esglise de Saint Saturnin de Tours'. Fol. 13v.
12. Varying the form of the swaddle could represent the ages when they lost these children. Those who died less than three months after birth would have been completely wrapped, like the child on fol. 2r (Fig. 1.1). The eldest daughter, Jehanne, who died at fifteen months could have been shown swaddled with allowance for her arms to move. Partial swaddling for older children is documented; see the façade reliefs on Bru-

nelleschi's Foundling Hospital in Florence.
13. Wieck used the phrase 'Accessory Texts' to include the Passion texts from the Gospels, Seven Verses of St Bernard, Joys of the Virgin and other popular components. R. Wieck, *Time Sanctified* (New York: George Braziller, 2001), pp. 157–67.
14. Avril and Reynaud, *Manuscrits*, pp. 130–9 and 147–52; Avril, *Jean Fouquet*, pp. 169–219, 252–8, 308–9, 328–35, 345–9, 354–74, 380–5 and 388–94; and S. Clancy, 'Books of Hours in the "Fouquet Style": The Relationship of Jean Fouquet and the Hours of Étienne Chevalier to French Manuscript Illumination of the Fifteenth Century' (PhD dissertation, Cornell University, 1988), pp. 182–201.
15. Hadley, 'Yale Missal', pp. 270–88.
16. Fols 3r–4r and 9v–14r.
17. Fols 17r–59r.
18. Fols 63r–111v and 115v–16v.
19. Fols 118r–20r.
20. Fols 120r–7v.
21. Fols 127v–33r.
22. Fols 135r–43v.
23. Fols 149r–64r and 171r–2r.
24. Fols 112r–15v, 143v–9r and 164v–70v.
25. '… pour memoire et souvenance'. Fol. 3r.
26. H. Bouchot, *Les primitifs français à la Bibliothèque nationale* (Paris: Bibliothèque nationale, 1904), p. 51, cat. 154.
27. Phrases such as 'tableau de famille' and the 'portrait de Macé Prestesaille' have been used. See A. Vallet de Viriville, 'Jean Fouquet, peintre français du xve siècle', *Revue de Paris*, 38 (1 August 1857), pp. 409–37, on pp. 433–4.
28. J. L. Deuffic, 'Paris, BnF, Lat. 1179: Les Heures de Macé Prestesaille: une affaire de famille', blog dated 17 September 2012 at http://blog.pecia.fr/post/2012/09/18/Paris,-BnF,-Lat.-1179-%3A-Les-Heures-de-Mac%C3%A9-Prestesaille-%3A-une-affaire-de-famille [accessed 6 January 2015]. Couderc's earlier transcription compares better to the manuscript.
29. Couderc, *Album*, pp. 52–4.
30. Avril and Reynaud, *Manuscrits*, p. 155.
31. For a review of his oeuvre, see Hadley, 'Yale Missal', pp. 25–33 and 64–91. This collective grouping has been discussed for decades via the shorthand of a conventional name. My arguments for removing multiple manuscripts from his oeuvre have proved fruitful. Recent work by Gras and Seidel, apart from their individualized elaborations or revisions and new artists' names, fundamentally derives from connoisseurial distinctions I introduced as: Associate of the Yale Missal Master and Master of the Laval Hours. S. Gras, 'Un livre d'heures à l'usage de Rome conservé à la Bibliothèque nationale d'Espagne', *Art de l'enluminure*, 50 (2014), pp. 2–73, on pp. 6–7, 17, 21–2, 26–7 and 71–2; and C. Seidel, *Jean Colombe, Guillaume Piqueau, Louis Fouquet (?)* (Ramsen: H. Tenschert, 2014), pp. 95–7, 105–9, 126–8 and 175. Note Guillaume Piqueau's name among possible candidates for identification with unsigned Turonian illumination of the Fouquet circle and compare with Hadley, 'Yale Missal', pp. 75–82, 273–4 and 278–88.
32. Fol. 3r.
33. Fols 13v–14r.
34. Charron recognized this similarity and suggested that black head coverings connote

deceased status. P. Charron, 'Livre de prières dit Heures de Macé Prestesaille', in *Tours 1500: Capitale des arts* (Paris: Somogy, 2012), pp. 354–5. Note that the eldest daughter, whose death notice appears on fol. 14r, is depicted with a pink head covering on fols 2r (Fig. 1.1) and 9r.

35. Ariès, *Centuries*, pp. 37, 40, 50 and 57. See also Averett's Introduction and Giuntini's chapter, 'Dressing the Part', in this volume, pp. 4 and 117–32.
36. This material form of legacy was recognized by fifteenth century authors, who also focused efforts on lasting fame through 'literary progeny'. G. McClure, 'The Art of Mourning: Autobiographical Writings on the Loss of a Son in Italian Humanist Thought (1400–1461)', *Renaissance Quarterly*, 39:3 (1986), pp. 440–75, on pp. 469–70.
37. M. L. King, *The Death of the Child Valerio Marcello* (Chicago, IL: University of Chicago Press, 1994), p. 173.
38. Prestesaille enjoyed relatively modest circumstances; see B. Chevalier, *Tours, ville royale (1356–1520)* (Louvain: Vander, 1975), p. 565.
39. Job 1.
40. Job 42:10–16. His 500 yoke of oxen, by contrast, were doubled precisely to 1,000.
41. Job 19:25.
42. Commentators such as Augustine, Gregory the Great and Anselm of Canterbury classified unbaptized babies as 'surely damned'. Peter Abelard and Peter Lombard argued against the automatic condemnation of these at-risk infants. Aquinas, then, pioneered using the term 'limbo of children'; D. Herlihy, *Women, Family and Society in Medieval Europe* (Providence, RI: Berghahn Books, 1995), pp. 227–8 and 237–8. Literary sources assert that unnamed and unbaptized souls would not enter heaven. D. Alighieri's *Inferno* places those without baptism in Limbo; Canto IV.25–39. Orme, for example, cites W. Langland's *Piers Plowman*, XV. 448 [see also XV.454–6]; and Orme, *From Childhood*, pp. 9–10.
43. Orme, *From Childhood*, p. 9; Musacchio, *Art and Ritual*, pp. 29–32, 182 n. 63 and 183 n. 72.
44. The sanctified status of baptized infants is asserted by the representation of a child in swaddling clothes, resting on Francesca Tornabuoni's chest, in a double funerary monument. This work was probably produced in Florence, dismantled and moved to the Minerva in Rome. Musacchio, *Art and Ritual*, pp. 30–2. If it was in Florence or Rome, Fouquet could have seen and sketched this model, giving his later emulators visual access to it in Tours. For discussion on the notion of Fouquet's sketchbook, see E. Inglis, *Jean Fouquet and the Invention of France: Art and Nation after the Hundred Years War* (New Haven, CT: Yale University Press, 2011), pp. 35–67.
45. Fol. 13v.
46. Hadley, 'Yale Missal', pp. 132–3.
47. S. Cassagnes-Brouquet, *Louis XI ou le mécénat bien tempéré* (Rennes: Presses universitaires de Rennes, 2007), pp. 44–5. Earlier youthful funerary monuments include those for two of St Louis's children, at the Abbey of Royaumont, that are now in the Basilica of St Denis. P.-Y. Le Pogam, *St Louis* (Paris: Éditions du patrimoine, 2014), pp. 72–4 and 224. Two sons of Queen Anne of Brittany (1477–1516) and King Charles VIII (1470–98) were later memorialized via child-sized monumental tombs in the Cathedral of St Gatien, Tours. B. de Chancel-Bardelot, 'Guillaume Regnault', in *Tours 1500: Capitale des arts* (Exhibition, Musée des Beaux-Arts, Tours; Paris: Somogy, 2012), pp. 192–4. The dauphins's effigies are illustrated online: http://www.patrimoine-histoire.

fr/Patrimoine/Tours/Tours-Saint-Gatien.htm [accessed 6 January 2015].
48. Fol. 14r.
49. M. Mead, 'The Swaddling Hypothesis: Its Reception', *American Anthropologist*, n.s. 56:3 (June 1954), pp. 395–409, on pp. 396 and 399–400.
50. Mead, 'Swaddling', p. 402.
51. Public displays of grief in representations of the *Crucifixion* and *Lamentation* offered models for 'extreme emotions' over the loss of a relative or close associate; McClure, 'Art of Mourning', p. 464.
52. Fol. 4r.
53. C. J. Sommerville, *The Rise and Fall of Childhood* (Beverly Hills, CA: Sage, 1982), p. 47.
54. Matthew 3:17.
55. 'Ie croy en dieu le pere omnipotent. Qui a cree et terre et firmament'. Fol. 149^{bis}r [n.p.].
56. 'Resuscita et monta sur les cieulx. Ou a dextre de dieu siet glorieulx. Iuger vendra vifs et mors iustement'. Fol. 149^{bis}v.
57. Some authors cite memorizing and learning to read with the Psalter. Ariès, *Centuries*, p. 141. Prestesaille's manuscript contains elements of the Psalter in its liturgical texts.
58. Wieck has identified texts for educating children in fifteenth-century French books of hours: Baltimore, Walters Art Museum, W.261 and W.268. R. Wieck, 'Special Children's Books of Hours in the Walters Art Museum', in B. Cardon (ed.), *Als ich can: Liber Amicorum in Memory of Prof. Dr Maurits Smeyers*, 2 vols (Louvain: Uitgeverij Peeters, 2002) vol. 2 pp. 1629–39, on pp. 1629, 1635 and 1637. James Marrow signaled another manuscript with children's texts: New York, New York Public Library, MA 45. J. J. G. Alexander, J. Marrow and L. Sandler, *The Splendor of the Word: Medieval and Renaissance Illuminated Manuscripts at the New York Public Library* (New York: Harvey Miller, 2005), p. 252.
59. Orme, *From Childhood*, p. 10; and S. Strocchia, 'Learning the Virtues: Convent Schools and Female Culture in Renaissance Florence', in B. Whitehead (ed.), *Women's Education in Early Modern Europe: A History, 1500–1800* (New York: Garland Publishing, Inc., 1999), pp. 3–46, on p. 19.
60. Note the Creed: fols 60r–v [in a later scribe's hand] and fols 149^{bis}r–v. See the *Pater Noster*: fol. 141r.
61. Fols 149r–v and 149^{bis}r. The *Alphabet of Christians* begins: 'De par dieu humblement te salue ... '.
62. Orme, *From Childhood*, p. 16.
63. Orme, *From Childhood*, pp. 129–30.
64. S. Jansen, *Anne of France: Lessons for my Daughter* (Cambridge: DS Brewer, 2004), pp. 32–3.
65. Beyond the Office of the Dead and the Mass for the Dead, Prestesaille included a translation of the 'In manus' prayer: "Sire en tes mains ie recommande mon ame. Rachate mas de linfernalle flamme"' (fol. 151r). Additionally, see: 'De morte et iudicio' (fol. 154r), 'Pene infernales' (fol. 154v) and 'Des ioyes de paradis' (fols 154v–5r).
66. Gerson also suggested a wide range of ancient secular authors from Aristotle to Seneca and Valerius Maximus to Titus Livius for Charles VI's sons. A. Thomas, *Jean de Gerson et l'éducation des dauphins de France* (Paris: Droz, 1930), pp. 14, 30 and 48–50.
67. Thomas, *Jean de Gerson*, p. 48.
68. Fols 63r–111v and 115v–16v.
69. Thomas, *Jean de Gerson*, pp. 49–50.

70. Fols 152r–v and 164v–72r.
71. Fols 155r–64r.
72. Jansen, *Anne of France*, p. 60.
73. Jansen, *Anne of France*, pp. 60–1.
74. Fols 150r–v and 151v.
75. Strocchia, 'Learning', p. 26.
76. Jansen, *Anne of France*, p. 60.
77. Fols 152v–4r.
78. 'Garde ton œil ... Voy en pitie com pour toy pend en croix. Meptz en ton cuer son langaige et sa voix. Et lembrasse par grant dilection en lequerant de toute affection'. Fols 151v–2r.
79. Strocchia, 'Learning', pp. 22 and 43 n. 77.
80. Orme, *From Childhood*, p. 10.
81. Fols 9v–13r.
82. Herlihy, *Women*, p. 219.
83. Fol. 4r.
84. 'Toutesvoies la regle de vivre nest mye a delaissier'. Fol. 155v.
85. A. Macfarlane, *Marriage and Love in England: Modes of Reproduction 1300–1840* (Oxford: Basil Blackwell, 1986), p. 51.
86. Fols 3r–4r and 9v–14r.
87. Fols 135r–43v. For commentary on laypeople's access to the mass liturgy, see Hadley, 'Yale Missal', pp. 98–117.
88. Fols 3r–4r.
89. Fols 13v–14r, 155r–64r and 171r–2r.
90. 'Les bons auront trescler vision de dieu amour ... agilite, impassibilite, subtilite ... immortalite, ioye sans fin, bonte, beaulte, richesse, puissance, honneur, sante, vertu, ieunesse, clarte, repos, seurete, paix, plaisir, gloire ... doulceur et tout aultre desir'. Fols 154v–5r.
91. McClure, 'Art of Mourning', pp. 450–1.

2 Tiffany, '"Little Idols": Royal Children and the Infant Jesus in the Devotional Practice of Sor Margarita de la Cruz (1567–1633)'

1. Research for this essay was made possible by a Long-Term Fellowship (funded by the National Endowment for the Humanities) at the John Carter Brown Library at Brown University and by a Research Growth Initiative Award from the University of Wisconsin-Milwaukee. Laura R. Bass generously provided valuable feedback. I dedicate the essay to Sanne, my thoroughly modern child.
2. J. de Palma, *Vida de la serenissima Infanta, Sor Margarita de la Cruz Religiosa descalça de S. Clara* (1636; Seville: Rodríguez de Abrego, 1653), fols. 50v–51r: 'No ha nacido ... Vuestra Alteza para si sola; para bien de muchos ha nacido'; 'a su casa le conuiene ... los Reynos lo piden'. See also M. Sánchez, *The Empress, the Queen, and the Nun: Women and Power at the Court of Philip III of Spain* (Baltimore, MD: Johns Hopkins University Press, 1998), p. 79; and H. Paravicino y Arteaga, *Margarita o Oracion funebre en las onras de la Serenissima Infanta ... Soror Margarita de la Cruz* (Madrid: Andrés de Parra, 1633), fols. 7v–8v.
3. On the profession, see C. van Wyhe, 'The Making and Meaning of the Monastic

Habit at Spanish Habsburg Courts', in A. Cruz and M. Stampino (eds), *Early Modern Habsburg Women: Transnational Contexts, Cultural Conflicts, Dynastic Continuities* (Farnham: Ashgate, 2013), pp. 250–6 (this is a revised version of C. van Wyhe, 'The Making and Meaning of the Monastic Habit at Spanish Habsburg Courts', in J. Colomer and A. Descalzo (eds), *Spanish Fashion at the Courts of Early Modern Europe*, 2 vols (Madrid: Centro de Estudios Europa Hispánica, 2014), vol. 1, pp. 261–6). See M. Sánchez, 'Where Palace and Convent Met: The Descalzas Reales in Madrid', *Sixteenth Century Journal*, forthcoming, on Philip II's lingering dismay at the rejected proposal; I am grateful to Magdalena Sánchez for sharing her essay with me.

4. Palma, *Vida*, esp. fols. 225r–27v. I am currently writing an essay on Sor Margarita's engagement with those images.

5. According to Joseph de Palafox (who edited Juan de Palafox's complete works), Juan de Palafox claimed that he composed the text based on 'materiales, y noticias' given to him by Palma; see Joseph de Palafox y Mendoza (ed.), *Obras del ilustrissimo, excelentissimo, y venerable siervo de Dios don Juan de Palafox y Mendoza*, 13 vols (Madrid: Gabriel Ramírez, 1762), vol. 9, p. 157. For the purposes of my argument, the question of who crafted the prose is less important than the fact that Palma, as Sor Margarita's confessor and confidant, provided the information on her religious practice.

6. 'Documentacion relativa al proceso de beatificacion de la Infanta Sor Margarita de la Cruz, fallecida y enterrada en la clausura de las Descalzas, iniciado por la comunidad y abadesa del citado monasterio, Sor Juana del Espiritu Santo (1689)', Archivo General del Palacio Real, Sección Patronatos, Fondo Descalzas, Caja 27, Exp. 1 (microfilm); I am grateful to María José del Río Barredo for sharing with me her copy of this document as well as her extraordinary knowledge of Sor Margarita and court culture. The proposed beatification is also mentioned in J. Hathaway, 'Spirituality and Devotional Music in the Royal Convent of the Descalzas, Madrid', *The Journal of Musicological Research*, 30:3 (2011), pp. 202–26, on p. 206.

7. F. de Jesús, prologue to Margarita de la Cruz, *Exercicios de devocion y oracion, para todo el discurso del año, del Real monasterio de las Descalças de Madrid* (Antwerp: Plantin, 1622), n.p.: 'el sentimiento tan vivo, tan devoto, y tan tierno'.

8. Sánchez, *Empress, Queen, Nun*, pp. 137–55; Sánchez, 'Palace and Convent'. On the 'permeable cloister', see E. Lehfeldt, *Religious Women in Golden Age Spain: The Permeable Cloister* (Aldershot: Ashgate, 2005).

9. M. Hoffman, *Raised to Rule: Educating Royalty at the Court of the Spanish Habsburgs, 1601–1634* (Baton Rouge, LA: Louisiana State University Press, 2011), esp. pp. 11, 12, 16–17; M. Hoffman, 'Childhood and Royalty at the Court of Philip III', in G. Coolidge (ed.), *The Formation of the Child in Early Modern Spain* (Farnham: Ashgate, 2014), pp. 123–42 (as a whole, Coolidge's volume places childhood in Spain within its broader early modern cultural context).

10. E. Goodman, 'Royal Piety: Faith, Religious Politics, and the Experience of Art at the Convent of the Descalzas Reales in Madrid' (PhD dissertation, New York University, 2001), pp. 147–81.

11. A. García Sanz, *El Niño Jesús en el Monasterio de las Descalzas Reales de Madrid* (Madrid: Patrimonio Nacional, 2010); A. García Sanz, 'La collezione dei Niños Jesús', in *Niños Jesús: Sculture policrome dalle collezioni reali di Madrid* (exh. cat., Milan: Basilica di Sant'Ambrogio, Oratorio della Passione, 1989), pp. 71–82; and A. García Sanz, 'La imagen y su contexto: Los Niños Jesús del Monasterio de las Descalzas Reales de Madrid', in Rafael Ramos Sosa (ed.), *Actas del Coloquio Internacional El Niño Jesús y la*

infancia en las artes plásticas, siglo XV al XVII: IV centenario del Niño Jesús del Sagrario, 1606–2006 (Seville: Archicofradía del Santísimo Sacramento del Sagrario de la Catedral de Sevilla, 2010), pp. 289–314. I thank Ana García Sanz for generously showing me the Descalzas's collections and sharing her incomparable knowledge of the convent's visual culture.

12. Sánchez, *Empress, Queen, Nun*, p. 118.
13. Sánchez, *Empress, Queen, Nun*, p. 71.
14. My discussion of the royal children in this paragraph is based on Hoffman, *Raised to Rule*, pp. 25–110.
15. Hoffman, *Raised to Rule*, p. 20.
16. G. de Quesada, *Exemplo de todas las virtudes y vida milagrosa de la venerable madre Geronyma de la Assumpción* (Madrid: Antonio Marín, 1717), p. 456: 'gran siervos de Dios'.
17. Hoffman, *Raised to Rule*, p. 12.
18. Margarita de la Cruz to Philip III, Día de todos santos [1 November], 1606, in 'Papeles del reinado de Felipe III' (Madrid, Biblioteca Nacional MSS/915), fol. 117r: 'comyo aqui sus sopicas muy bien y despues estuvo haciendome merced de entretenerse conmigo hasta que fue ora de mamar. Diyeronle el pecho y adormyose como un angel. Hecharonle en su cuna ... estuvele yo meciendo un buen rato' (punctuation added). The letter is published in M. Serrano y Sanz, *Apuntes para una biblioteca de escritoras españolas desde el año 1401 al 1833*, 2 vols (Madrid: Sucesores de Rivadeneyra, 1903), vol. 1, p. 89.
19. Margarita de la Cruz to Philip III, in 'Papeles del reinado', fol. 117r: 'tuve muy lindo dia ... aunq[ue] ... tuve harta soledad de la infante'.
20. Margarita de la Cruz to Philip III, in 'Papeles del reinado', fol. 117v: 'La infante doña M^a me dixo la de Altamira q[ue] estava muy linda y ya con los braços fuera que otro dia me la trayera'. The Countess of Altamira was 'the primary caretaker of the royal children', as explained in Hoffman, *Raised to Rule*, p. 29.
21. Palma, *Vida*, fol. 141v: 'oficios de madre'; see also Hoffman, *Raised to Rule*, pp. 16–17.
22. Palma, *Vida*, fol. 141v: 'mirauan como à madre a su tia'.
23. R. Martorell Téllez-Girón (ed.), *Cartas de Felipe III a su hija Ana, reina de Francia (1616–1618)* (Madrid: Imprenta helénica, 1929), pp. 44, 47: 'para que la viese' (p. 47). See also Hoffman, *Raised to Rule*, p. 11.
24. A. Álvarez, 'Curioso epistolario en torno a la Infanta Sor Margarita de la Cruz', *Hispania Sacra*, 24 (1971), pp. 187–234, on p. 205: 'la norabuena que V. A. me da del cumplimiento de sus 12 años ... el miercoles espero ver a V. A., para que voy muy alvoroçado y llevare el prinçipe conmigo'. See also Sánchez, 'Palace and Convent'.
25. Álvarez, 'Curioso epistolario', p. 205: 'la imagen que pinto el principe para V. A. ... de la Conçepçion'. On Immaculist devotion in Philip III's Spain, see S. Stratton, *The Immaculate Conception in Spanish Art* (Cambridge: Cambridge University Press, 1994), pp. 67–87. See also J. Gállego, 'Felipe IV, pintor', in *Estudios sobre literatura y arte dedicados al profesor Emilio Orozco Díaz*, 3 vols (Granada: Secretariado de Publicaciones de la Universidad, 1979), vol. 1, pp. 533–40.
26. Álvarez, 'Curioso epistolario', pp. 211–12.
27. On the marriage, see Hoffman, *Raised to Rule*, pp. 137–46; and Sánchez, *Empress, Queen, Nun*, p. 116. On the proposed marriage to the Prince of Wales, see G. Redworth, *The Prince and the Infanta: The Cultural Politics of the Spanish Match* (New Haven, CT: Yale University Press, 2003); F. de Jesús, *El hecho de los tratados del matri-*

monio pretendido por el Principe de Gales con la serenissima infante de Espana, Maria, ed. S. Gardiner (Westminster: Camden Society, 1869), which was written by the same cleric who wrote the prologue to Sor Margarita's *Exercicios*.

28. Archivo Histórico Nacional, Consejos, Cámara de Castilla, libro de cédulas de paso (pasaportes), libro 635 (1622–9), fols. 234v–40r, Madrid, 22 July 1625: 'dos muñecas vestidas' (fol. 239r); see Sánchez, 'Palace and Convent', on this document and on various gifts exchanged between Sor Margarita and family members.
29. Álvarez, 'Curioso epistolario', pp. 232–4.
30. Palma, *Vida*, fol. 179v: 'los primeros paños, que se ha de vestir el Principe'.
31. Palma, *Vida*, fol. 180r: 'Hizo bendecir los habitos, y que se dixessen muchas Missas por este sucesso; y tuuo todas estas cosas sobre vn Altar de Nuestra Señora nueue dias'.
32. See F. Marías, 'Juan Pantoja de la Cruz: El arte cortesano de la imagen y las devociones femeninas', in *La mujer en el arte español: VIII jornadas de arte* (Madrid: Alpuerto, 1997), pp. 103–116, on p. 108. As Marías notes, Pantoja painted six versions of the portrait – probably including the Descalzas version – soon after the baby's death in 1603, and another version in 1607. See also M. Kusche, *Juan Pantoja de la Cruz y sus seguidores: B. González, R. de Villandrando y A. López Polanco* (Madrid: Fundación Arte Hispánico, 2007), pp. 137–41.
33. Marías, 'Pantoja', p. 108.
34. Palma, *Vida*, fols. 179v–180r.
35. Palma, *Vida*, fols. 223r–23v: 'siendo muy niños ... era cosa notable las caricias que les hazia, en orden à los espirituales sentimientos, que tenia de la memoria del niño Iesus'. The chapter is entitled 'El amor, y deuocion que tuuo al Niño Iesus' (fol. 222r). Palma also emphasizes Sor Margarita's affection for other children, relatives of the Habsburgs, who took up permanent residence at the Descalzas: Catalina d'Este and Ana Dorotea de Austria, illegitimate daughter of the nun's brother, Rudolf II; Palma, *Vida*, fols. 145r–45v, 151v–57v.
36. Palma, *Vida*, fol. 223v: 'Dezianla algunas Religiosas: Señora mire V. A. que se dexa lleuar mucho destas criaturas, guarde que son idolillos que lleuan el coraçon, y dexan seca el alma'.
37. Palma, *Vida*, fol. 223v: 'sucede muy al contrario ... con su hermosura, y su gracia, me ayudan à la memoria del niño Iesus, y cada vno dellos me parece que lo representa, que son Imagenes viuas suyas, y como à tales les siruo'.
38. Palma, *Vida*, fol. 223r: 'Imitaua en esto à mi Seraphico P. S. Fra[n]cisco, como buena hija, q[ue] no podia sufrir que delante del matassen corderos, acorda[n]dose del cordero de Dios; y assi como S. Fra[n]cisco mi padre amaua al cordero mistico, en los corderos naturales, amaua su A. al niño Iesus en los niños'.
39. See Goodman, 'Royal Piety', pp. 166–7. Among seventeenth-century Spanish sources on Franciscan devotion to the Child, see P. de Ribadeneyra, *Flos sanctorum: Libro de las vidas de los santos* (Madrid: Imprenta Real, 1675), esp. p. 308.
40. Palma, *Vida*, fols. 223r, 12r, respectively: 'Tenia mas aficio[n] à los pobrecitos, porq[ue] estos, dezia, parecian mas al niño Iesus'; 'la inocencia de Christo, pobre, y humilde'.
41. Palma, *Vida*, fol. 223r: 'Como sabia[n] el gusto q[ue] en esto tenia, traìa[n]le algunos niños, y les hazia muchas caricias, y mandaua q[ue] los vistiessen'.
42. Palma, *Vida*, fol. 223r: 'algunas vezes, por ver lo q[ue] hazia, obligaua[n] à los niños q[ue] llorassen, y qua[n]do lo oîa, era tan gra[n]de su co[m]passion, q[ue] lloraua ta[m]bien, y dezia: Valgame Dios, porque haze[n] llorar à esse angelico? Assi lloraria el niño Iesus en el pesebre'.

43. Margarita de la Cruz, *Exercicios*, p. 62: 'todos los niños, que viere, ù oyere llorar, me despertaràn el afecto, para que no me descuide de alabar al que por mi llora'.
44. R. de Aguirre, 'Documentos relativos a la pintura en España: Juan Pantoja de la Cruz, pintor de cámara', *Boletín de la Sociedad española de excursiones*, 30 (1922), pp. 17–22, on p. 18: 'bestido [sic] de berde'.
45. A. García Sanz and L. Ruiz, 'Linaje regio y monacal: La galería de retratos de las Descalzas Reales', in *El Linaje del emperador* (exh. cat., Cáceres: Iglesia de la Preciosa Sangre, Centro de Exposiciones San Jorge, 2000), pp. 146–50.
46. M. de Carlos Varona, 'Representar el nacimiento: Imágenes y cultura material de un espacio de sociabilidad femenina en la España altomoderna', *Goya: Revista de arte*, 319 (2007), pp. 231–45 (see also the abbreviated English version: M. de Carlos Varona, 'Giving Birth at the Habsburg Court: Visual and Material Culture', in Cruz and Stampino (eds), *Habsburg Women*, pp. 151–73); and Marías, 'Pantoja', pp. 103–16.
47. On such accoutrements, see García Sanz, *Niño Jesús*, pp. 160–207.
48. Palma, *Vida*, fol. 225r.
49. García Sanz, *Niño Jesús*, pp. 177, 184–99.
50. Margarita de la Cruz to Philip III, in 'Papeles del reinado', fol. 117r.
51. See Kusche, *Pantoja*, p. 137 (on the image of Ana); García Sanz, *Niño Jesús*, pp. 161–5 (on the images of Ana and the Christ Child).
52. E. Scheicher, 'Coral', *Grove Art Online. Oxford Art Online* (Oxford University Press), at http://www.oxfordartonline.com/subscriber/article/grove/art/T019410 [accessed 2 January 2015].
53. H. Friedmann, *The Symbolic Goldfinch, Its History and Significance in European Devotional Art* (Washington: Pantheon Books, 1946), pp. 1–51. For images in the Descalzas of the Christ Child with the orb, see García Sanz, *Niño Jesús*, pp. 211–37.
54. For those portraits, see Kusche, *Pantoja*, pp. 262–5. Although Velázquez's portraits of Philip IV's children were not explicitly religious, he used apotropaic elements in a portrait of Prince Felipe Próspero; see García Sanz and Ruiz, 'Linaje regio', p. 146; and Javier Portús Pérez (ed.), *Velazquez: Las Meninas and the Late Royal Portraits* (exh. cat., Madrid: Museo Nacional del Prado, 2013), pp. 131–2.
55. Marías, 'Pantoja', pp. 103–16.
56. García Sanz, *Niño Jesús*, p. 161.
57. Palma, *Vida*, fol. 223v.
58. García Sanz, *Niño Jesús*, pp. 184–99; and P. Junquera, 'Belenes monásticos del Patrimonio Nacional', *Reales sitios*, 5 (1968), pp. 24–36.
59. A number of these works are illustrated in E. Tormo y Monzó, *En las Descalzas Reales: Estudios históricos, iconográficos y artísticos*, 2 vols in 3 (Madrid: Blass, 1917–45), vol. 2.
60. Palma, *Vida*, fol. 223r.
61. García Sanz, *Niño Jesús*, p. 163, specifically describes the iconographical type as a 'Niño Jesús de Praga'.
62. Álvarez, 'Curioso epistolario', p. 224.
63. Álvarez, 'Curioso epistolario', p. 224: 'conociera poco'.
64. The city closely resembles Vienna as depicted in an engraving of 1663 (itself based on an example from 1602): Paul Fürst, *Conterfactvr wie die havptstad Wien in Österreich vom Tvrucken ist belegert gewest anno 1529*, 1663, at http://vc.lib.harvard.edu/vc/deliver/~maps/010590389 [accessed 2 January 2015].
65. Álvarez, 'Curioso epistolario', p. 233: 'el dolor que yo tengo siempre este dia de no allarme en la fiesta de la Concesion [apparently, the day the nun received the habit] de las

Descalças'. Sor Margarita took the habit on her birthday; Palma, *Vida*, fol. 62r.
66. Palma, *Vida*, fols. 166r, 168r.
67. Palma, *Vida*, fol. 282v.
68. See the front matter of Paravicino y Arteaga, *Margarita*.
69. For a recent discussion, see Mercedes Llorente, 'Portraits of Children at the Spanish Court in the Seventeenth Century: The Infanta Margarita and the Young King Carlos II', *Bulletin of Spanish and Portuguese Historical Studies*, 35:1 (2011), pp. 30–47.
70. See S. Schroth, 'A New Style of Grandeur: Politics and Patronage at the Court of Philip III', in S. Schroth and R. Baer (eds), *El Greco to Velázquez: Art During the Reign of Philip III* (exh. cat., Boston, MA: Museum of Fine Arts, 2008), pp. 77–120; J. Brown and J. Elliott, *A Palace for a King: The Buen Retiro and the Court of Philip IV*, rev. edn (New Haven, CT: Yale University Press, 2003), pp. 7–30; and J. Brown, 'Enemies of Flattery: Velázquez' Portraits of Philip IV', *Journal of Interdisciplinary History*, 17:1 (1986), pp. 137–54.
71. On the frescoes, their attribution and dating (the decoration may have been completed in various phases), see especially Goodman, 'Royal Piety', pp. 144–5. See also Tormo, *Descalzas*, vol. 1, pp. 31–40; and A. García Sanz and M. Sánchez Hernández, *Conventos de las Descalzas Reales y de la Encarnación: Dos clausuras de Madrid* (Madrid: Patrimonio Nacional, 1999), pp. 28–30.
72. Goodman, 'Royal Piety', pp. 144–5.

3 Flansburg, '*E Riluttante Ragazzotti*: Youths as Hesitant Participants in the Crucifixion'

1. A. Derbes, *Picturing the Passion in Late Medieval Italy: Narrative Painting, Franciscan Ideologies, and the Levant* (Cambridge: Cambridge University, 1996), p. 1.
2. One example is the episode in Luke 18:15–17 when Jesus called his disciples to him and said, 'Suffer the little children to come unto me and forbid them not: for of such is the kingdom of God'.
3. There are brief admonitions to children to obey their parents. In 2 Kings 2:23–4 bad children mock Elisha and forty-two are eaten by bears.
4. A. Neff, 'Wicked Children on Calvary and the Baldness of St. Francis', *Mitteilungen des Kunsthistorischen Institut in Florenz*, 34 (1990), pp. 217–44.
5. Neff 'Wicked Children', pp. 221–2.
6. Derbes, *Picturing the Passion*, pp. 12–16.
7. H. Maginnis, *The World of the Early Sienese Painter* (University Park, PA: Pennsylvania State University Press, 2001), pp. 3–4.
8. John of Caulibus, *Meditations on the Life of Christ*, trans. F. Taney, A. Miller and C. Mary Stallings-Taney (Asheville, NC: University of North Carolina at Asheville, 2000), pp. 176–7.
9. A. McNeary-Neff, *The Supplicationes Variae in Florence: A Late Dugento Manuscript* (dissertation, University of Pennsylvania, Ann Arbor, MI: Xerox University Microfilms, 1977), pp. 38–88.
10. McNeary-Neff, *Supplicationes*, p. 7.
11. McNeary-Neff, *Supplicationes*, p. 41.
12. 'Bad' children also appear in Giotto's fresco of Francis Renouncing his Inheritance, in the Bardi Chapel at Santa Croce in Florence (*c.* 1320) and in the Upper Church

in Assisi, by a follower of Giotto (late 1320s). Francis was seen as the New Christ in Franciscan literature. In the Bardi Chapel scene, a pair of unruly boys struggle with their mothers to hurl the stones that they have collected; one holds his in his tunic skirt and the other in a satchel. The mothers grasp handfuls of the boys' hair in what is surely a reference to the baldness of Elisha, as well as the *Dialogus de Passione Domini*. In the same subject, at the Upper Church at Assisi, two boys stand side by side in conversation, watching the scene. They gather their skirts to possibly hold stones but do not appear inclined to throw them.

13. Neff, 'Wicked Children', p. 239 notes a panel credited to Duccio in the Hermitage that shows four children, two 'perhaps innocent' stand near the Virgin.
14. Neff, 'Wicked Children', pp. 239–40. In addition to works to be discussed here – a Giotto panel in Berlin (two grieving children, a follower of Triani in Pisa; several children, some 'apparently innocent'), Andrea Orcagna and Nardo di Cione at S. Spirito in Florence (two children), Roberto d'Oderisio in the Louvre (eight children), so called Barna da Siena in San Gimignano (seven children – three watching the swooning Virgin, four watching the Cross and the dividing of the robe), a Geri di Lapo embroidered altar hanging in the Manresa Cathedral (two children probably with stones), Andrea di Firenzi in the Spanish Chapel at S. Maria Novella in Florence (six children – two walk in the procession to Golgatha, two watch, two in dorsal position stand before the cross – one holds up his hand in a gesture of derision), Altichiero at the Basilica del Santo in Padua (one child), Andrea di Bartolo at the Metropolitan Museum in New York (several watching the Virgin, two near the Cross and two watching the dividing of Christ's robe), Veneziano in the Cappella di San Blas, Toledo (two boys) and one innocent child in a pinnacle panel in the Galleria Nazionale delle Marche in Urbino to be discussed here.
15. G. Schiller, *Iconography of Christian Art*, 2 vols (Greenwich: Conan, 1968), vol. 2, p. 91.
16. John 19:23–9.
17. Schiller, *Iconography*, p. 89.
18. See B. Berenson, *Italian Pictures of the Renaissance* (Oxford: Clarendon Press, 1932); C. Volpe, *La Pittura Riminese del Trecento* (Milan: Fratelli Fabbri, 1965); J. White, *Art and Architecture in Italy, 1250–1400* (New Haven, CT: Yale University Press Pelican History of Art, 1993); M. Salmi, 'La Scuola de Rimini', 3, *Instituto di Archeologia e Storia dell'Arte,* (1931–2), pp. 238–42; M. Boskovits, 'Per la storia della pittura tra la Romagna e le Marche ai primi del' 300–1 and 2 *Arte Cristiana*, 81 (1993); F. Zeri, 'Un'affresco del Maestro del Incoronazione di Urbino', *Proporzioni, Studi di storia dell'Arte,* ed. R. Longhi, 3 (Florence: Sansoni Editore, 1950), pp. 230–45; and A. Volpe, *Giotto e Riminese: Il gothic e lattice nelle picture di primo Trecento* (Milan: Federico Motto Editor, 2001).
19. A. Marchi, *Il Trecento Riminese: Maestri e Botteghe tra Romagna e Marche,* ed. D. Benati (Milan: Electra, 1995).
20. J. Stubblebine, *Assisi and the Rise of Vernacular Art* (New York, Cambridge: Harper and Row Publishers, 1985), p.72.
21. Alison C. Fleming has suggested that the date is *c.* 1350–60 and the artist is Giovanni Baronzio in 'Maiden or Matron? The Unusual Iconography of the Virgin Mary with the Long Flowing Hair', *Nierika Journal of Art Studies* (August–December 2012), pp. 32–41. In unpublished conference papers, I have argued that the date is after 1365 based on the history of the church building. See Flansburg 'The Dominican Agenda in Trecento Fabriano and the Boston Museum of Art's *Crucifixion Fresco*' presented at

the Renaissance Society of America Conference in Cambridge, 2005; 'The *Crucifixion Fresco* in Boston and the *Meditiones Vite Christe* of Pseudo-Bonaventura' presented at the Oklahoma Conference of Art Historians at the University of Tulsa, 2012. See also Salmi, 'La Scuola de Rimini', p. 238.

22. G. Constable, 'A Fresco of the School of Rimini', *Bulletin of the Museum of Fine Arts*, 39:243 (August 1941), pp. 48–54.
23. Dating is often unclear and progression of influences and images is hard to determine.
24. The painting is also attributed to the Master of the Urbino Coronation by C. Volpe, *Giotto e Riminese*, p. 50, figure 294.
25. For the meaning of the pruned tree, see the meanings of Christ as the Tree of Life. I have explored this motif, which occurs surprisingly often in riminese art. See unpublished paper presented for the Renaissance Society of America, 2005 (see note 21 above).
26. Stubblebine, *Assisi and the Rise of Vernacular Art*, p. 72.
27. A source for this may be found in late Byzantine manuscript drolleries with twisted and contorted bodies.
28. Boskovits credited it to Francesco da Rimini, 2, p. 166.
29. A. Smart argues that the inscribed date should be read as 1340 in *The Dawn of Italian Painting 1250-1400* (Ithaca, NY: Cornell University Press, 1978), p. 72.

4 Chantos, '"These Stories Are Not for Children": Misbehaving Children in "World Upside Down" Prints and the Origins of Folk Tales'

1. David Kunzle is the leading pioneer in popular prints, and he first broached the subject of the *World Upside Down* in his 1972 chapter, '"World Upsides Down": The Iconography of a European Broadsheet Type', in *The Reversible World*, followed by his seminal 1973 text, *The Early Comic Strip* (Berkeley, CA: University of California Press, 1973). Other major contributors to the genre include B. Scribner, 'Reformation, Carnival and the World Turned Upside Down', *Social History*, 3:3 (October 1978), pp. 303–29; and P. Burke, *Popular Culture in Early Modern Europe* (Aldershot: Ashgate, 1978).
2. D. Kunzle, 'Bruegel's Proverb Painting and the World Upside Down', *Art Bulletin*, 59:2 (June 1977), pp. 197–202, on p. 198.
3. For more on the development of broadsheets, see Kunzle, *The Early Comic Strip*.
4. Kunzle, 'Bruegel's Proverb Painting', p. 202.
5. D.Kunzle, 'World Upside Down: The Iconography of a European Broadsheet Type', in *The Reversible World*, ed. Barbara Babcock (Ithaca, NY and London: Cornell University Press, 1972), pp. 39–94, on p. 39.
6. Kunzle has noted the important theme of animals, in *World Upside Down* prints, in relationship to peasant discontent, as peasants were not allowed to kill the game that continuously destroyed their crops due to feudal laws. See 'World Upside Down', p. 61–3 for more on animals as a rhetorical device for peasant unrest.
7. Kunzle, 'Bruegel's Proverb Painting', p. 202. Peter Burke notes that a particularly regular outbreak of violence was by apprentices, explained to be 'as regular as pancake-eating', a notably common food served during Carnival. See Burke, *Popular Culture*, p. 188.
8. B. Scribner, 'Reformation, Carnival', pp. 303–4, 312. Ironically, Martin Luther himself was attacked for 'turning the world upside down' and, subsequently, blamed for inciting

the Peasant Revolt of 1525. See Burke, *Popular Culture*, p. 189.
9. Kunzle, 'World Upside Down', pp. 42–3. Another major theme is that of Fortuna turning her wheel, although this pagan image was largely suppressed after the late sixteenth century.
10. See N. Davis, 'The Reasons of Misrule: Youth Groups and Charivaris in Sixteenth-Century France', *Past and Present*, 50 (February 1971), pp. 41–75.
11. Scribner, 'Reformation, Carnival', p. 316.
12. Kunzle, 'World Upside Down', p. 50.
13. Although there are elements of folk tales found in England as early as Chaucer (*c.* 1400) and developed later by Shakespeare and Spenser (*c.* 1590), the English fairy tale tradition was largely stymied by the Puritans in the seventeenth century. See J. Zipes, *When Dreams Came True: Classical Fairy Tales and Their Tradition* (New York and London: Routledge, 1999), p. 11.
14. I prefer to use the terminology of 'folk tale' versus 'fairy tale', as the majority of early modern tales do not feature fairies, which is a more prominent aspect in English literature. For more on the conflation of folk tales and fairy tales, see the the author's introduction in R. B. Bottigheimer's *Fairy Tales: A New History* (Albany, NY: State University of New York Press, 2009).
15. The link between these two genres was solidified further in the beginning of the eighteenth century, when the folk tale *Puss in Boots* was disseminated through chapbooks and broadsides in England and Germany. Now widely known by its English name, the original Italian version, *Costantino Fortunato*, was published by Straparola in 1553. See J. Zipes, 'Of Cats and Men: Framing the Civilizing Discourse of the Fairy Tale', in *The Origins of the Literary Fairy Tale in Italy and France*, ed. N. L. Canepa (Detroit, MI: Wayne State University Press, 1997), pp. 176–193.
16. R. B. Bottigheimer, *Fairy Godfather: Straparola, Venice, and the Fairy Tale Tradition* (Phildelphia, PA: University of Pennsylvania Press, 2002), p. 5.
17. Bottigheimer, *Fairy Godfather*, p. 122. In the introduction of the tale, the narrator warns the audience that this tale is about a son who does not follow his father's wishes, thus in effect disobeying the commandments of God. For the full English translation, see *The Pleasant Nights*, ed. D. Beecher (Toronto: University of Toronto Press, 2012).
18. For more on this, see M. Cottino-Jones, 'Medieval Fantasies: Other Worlds and the Role of the Other in the "Decameron"', in *Approaches to Teaching World Literature*, 69 (2000), pp. 87–94.
19. J. Zipes, *Breaking the Magic Spell: Radical Theories of Folk and Fairy Tales* (Austin, TX: University of Texas, 1979), pp. 5–6.
20. J. Zipes, *Fairy Tales and the Art of Subversion* (New York: Routledge, 2006), p. 14. The audience were also likely drawn to the use of erotic and obscene riddles in the narrative, as well as an interest in magic and the supernatural. See S. Magnanini, *Fairy Tale Science: Monstrous Generation in the Tales of Straparola and Basile* (Toronto: University of Toronto, 2008).
21. Bottigheimer, *Fairy Godfather*, p. 120.
22. The multiple reprints of Basile's tales is a testament to his popularity, despite the fact that the Neapolitan dialect was difficult for a wider Italian audience outside of Naples. Zipes, *Fairy Tales and the Art of Subversion*, pp. 16–18.
23. McGlathery argues that the tales often focus on courtship and marriage because they are the most exciting and the focal point of a girl's life and as a result, fairy tales are the ancestor of popular romances for women. See J. M. McGlathery, *Fairy Tale Romance:*

The Grimms, Basile, and Perrault (Chicago, IL: University of Illinois Press, 1991), pp. 10, 14–15.

24. For a seminal study dedicated to the many ways the tale has been interpreted, revised and parodied, see R. Böhm-Korff, *Deutung und Bedeutung von 'Hansel und Gretel': eine Fallstudie* (Frankfurt am Main and New York: Peter Lang, 1991).

25. For an interesting study on the abandonment of children, see J. Boswell, *The Kindness of Strangers: The Abandonment of Children in Western Europe from Late Antiquity to the Renaissance* (New York: Pantheon Books, 1988).

26. In a similar tale, *Cecino (Little Chick-Pea)*, the Tuscan predecessor to the English *Tom Thumb*, magic peas are turned into tiny sons for a poor carpenter and his wife. Even though the father sells Cecino for money, the young son returns home with a bag of money for his father. T. F. Crane, *Italian Popular Tales*, ed. J. Zipes (Santa Barbara, CA: ABC Clio, 2001), pp. 195–8. Similar to *Nennillo and Nennella*, these tales seek to strengthen the symbolic role of the father, often in spite of the children or his treatment of them. In all nineteenth-century literary versions, Zipes notes that poverty drives the abandonment of children, coinciding with many famines between 1810–57 across Europe. The Grimm brothers had themselves lost their own father at a young age and vowed never to separate and, as Wilhelm did not scribe the oral tale but rather wrote from memory, the story easily reveals his own subconscious. See J. Zipes, *Happily Ever After* (New York: Routledge, 1997), pp. 48–9, 52–3.

27. R. Darnton, *The Great Cat Massacre* (New York: Basic Books, 1984), pp. 18, 29.

28. See R. Steinlein, *Die domestizierte Phantasie: Studien zur Kinderliteratur, Kinderlektüre und Literaturpädagogik des 18. und frühen 19. Jahrhundert* (Heidelberg: Universitätsverl, 1987).

29. Zipes, *Happily Ever After*, p. 49. Zipes notes that in the earliest versions of *Hansel and Gretel*, the witch's house is described as made of bread, not gingerbread.

30. For more on domestic violence, see K. Moxey, 'The Battle of the Sexes and the World Upside Down', in *That Gentle Strength: Historical Perspectives on Women in Christianity*, eds L. L. Cool, K. J. Haldane and E. W. Sommer (Charlottesville, VA and London: University Press of Virginia, 1990) and L. Roper, *The Holy Household: Women and Morals in Reformation Augsburg* (Oxford: Clarendon Press, 1989).

31. N. Schlinder, *Rebellion, Community, and Custom in Early Modern Germany*, trans. P. E. Selwyn (Cambridge: Cambridge University Press, 2002), pp. 93–6. The connection of carnival to prints and folk tales is mine, not Schlinder's. Schlinder's argument is largely focused on the role of carnival to the theological concerns of the Church.

32. The dynamic of father and son is also paralleled in folk tales in the role of master and apprentice, such as Straparola's story of the *Tailor's Apprentice*, Night Eight, Story Four.

33. Bottigheimer, *Fairy Tales*, p. 24. According to Magnanini, metamorphosis is one of the hallmarks of the literary fairy tale, such as pumpkins turning into elegant coaches and she notes that Straparola offers his non-aristocratic audience a fantasy of assuming social roles from which they were legally excluded. See Magnanini, *Fairy Tale Science*, p. 52.

34. Schlinder, *Rebellion, Community and Custom*, pp. 106–7.

35. N. L. Canepa, 'Quanto "nc'e da cca a lo luoco dove aggio da ire?": Giambattista Basile's Quest for the Literary Fairy Tale', in *The Origins of the Literary Fairy Tale in Italy and France*, ed. N. L. Canepa (Detroit, MI: Wayne State University Press, 1997), p. 48. Dieter Richter and Johannes Merkel have noted that folk tales were often censored and outlawed during the early phase of the bourgeoisie's rise to power because they were

perceived to encourage fantasy, as well as serve as a threat to capitalist and Protestant principles. See Richter and Merkel, *Märchen, Phantasie und soziales Lernen* (Berlin: Basis-Verlag, 1974).
36. Protestant Reformers compared the gluttony of Carnival, particularly the emphasis on food, sex and violence, to the ancient Bacchanalia. For more on Carnival theme, see K. Eisenbichler, *Carnival and The Carnivalesque: The Fool, The Reformer, The Wildman, and Others in Early Modern Theatre* (Amsterdam: Rodopi, 1999). Catholic reformers of Carnival existed prior to the Reformation, such as Savonarola, and from the 1560s on, popular religious figures such as Carlo Borromeo and Gabriele Paleotti were described as being 'enemies of Carnival'. See Burke, *Popular Culture*, pp. 220–1.
37. Schlinder, *Rebellion, Community, and Custom*, pp. 110, 128–9.
38. Carnival is the most famous of religious festivals celebrated in Europe and Peter Burke has noted that half of the household goods were reserved for such an occasion, which provides insight into how important these rituals were to early modern folk. See Burke, *Popular Culture*, pp. 178–82.
39. Burke, *Popular Culture*, p. 193.
40. For more on this tradition, see M. Harris, *Sacred Folly: A New History of the Feast of Fools* (Ithaca, NY: Cornell University Press, 2011), pp. 135–6. The religious play began as an enactment of a 'Herod game', in which young boys mutinied against Herod, the earliest recorded event being thirteenth-century Padua, although the first Feast of Fools was recorded in twelfth-century France. Harris, *Sacred Folly*, pp. 41–4, 66.
41. Harris, *Sacred Folly*, p. 239.
42. Harris, *Sacred Folly*, p. 116.
43. T. S. R. Boase notes that the parable of Lazarus and the rich man was the most popular New Testament in the later middle ages. See T. S. R. Boase, *Death in the Middle Ages: Mortality, Judgment, and Remembrance* (New York: McGraw-Hill, 1972), pp. 28–35, 45.
44. Scribner, 'Reformation, Carnival', p. 327.
45. Zipes notes that the literary institution of the folk tale itself assumes a secular religious purpose, presenting a moral and political critique of society at the same time that it seeks to reunite an overwrought protagonist with society. See J. Zipes, *The Brothers Grimm: From Enchanted Forests to the Modern World* (New York: Palgrave Macmillian, 2002), p. 118. Harris notes that thirteenth-century records reveal that the Feast of Innocents was a day of highly controlled liturgical play, preparing young men for their future roles, not mocking but practicing for their own education. See Harris, *Sacred Folly*, p. 145.
46. D. Herlihy, *Medieval Households* (Cambridge, MA: Harvard University Press, 1985), p. 27.
47. C. C. Frick, 'Boys to Men: Codpieces and Masculinity in Sixteenth-Century Europe', in *Gender and Early Modern Constructions of Childhood*, eds N. J. Miller and N. Yavneh (Burlington, VT: Ashgate, 2011), pp. 165–9. See also W. Fisher, *Materializing Gender in Early Modern English Literature and Culture* (New York: Cambridge University Press, 2006), on pp. 68–9.
48. For more on the appearance of soldiers in Renaissance art, see K. Moxey, *Peasants, Warriors, and Wives: Popular Imagery in the Reformation* (Chicago, IL: University of Chicago Press, 1989). For more on codpieces and foot soldiers, see J. R. Hale, 'The Soldier in Germanic Graphic Art of the Renaissance', *Journal of Interdisciplinary History* 17/1 (Summer 1986), pp. 85–114, on pp. 86, 102–5.

49. By the twentieth century, fairy tales were transformed into a family genre with the introduction of film, particularly the creations of Walt Disney. Zipes, *Happily Ever After*, pp. 65 and 67. For a survey of films, see P. Greenhill and S. E. Matrix (eds), *Fairy Tale Films: Visions of Ambiguity* (Logan, UT: Utah State University Press, 2010).
50. See N. Elias, E. Dunning and E. Jephcott, *The Civilizing Process: Sociogenetic and Pyschogenetic Investigation*, rev. edn (Malden, MA: Blackwell, 2010).
51. Some of the most famous examples include Castiglione's *Book of the Courtier*, c.1528, and Erasmus's *De civilitate morum puerilium*, c.1530. A less famous example, aimed at ordinary citizens, unlike Castiglione's text, was Giovanni della Casa's *Il Galateo, overo de' costumi* (Galateo: The Rules of Polite Behavior), published in Venice, in 1558. This courtesy book was so well known that if one did 'not know the Galateo', it inferred the rudeness and impoliteness of the individual. For more on *Il Galateo*, see G. della Casa, *Galateo: a Renaissance treatise on manners*, eds K. Eisenbichler and K. R. Bartlett (Toronto: Centre for Reformation and Renaissance Studies, 1994).
52. Zipes, *Fairy Tales and the Art of Subversion*, p. 16.
53. Zipes, *Happily Ever After*, pp. 64–5.
54. Zipes, *Fairy Tales and the Art of Subversion*, p. 19.
55. Victorian culture embraced folk tales for their oversimplification of moral issues, while proponents of Romanticism were fascinated by their elements of primitivism, childhood and peasant folklore. For more on this, see N. Auerback and U. C. Knoepflmacher, *Forbidden Journeys: Fairy Tales and Fantasies by Victorian Women Writers* (Chicago, IL: University of Chicago Press, 1993); and J. Zipes, *Victorian Fairy Tales: The Revolt of the Fairies and Elves* (New York: Routledge, 1989). For an interesting study on the rise of children's literature in the nineteenth century, largely connected to folk tale traditions, see M. Gubar, *Artful Dodgers: Reconceiving the Golden Age of Children's Literature* (New York: Oxford University Press, 2010).
56. Kunzle, 'World Upside Down', pp. 84–9.

5 Cyril, 'Dynastic Identity in Renaissance Court Life: Dynastic Privilege in Portraits of Children'

1. C. B. Rose, *Dynastic Commemoration and Imperial Portraiture in the Julio-Claudian Period* (Cambridge: Cambridge University Press, 1997), pp. 11–21, Plate numbers (hereafter Pl.) 105–110.
2. K. Christiansen and S. Wappelmann (eds), *The Renaissance Portrait from Donatello to Bellini* (New York: The Metropolian Museum of Art, 2011), pp. 40–5.
3. Christiansen and Wappelmann, *Renaissance Portrait*, pp. 287–90, Pl. 120.
4. S. Campbell and M. Cole, *Italian Renaissance Art* (New York: Thames and Hudson, 2012), pp. 225–7, Pl 8.28, 8.29. Also J. Pope-Hennessy, *The Portrait in the Renaissance*, 2nd edn (1966; Princeton, NJ: Princeton University Press, 1989), pp. 17–18, Pl. 16.
5. Christiansen and Wappelmann, *Renaissance Portrait*, pp. 24–5, fig. 8.
6. Pope-Hennessy, *The Portrait in the Renaissance*, pp. 17–18, Pl. 16.
7. F. Münzer, *Roman Aristocratic Parties and Families* (Baltimore, MD: Johns Hopkins University Press, 1999).
8. Rose, *Dynastic Commemoration*, pp. 12–13.
9. Rose, *Dynastic Commemoration*, pp. 15–16.
10. Rose, *Dynastic Commemoration*, p. 20.

11. J. Pollini, *From Republic to Empire: Rhetoric, Religion, and Power in the Visual Culture of Ancient Rome* (Norman, OK: Oklahoma University Press, 2012), p. 225, fig. V, 15.
12. Pollini, *From Republic to Empire*, pp. 220–1, 247, fig. V. 11a.; and J. M. C. Toynbee, *The Ara Pacis Reconsidered and Historical Art in Roman Italy* (London: n. p., 1954), pp. 82, 84–7.
13. C. Richardson (ed.), *Locating Renaissance Art*. (New Haven, CT and London: Yale University Press, 2007), pp. 25–6. Her inclusion of the dialogue emphasized the link that Humanists felt between Rome and Florence, or antiquity and the Quattrocento.
14. J. Polzer, 'Andrea Di Bonaiuto's Via Veritatis and Dominican Thought in Late Medieval Italy', *The Art Bulletin*, ed. J. Shapley et al., (1995), pp. 263–89, on pp. 270–2.
15. C. Frugoni and A. Frugoni, *A Day in a Medieval City* (Chicago, IL: University of Chicago Press, 2005), pp. 74–5, fig. 56.
16. Richardson, *Locating Renaissance Art*, pp. 149–59, Pl. 4.15, 4.16, 4.17, 4.22. The frescoes detail the charitable care of orphans in the Sienese contado.
17. A. V. Coonin, 'Portrait Busts of Children in Quattrocento Florence', *Metropolitan Museum Journal* (Metropolitan Museum of Art: New York, 1995), pp. 61 and 67, figs 1, 5 and 7.
18. Coonin, 'Portrait Busts of Children', pp. 64–6. Coonin quotes from *I Libri Della Famiglia*, by Leon Battista Alberti, date from 1434–7, when he was a secretary to the Papal Curia. Although Alberti was childless, the circumstances of his life as an illegitimate son of a noble family, informed his ideas about the care and education of the future members of the civic entity.
19. L. B. Alberti, *The Family in the Renaissance Florence, Books One – Four*, trans. R. N. Watkins (1969; Long Grove, IL: Waveland Press, 2004), p. 5.
20. Alberti, *The Family in the Renaissance Florence*, pp. 80–1.
21. Alberti, *The Family in the Renaissance Florence*, pp. 83–4
22. 2nd Cen. Roman sarcophagus, exhibition, Colosseum, Rome, on Ancient Libraries. 'La Biblioteca Infinita' – the Infinite Library.
23. Christiansen and Wappelmann, *Renaissance Portrait*, pp. 302–6, figs 128, 129 and 130. There is no credible manner to identify the subjects, yet every detail of features, dress and hairstyle strongly suggest these are definite individual portraits and not generic youthful busts.
24. S. R. Miller, 'A Material Distinction: Fifteenth-Century Tin-Glazed Terracotta Portraits in Italy', *Sculpture Journal*, 22:1 (2013), pp. 7–20, on pp. 13–15, fig. 4, 5, and 6.
25. Miller, *Sculpture Journal*, p. 14, and n. 46 and 47.
26. R. Hatfield, 'The Compagnia De' Magi', *Journal of the Warburg and Courtauld Institutes*, 33 (1970), pp. 107–61. Hatfield's study is the seminal work on this frescoed panoramic representation.
27. Hatfield, 'The Compagnia De' Magi', p. 111, n. 21.
28. R. Trexler, *The Children of Florence, Power and Dependence in Renaissance Florence* (1993; Asheville, NC: Pegasus Press, 1998), p. 58.
29. Trexler, *The Children of Florence*, p. 60.
30. Hatfield, 'The Compagnia De' Magi', p. 138.
31. Campbell and Cole, *Italian Renaissance Art*, p. 226.
32. Campbell and Cole, *Italian Renaissance Art*, p. 226.
33. G. Langdon, *Medici Women: Portraits of Power, Love and Betrayal From the Court of Duke Cosimo I* (Toronto: University of Toronto Press, 2006), pp. 105–6.
34. Christiansen and Wappelmann, pp. 24–5, fig. 8; and P. L. Rubin, *Images and Identity in*

Fifteenth-Century Florence (New Haven, CT: Yale University Press, 2007), pp. 120–30, figs 107–11.
35. Rubin, *Images and Identity*, p. 129.
36. Alberti, *The Family in the Renaissance Florence*, pp. 80–1. Especially, 'Try to make your civil life shine by your splendid character'.
37. Rubin, *Images and Identity*, p. 335, citing E. Borsook and J. Offerhaus, *Francesco Sassetti and Ghirlandaio at Santa Trinità, Florence: History and Legend in a Renaissance Chapel* (Doornspijk, Holland: Davaco Publishers, 1981), for the entire program of the chapel and Sassetti's unique role as iconographer in directing Ghirlandaio to realize this new vision of magic realism.
38. A. Warburg, *Gesammelte Schriften, I* (Berlin: B. G. Teuber, 1932), pp. 101–8. Later updated by E. H. Gombrich, 'The Sassetti Chapel Revisited: Santa Trinita and Lorenzo De' Medici', *I Tatti Studies; Villa I Tatti, the Harvard University Center for Italian Renaissance Studies* (1997) pp. 11–35.
39. Christiansen and Wappelmann, *The Renaissance Portrait*, pp. 40–5.
40. Christiansen and Wappelmann, *The Renaissance Portrait*, p. 39.
41. Trexler, *The Children of Florence*, pp. 88–95.
42. Trexler, *The Children of Florence*, p. 88, n. 144 and 145.
43. Christiansen and Wappelmann, *The Renaissance Portrait*, p. 41.
44. K. Christiansen, *The Genius of Mantegna* (New York: Metropolitan Museum of Art, 2009), pp. 28–30. He includes a view of the Ara Pacis Augustae for comparison.
45. Christiansen and Wappelmann *The Renaissance Portrait*, pp. 287–90, Pl. 120; and L. Campbell, M. Faolmir, J. Fletcher and L. Syson (eds), *Renaissance Faces: Van Eyck to Titian* (2008; London: National Gallery, 2010), pp. 190–1, Pl. 190. Christiansen and Wappelmann identify the artist as Pietro de Spagna, while Campbell et al., names Justus of Ghent as the painter based on Vespasiano da Bisticci's memorie.
46. Campbell, et al., *Italian Renaissance Art*, p. 190.
47. Christiansen and Wappelmann, *The Renaissance Portrait*, p. 187–8.
48. D. Katz, 'The Contours of Tolerance: Jews and Corpus Domini Altarpiece in Urbino', *Art Bulletin*, 63:4 (2003), pp. 646–61, fig. 1, main panel, fig. 15, detail.

6 Lacouture, '"You Will Be a Man, my Son": Signs of Masculinity and Virility in Italian Renaissance Paintings of Boys'

1. MAP (*Mediceo avanti il Principato*), XXVII, p. 192, quoted by Jacqueline Marie Musacchio, *The Art and Ritual of Childbirth in Renaissance Italy* (New Haven, CT & London: Yale University Press, 1999), p. 21.
2. See J. B. Ross, 'The Middle-Class Child in Urban Italy, Fourteenth to Early Sixteenth Century', in *The History of Childhood*, ed. Lloyd de Mause (New York: Psychohistory Press, 1974), p. 206.
3. About the increasing of dowries, see (among others) E. L'Estrange, 'Deschi da parto and Topsy-Turvy Gender Relations in Fifteenth-Century Italian Household', in *Representing European Genders and Sexualities, 600–1530: Construction, Transformation, and Subversion*, ed. A. More and E. L'Estrange (Aldershot: Ashgate, 2011), p. 131; and S. Chojnacki, *Women and Men in Renaissance Venice: Twelve Essays on Patrician Society* (Baltimore, MD: Johns Hopkins University Press, 2000).
4. Aritotle's *Oeconomica* has been rediscovered first translated and commented by Leon-

ardo Bruni in Florence in the 1420s. It codifies a series of precepts and observations about family life already presents in the earlier Greek culture, in particular in Xenophon's *Oeconomicus*. This dialogue had had a great influence on the treaties of the time, thanks to the translation made by Alessandro Piccolomini: *La Economica di Xenofonte, tradotta di lingua greca in lingua toscana, dal s. Alessandro Piccolomini, altrimenti lo Stordito Intronato* (1540; Venezia: Sessa, 1546).

5. Leon Battista Alberti, *I Libri della Famiglia*, 1431: *Liber primus familie: de officio senum erga iuvenes et minorum erga maiores et de educandis liberis*. These texts have only been published as a book for the first time in the nineteeth century. In a manuscrite form, they could not have circulated and been know by the majority. The immediate influence of Alberti's text must be reduced, but it's importance was – and should remain – worth of mentioning. Indeed, the text is a synthesis of all the literature produced on the family and the regulation of the household until then.

6. For a precise study of the vocabulary used to designate children in Renaissance Italy, see I.Taddei, 'Puerizia, adolescenza and giovinezza: Images and Conceptions of Youth in Florentine Society During the Renaissance' in *The Premodern Teenager: Youth in Society 1150–1650*, ed. K. Eisenbichler (Toronto: Centre for Reformation and Renaissance Studies, 2002).

7. L. B. Alberti, *De la famille*, 55:71 (Paris: Les Belles Lettres, 2013) [Translated by the author]: 'This is a clear sign of a virile soul if a child is swift in his answers, bold in appearing among men, with no incivility or other fear significant of a villain'. / 'You said, Lionardo, a man has to understand where the nature calls his children; then you said it was good for them to do some physical exercises, and we have to lead them to a greater virility and a fortitude of soul as perfect and vast as possible'.

8. I do not want to deny the presence of little girls, young girls or women in the visual culture of the Renaissance, and a similar study could be led about the signs of femininity. My choice went to the representations of boys and young men because the corpus is much larger and the signs much more numerous, which allows me to analyse these images across a broader theorical spectrum.

9. Isidore of Seville's categorization in the *Etymologiae Origines* (written near 630 and republished several times, specially during the Renaissance, received the biggest success). The Spanish bishop proposes six ages of life, and three correspond to childhood. The first, *Infanzia*, whose etymology comes from the expression *non fari* (literally 'who does not speak'), goes from the birth to the age of seven. The second period, the *puerizia*, goes from seven to fourteen years old (twelve for the girls). The third, the *adolescenza*, goes from fourteen and could last until twenty-eight. Let us note that for the first two periods, Isidore of Seville takes the limits established by Roman Law.

10. G. Vigarello, *Histoire de la virilité. 1, De l'Antiquité aux Lumières: l'invention de la virilité* (Paris: Éd. du Seuil, DL 2011), p. 7.

11. As previously mentioned, the Christ-Child is not part of my field of research. I have nonetheless, to quote about this topic of the displaying of Jesus's genitals as a way to stress the miracle of the Incarnation, L. Steinberg's founding book, *The Sexuality of Christ in Renaissance Art and in Modern Oblivion* (New York: Pantheon books, 1983). I would also quote Jean-Claude Schmitt & Jérôme Baschet's answer, 'La "sexualité" du Christ', in *Annales. Économies, Sociétés, Civilisations*, 46:2 (1991), pp. 337–46.

12. Christiane Klapisch-Zuber mentions a statistical study about almost one thousand children born between 1300 and 1550. The results of this inquiry underline the high infantile mortality rate in Florence (but this was the same in other cities) and shows

that about 20 per cent of children born during this period died before the age of three, when they came back from the nurse, 30 per cent before the age of ten and 34 per cent before turning fifteen. See C. Klapisch-Zuber, 'L'enfant, la mémoire et la mort dans l'Italie des XIVe et XVe siècles', in *Histoire de l'enfance en Occident – Tome I: De l'Antiquité au XVIIe siècle*, ed. E. Becchi and D. Julia (Paris: Seuil, 1998), p. 226.

13. 'The fact that procreation was advocated by both Bernardino, a preacher to the masses, as well as by Alberti, illegitimately born but an architect and intellect of great sophistication, indicates that it was not simply a humanist tenet upheld by a small and elite percentage of the population, but a general stance advocated in even the more popular guides to matrimony. One such text was Fra Cherubino of Spoleto's *Regole della vita matrimoniale* (1490) [which] emphasized the importance of childbearing as reason to marry', in Musacchio, *Art and Ritual*, pp. 19–20.

14. L. Haas, 'Women and Childbearing in Medieval Florence', in *Medieval Family Roles. A Book of Essays*, ed. C. J. Itnyre (New York and London; Garland Publishing, 1996), p. 89.

15. For more information about birth in the Renaissance, see mostly Musacchio, *Art and Ritual*; see also A. W. B. Randolph, 'Gendering The Period Eye: *Deschi Da Parto* And Renaissance Visual Culture', *Art History*, 27 (2004), pp. 538–62.

16. In his *Lives of the Most Excellent Architects, Painters, and Sculptors*, Vasari described a drawing made by the painter Francesco Salviati (1501–63) in the early 1540s, which was used 'to paint on one of those round panels on which one carries food to confined women'. See J. M. Musacchio, 'The Medici-Tornabuoni Desco da parto in context', *Metropolitan Museum Journal*, 33 (1998), p. 141 and n. 25.

17. For a large bibliography about *deschi da parto* as a gendered *genre*, I refer to Randolph's article, 'Gendering The Period Eye', pp. 546–7 and particularly n. 23.

18. See D. C. Ahl, 'Renaissance Birth Salvers and the Richmond Judgment of Salomon', *Studies in Iconography*, 7–8 (1981–2), pp. 157–84.

19. Musacchio, *Art and Ritual*, p. 41.

20. B. da Fruosino, *Desco da Parto with seated 'putto'*, c. 1400–5, Collezione Borromeo; *Desco da parto with putto pissatore* (New York Historical Society, c. 1428).

21. The tray of the New York Historical Society has been painted for the birth of Tommaso Montauri, 25 April 1428. It shows on one side a confinement room and the care given to the newborn and to the mother, and on the other the child, a bit older, sitting on a boulder, naked, releasing a spurt of urine, action related to a part of the circular inscription: 'I AM A BABY WHO LIVES ... AND I MAKE URINE OF SILVER AND GOLD'. According Nadeije Laneyrie-Dagen, this statement is a pun about the name of the boy: Mont (the rock) Auri (the gold). The painter suggested the urine by golden threads that today completely disappeared. Tommaso's father was a goldsmith, and the child, logically, should soon be his successor: gold and silver are materials related to his future profession. See N. Laneyrie-Dagen, *L'Enfant dans la peinture* (Paris: Citadelle & Mazenod, 2011), p. 45.

22. Laneyrie-Dagen, *L'Enfant dans la peinture*, p. 45.

23. A. di Giovanni di Tomaso (workshop), *Desco da Parto*, c. 1450–60 (North Carolina Museum of Art, Raleigh).

24. Obviously some of these objects were kept after the postnatal ceremony. Several clues allow us to think they were then hung on the walls of the household and turned around regularly so that both sides would be visible. See Randolph, 'Gendering the Period Eye', n. 27; and Musacchio, *Art and Ritual*, p. 61.

25. 'But every time someone talk about the family – precised Tommasi – it is the perfect family, the one which has received the perfection by having given birth to boys'. Tommasi, *Reggimento*, p. 38, mentioned by D. Frigo, *Il padre di famiglia: governo della casa e governo civile nella tradizione dell 'economica' tra Cinque e Seicento* (Rome: Bulzoni, 1985), p. 72.
26. 'If we can bring up children separately, boys away from girls, they would grow up better ... Make them [boys] dance with young girls, it would be the same than giving them rotten meat'. G. Dominici, *Regola del Governo di Cura Familiare, a cura di Donato Salvi* (Firenze: A. Garinei, 1860), pp. 144 and 146. L. B. Alberti, *De la famille*, p. 56, translated by the author: 'You have to accustom the young boys, from the first day, to be among men ... and take them away from the customs and the attitudes of women'.
27. Veronese, *Portrait of Count Giuseppe da Porto with his Son Adriano / Livia da Porto Thiene and her Daughter Porzia* (1551–2) Private Collection / Walters Art Museum, Baltimore, MD.
28. Alberti, *De la famille*, p. 35, translated by the author: 'But it is by nature in fathers, I do not know how, a greater necessity, an appetite for having and raising children and then enjoying seeing in them the reflection of their own image and the resemblance with their own features: they base all their hopes on their children, and then, in their old age, wait for them to be a strong defence and support for their age now weak and exhausted'.
29. Titian, *The Marchese del Vasto Addressing his Troops* (1539–41), Museo del Prado, Madrid.
30. Francesco Valori, gonfaloniere of the République of Florence, in 1496, quoted from L. Sebregondi, 'Clothes and Teenagers: What Young Men Wore in Fifteenth-Century Florence', in K. Eisenbichler, *The Premodern Teenager: Youth in Society, 1150-1650* (Toronto: Centre for Reformation and Renaissance Studies, 2002), p. 29.
31. Titian, *Ranuccio Farnese* (1542) National Gallery of Art, Washington.
32. David Jaffé (ed.), *Titian* (London: Yale University Press, 2003), p. 136.
33. P. Ariès, *L'Enfant et la vie familiale sous l'Ancien régime* (Paris: Éditions du Seuil, 1973), p. 48.
34. G. Vigarello, *Histoire du corps, 1. De la Renaissance aux Lumières* (Paris: Éd. du Seuil, 2005), p. 337.
35. Vigarello, *Histoire de la virilité*, p. 7.
36. The Economic, which comes from the rediscovery and translation of Xenophon and Aristotle's texts (see *supra* note 4), looks to transcribe the founding principles of the civic life in a language and a set of clear precepts, understandable by a wide audience made of noblemen, gentlemen, officers, high merchants and landholders. The Economic thought is a practical science of the good administration of the household, and builds the project of an efficient codification of an ideal of nobility, which seeks to stand its own hegemony in the conduct of the public life, in the cities of Renaissance Italy.
37. Pontormo, *Portrait of a Halberdier* (Francesco Guardi, 1528–30), The J. Paul Getty Museum, Los Angeles.
38. Veronese, *Boy with a Greyhound* (c.1570), Metropolitan Museum of Art, New York.
39. For a study of the links between dogs and virility, see N. Laneyrie-Dagen, 'Le témoignage de la peinture', in Vigarello, *Histoire de la virilité*, pp. 383–7.
40. P. Caggio, *Iconomica* (Venezia, 1552), p. 27, mentioned by D. Frigo, *Il padre di famiglia*, p. 119.
41. Bronzino, *Portrait of a Young Man* (c.1530), Metropolitan Museum of New York. In all probability this painting has been made in two campaigns of work. See M. Brock,

Bronzino (Paris: Éd. du Regard, 2002), 110–11.

42. 'The deformed head at the bottom of the *Portrait of the Young Man with a Book* are, along with the book itself, clues of his belonging to the literary circle of courtiers Bronzino frequented, and which liked farcical humour'. See P. Martin, 'La transparente opacité du masque ironique. Bronzino à l'épreuve de l'ironie figurative', *Images Re-vues*, 1 (2005), on http:// imagesrevues.revues.org/320 [accessed 18 May 2014] – quotation translated by the author. The emphasis on the apprenticeship of the civility through the study of literature is also underlined by Maurice Brock about the *Portrait of Ugolino Martelli*, in which Bronzino painted the young man with three books (Virgile, Bembo and Homer) around him. For a complete analysis of this painting, see Brock, *Bronzino*, pp. 124–32.
43. For information about the Barbaro family and above that a precise study of the iconographical program of the villa, see M. Rogers, 'An Ideal Wife at the Villa Maser: Veronese, the Barbaros and Renaissance Theorists of Marriage', *Renaissance Studies*, 7:4 (1993), pp. 379–97.
44. B. Castiglione, *Le livre du Courtisan*, trans. Alain Pons (Paris: G. Lebovici, 1987), p. 140.
45. Brock, *Bronzino*, p. 142.
46. Bronzino, *Guidobaldo della Rovere* (1531–2), Palazzo Pitti, Florence.
47. E. Jollet, *Jean & François Clouet* (Paris: Lagune, 1997), p. 118, quoted by N. Laneyrie-Dagen, 'Le témoignage de la peinture', p. 372.
48. I will not stay on this detail in order not to infringe upon the researches currently lead by Gaylord Brouhot, graduate student at the University Paris I Pantheon-Sorbonne.

7 Giuntini, 'Dressing the Part: Picturing and Promoting the Early Modern Child'

1. The three major exceptions to this study are the Amish, Orthodox Jews and Muslims. Girls and women belonging to these groups follow specific guidelines for dress that are determined by religious or cultural rules that are only marginally influenced by mainstream American fashion styles.
2. Female artists did paint and exhibit ninety-two portraits of children between 1770 and 1792 when Reynolds was President of the Royal Academy. Most of these were amateur artists, their works were not reviewed, rarely hung in the main room and they had no discernable influence on the new ideal. The most prestigious female Royal Academician (of the two who were admitted) was Angelica Kauffman who specialized in history paintings. Although she did paint several family portraits with young children, she did not want to be perceived as a portraitist. She eventually left England and went to Italy where there was a better market for history paintings. See W. W. Roworth (ed.), *Angelica Kauffman: A Continental Artist in Georgian England* (London: Reackion Books, 1992).
3. J. Northcote, *The Life of Sir Joshua Reynolds*, 8 vols (London, 1818) vol. 1, p. 44.
4. D. Sutton, 'Principles and Priorities in British Art', *Apollo*, 122 (September 1985), pp. 172–97, on p. 184.
5. M. Pointon, *Hanging the Head: Portraiture and Social Formation in Eighteenth-Century England* (New Haven, CT and London: Yale University Press, 1993), pp. 177–226.
6. John Locke's *Some Thoughts Concerning Education* had been continuously in print since

1693 and was considered the primary reference for subsequent childrearing advice. Jean-Jacques Rousseau's *Emile or an Essay on Education* was available in both French and English in 1763 and many of his ideas echoed those of Locke's earlier work. Both a novel and a social critique on contemporary French aristocratic child-rearing practices, *Emile* became so popular in England that it was serialized in *The Lady's Magazine*.

7. W. Buchan, *Domestic Medicine* (Walterford: James Lynn and Co., 1769) and *Advice to Mothers* (London: T. Cadwell and W. Davies, 1769); and W.Cadogan, *An Essay Upon Nursing and the Management of Children from their Birth until Three Years of Age* (London: J. Roberts, 1784). Although more elite texts grounded the philosophical discourse of domestic life and child rearing, these medical books were written with an educated, lay audience in mind. Both physicians were well known in London, with established practices and experience in pro bono work as well.

8. Not to be confused with contemporary swaddling, which means wrapping infants in lightweight blankets for several weeks to recreate the familiar womb-like comfort, eighteenth-century swaddling meant stretching a newborn out and immobilizing the body in yards of tightly wound cloth that encircled the child from head to feet and did not allow any movement at all. Infants were tightly wrapped like mummies immediately after birth for three months, after which their arms were released; their torsos and legs remained swaddled for another three to six months.

9. Buchan, *Domestic Medicine*, p. 2.

10. Breastfeeding was by far the single most controversial issue of the new maternal model. Although it was linked with better infant health and greater emotional benefits, a wide variety of reasons deterred gentry and aristocratic women, not the least of which was the need to become pregnant following the birth of a girl, when a male heir was still needed. Wet nurses worked continually without getting pregnant, often with several children in residence and that led to a common belief that breastfeeding inhibited pregnancy. Additionally, maternal breastfeeding restricted social activities and had lower class associations. Wet nursing was an established profession, but only the very wealthy could afford to have a wet nurse live in. Although Buchan was the most extreme in his stance, arguing that women who did not nurse their children should not be allowed to breed (Buchan, *Domestic Medicine*, p. 2), it is highly doubtful that most women believed maternal love primarily depended on breastfeeding or considered the only good mothers to be nursing mothers. Queen Charlotte approved of John Locke's strictures, even going so far a to have his book painted into one of her mother and child portraits. Nevertheless, she employed wet nurses for all her children.

11. *The Exemplary Mother; or, Letters Between Mrs. Villars and her Family*, published by a lady, 2 vols (London: T. Becket and P. A. Hondt, 1769), vol. 1, pp. 8–9.

12. Hon. J. S. Seymour, *On the Management and Education of Children, A Series of Letters Written to a Niece* (London: Baldwin, 1754)

13. L. Davidoff and C. Hall, *Family Fortunes: Men and Women of the English Middle Class, 1780–1850* (Chicago, IL: University of Chicago Press, 1987), p. 388.

14. See M. Girouard, *The Town and Country House* (New Haven, CT: Yale University Press, 1978) for an overview of new domestic architectural trends that included separate and dedicated domestic spaces. The best illustration of new and renovated homes appears in J. Paine's *Plans, Elevations, and Sections of Noblemen and Gentlemen's Houses* (London: James Paine, 1783). New homes were frequently designed with two wings, one of which accommodated family bedrooms, dressing, sitting and drawing rooms. These spaces were often decorated with domestic portraits and Paine, a member of the

Society of Artists, occasionally included the placement of family paintings in his design scheme.
15. J. Farrington, *The Diary of Joseph Farrington*, ed. K. Garlick and A. MacIntrye, 17 vols (New Haven, CT and London: Yale University Press, 1978), vol. 4, p. 129.
16. Pointon, *Hanging the Head*, p. 2.
17. At the 1769 inaugural Royal Academy exhibition, portraits accounted for a quarter of all pictures displayed; by 1773, the number had risen to a third. For the balance of the century, percentages hovered between these ratios, occasionally rising suddenly as in 1795 when portraits accounted for 41 per cent of exhibited works. Figures based on Royal Academy exhibition catalogues from 1769–1800.
18. Anon., *The Conduct of the Royal Academicians, while members of the Incorporated Society of Artists of Great Britain, viz, From the year 1760, to their Expulsion in the Year 1769* (London: J. Dixwell, 1771), p. 12. Although the Society of Artists held successful exhibitions beginning in 1761, the membership was bitterly divided over administration and exhibition organization between a small group of prestigious artists who dominated the leadership and the majority of the large membership who were minor painters and amateurs.
19. *London Chronicle, Whitehall Evening-Post, The Gazetteer* and *New Daily Advertiser*, 1 June 1769.
20. Anon.,*Letters Concerning the Present State of England. Particularly Respecting the Politics, Arts, Manners, and Literature of the Time* (London: J. Almon, 1772), p. 247.
21. *Catalogue of the Free Society of Artists*, 1783.
22. Admission was fixed at 1 shilling until 1798 when an additional 6 pence was charged for the catalogue. Patrons and potential clients were able to see work throughout the year in the artists' studio where finished paintings were typically displayed.
23. The Royal Academy Council and a rotating hanging committee strictly controlled selecting works for exhibition and determining their hanging placement. This could be and often was contentious, even for academicians who received special consideration. James Barry and Thomas Gainsborough both stopped showing in the annual exhibition because they were displeased with their requests for picture placement. As president for life, Reynolds had a permanent vote in any decision regarding acceptance, rejection and placement of pictures. For a more complete explanation see A. Pasquin, *A Critical Guide to the Royal Academy for 1796* (London: Symonds, 1796).
24. The four categories of domestic portraiture used by the Royal Academy in the eighteenth century were 1) Child or children with both parents, referred to as a family group; 2) Mother and child/children; 3) Father and child/children; 4) Children, either individual or in sibling groups. The most popular category was Number Four, portraits of children, followed by Number Two, children with their mothers, and Number One, family group portraits. The least popular category was that of father and child. Reynolds painted and exhibited in all categories.
25. Along with portraits, there were two other categories in which children appeared: History paintings and Fancy Pictures. Although Reynolds dominated those categories as well, the child sitters were generally dressed in historical costumes and do not align with the focus on contemporary dress.
26. S. Tytler, *Childhood a Hundred Years Ago* (London: Marcus and Ward, 1877), p. 10. Sarah Tytler was the pen name for Henrietta Keddie, a Scottish novelist.
27. E. Wind, *Hume and the Heroic Portrait. Studies in Eighteenth-Century Imagery*, ed. J. Anderson (Oxford: Clarendon Press, 1986), pp. 23–5.

28. Initially, Reynolds delivered the Discourses as an annual address to the Academy, but they were also published and made available to a wider readership.
29. Although audiences today often find it difficult to determine gender in paintings, of very young children, there is no indication that eighteenth-century audiences had that problem even when children of both sexes were dressed in the same kind of clothing and when exhibited portraits were often given generic titles such as *Painting of a Child*. Gender was visually communicated through a variety of details ranging from hair, bonnets, toys and animals to differences in gestures, poses and compositional placement.
30. Babies are excluded from this group because they were not typically included in portraits although Reynolds did paint several of them with their mothers. Infants wore gowns that extended well past their feet until they were about nine months old when they switched to ankle length gowns so they could learn to walk. The most famous contemporary portraits by Reynolds with babies, that were exhibited at the Royal Academy, engraved and published were *Lady Cockburn and her Children* (1774) in which all the children are shown semi-nude with drapery and *The Duchess of Devonshire and her Daughter* (1786), in which the baby wears the contemporary and fashionable white dress and sash.
31. Northcote, *The Life of Sir Joshua Reynolds*, p. 280.
32. L. Martin, *The Way We Wore: Fashion Illustrations of Children's Wear 1870–1970* (New York: Charles Scribner's Sons, 1978), p. 105. The tag accompanied an advertisement for girls' plaid gingham dresses, aged eight to fourteen.
33. Included in the mainstream group is an established category called 'tweens' which constitutes girls between the ages of eight and twelve who are identifiable by common factors, such as an aspiration to be older than their age, high comfort levels with information technology and some discretionary income. They also represent a distinct and identifiable advertising demographic. See J. Rosenberg, 'Brand Loyalty Begins Early', *Advertising Age*, 72:7 (12 February 2001), S2; and H. Chaplin 'Tween Picks', *American Demographics*, 21:12 (December 1999), pp. 66–7.
34. The Florence Eiseman Company designs and manufactures clothing for both boys and girls.
35. Interview with Terri Shapiro, Frank Butler and Lawrence Eiseman, 19 July 2001.
36. While classic clothing is designed with a variety of fabrics and colours, white is still the most mandated colour for First Communions and flower girl dresses and these constitute a large portion of special occasion dresses.
37. Knits, combed cotton, denim and synthetic fabrics are the most common materials for mainstream girls' clothing, including dresses. They are easily embellished, available in prints or solids and generally washable and these are the expected characteristics of everyday age appropriate clothing.
38. The only close design competition to the classic eighteenth century model is the A-line dress that originated in the late 1960s as an adult style and has become a modern classic option although it is a less flattering or popular choice for all body types and ages under consideration.
39. This is true regardless of cost. Many of the Calabrese designs can be ordered in infant through teen sizes. Seasonal special occasion clothing is widely available on the Internet in the same size range although less common in site specific retail stores which often cater to specific age groups.

8 Tom, 'Princely Portraits of Adolescence in the Habsburg Court of Philip II in the Mid-Sixteenth Century'

1. M. Kusche, *Retratos y retratadores Alonso Sánchez Coello y sus competidores Sofonisba Anguissola, Jorge de la Rúa y Rolán Moys* (Madrid: Fundación de Apoyo a la Historia del Arte Hispánico, 2003).
2. Kusche, *Retratos y retratadores*, p. 151.
3. H. Gamrath, *Farnese: Pomp, Power and Politics in Renaissance Italy* (Rome: L'Erma' di Bretschneider, 2007); E. M. Rocca, *I Farnese* (Milan: Dall'Oglio, 1969); and G. Drei, *I Farnese: Grandezza e decadenza di una dinastia italiana* (Rome: La Libreria dello Stato, 1954).
4. Giorgio Vasari mentions Margaret's commission of the work and provides a very brief description of it. Vasari, *Le Vite de' più eccellenti pittori scultori ed architettori*, ed. G. Milanesi, 5:236 (1568); L. F. and N. S. Schianchi (eds), *Galleria Nazionale di Parma, Catalogo della opera del Cinquecento e iconografia farnesiana*, 9 vols (Milan: Franco Maria Ricci, 1998), vol. 2, p. 68, n. 188; and L. F. and N. S. Schianchi (eds), *I Farnese: arte e collezionismo* (Milan: Electa, 1995), pp. 226–8, n. 39.
5. Schianchi, *I Farnese*, p. 228; and A. O. Quintavalle, *Mostra Parmense di dipinti noti ed ignoti dal XIV al XVIII secolo* (Parma: Ente provenciale, 1948), p. 48.
6. D. Ekserdjian, *Parmigianino* (New Haven, CT: Yale University Press, 2006), pp. 9, 142–4; and L. F. Schianchi, *Parmigianino e il Manierismo Europeo* (Milan: Silvana, 2003), pp. 226–7.
7. P. Attwood, *Italian Medals, c.1530–1600 in British Public Collections* (London: British Museum Press, 2003), vol. 1, cat. no. 1080, p. 434; vol. 2, Pl. 225.
8. A. Caro, *Lettere familiari*, A. Greco (ed.) (Florence, 1957–61) vol. 2, p. 251, letter 490; vol. 3, p. 146, letter 680.
9. Kusche, *Retratos y retratadores*, pp. 96–7.
10. Kusche, *Retratos y retratadores*, p. 96.
11. Schianchi, *Galleria Nazionale di Parma*, vol. 2, p. 127. There are at least two copies of the portrait of Philip II, one in the Palazzo Pitti in Florence and another in the Capodimonte in Naples. M. Falomir, 'Titian's Last Portraits', in Sylvia Ferino-Pagden (ed.) *Late Titian and the Sensuality of Painting* (Venice: Marsilio, 2008), p. 141.
12. 'Et ben aventurata sarà quella pittura che rapresenterà un Prencipe di tanta speranza, affinata dal giudicio di un tanto Re'. Letter by Francesco Luisino to Ottavio Farnese, dated 6 February 1557. G. Bertini, 'Felipe II y el retrato de Alejandro de Farnesio por Antonio Moro', *Reales Sitios*, 41:3 (2004), pp. 71–3, on pp. 72–3.
13. J. Woodall, *Anthonis Mor: Art and Authority* (Zwolle: Waanders, 2007), pp. 394–7.
14. Until quite recently, the portrait was attributed to Alonso Sanchez Coello. The work is now attributed to Sofonisba Anguissola by museum curators and scholars. See Kusche, *Retratos y retratadores*, pp. 211–12.
15. I. S. Perlingieiri, *Sofonisba Anguissola: The First Great Woman Artist of the Renaissance* (New York: Rizzoli, 1992), pp. 117–67.
16. Kusche, *Retratos y retratadores*, p. 209.
17. The painting is owned by a private collector in New York. Kusche, *Retratos y retratadores*, pp. 210–12, 356–9.
18. The panel *Alessandro Farnese and his Brother Ottavio Present a Gift to Pope Julius III* (1557–66), is an imagined retelling of the moment, as Alessandro would have been a very young boy at the time. Kusche, *Retratos y retratadores*, pp. 212–13; and L.

Partridge, 'Divinity and Dynasty at Caprarola: Perfect History in the Room of Farnese Deeds', *Art Bulletin*, 60:3 (September 1978), pp. 494–530.
19. J. M. Serrera,'*Alonso Sanchez Coello* y la mecánica del retrato de corte', in *Alonso Sanchez Coello: Vida y obra* (Madrid: Museo del Prado, 1990), p. 53.
20. K. Johannesson,'The Portrait of the Prince as a Rhetorical Genre', in A. Ellenius (ed.), *Iconography, Propaganda and Legitimation* (Oxford: Clarendon Press, 1998), pp. 11–36. Also see S. Schroth, 'Veneration of Beauty: Messages in the Image of the King in the Sixteenth and Seventeenth Centuries', in (ed.) Chiyo Ishikawa, *Spain in the Age of Exploration, 1492–1819* (Lincoln, NE: University of Nebraska Press, 2004), pp. 103–38.
21. R. Mulcahy, *Philip II of Spain, Patron of the Arts* (Dublin: Four Courts, 2004), p. 268.
22. M. Falomir, 'The Court Portrait', in L. Campbell, M. Falomir, J. Fletcher and L. Syson (eds), *Renaissance Faces: van Eyck to Titian* (London: National Gallery, 2011), pp. 71–9.
23. Kusche, *Retratos y retratadores*, p. 135; and S. Saavedra (ed), *Alonso Sánchez Coello y el Retrato en la corte de Felipe II* (Madrid: Museo del Prado, 1990), cat. no. 30, p. 147–8.
24. A. S. del Campo, *The Art of Power: Royal Armor and Portraits from Imperial Spain* (Madrid: Sociedad Estatal para la Acción Cultural Exterior, 2009), cat. no. 51, p. 239; and Woodall, *Anthonis Mor*, pp. 339–62.
25. del Campo, *The Art of Power*, cat. no. 25, p. 223–5.
26. F. Buranelli (ed.), *Palazzo Farnese: dale collezioni rnascimentali ad Ambasciata di Francia* (Rome: Giunta, 2010), cat. no. 72, p. 356–7; Kusche *Retratos y retratadores*, p. 354; and Schianchi, *Galleria Nazionale di Parma*, vol. 2, p. 128, n. 275.
27. E. Horowitz, 'The New World and the Changing Face of Europe', *Sixteenth Century Journal*, 28:4 (Winter 1997), pp. 1181–201.
28. D. Biow, 'The Beard in Sixteenth-Century Italy', in J. L. Hairston, W. Stephens (eds), *The Body in Early Modern Italy* (Baltimore, MD: John Hopkins University Press, 2010), pp. 176–94.
29. A. Jordan, 'Alonso Sánchez Coello y Juan de Austria: Un Retrato de Corte Reduscubierto', *Archivo español de arte*, 72:286 (1999), p. 187; and Kusche, *Retratos y retratadores*, pp. 130–1.
30. A. J. Cruz, 'Juana of Austria: Patron of the Arts and Regent of Spain, 1554–59', in A. J. Cruz and M. Suzuki (eds), *The Rule of Women in Early Modern Europe* (Urbana-Champaign, IL: University of Illinois Press, 2009), pp. 103–22.
31. J. Spicer, 'The Renaissance Elbow', in J. Bremmer and H. Roodenburg (eds), *A Cultural History of Gesture* (Ithaca, NY: Cornell University Press, 1991), pp. 84–128.
32. Kusche, *Retratos y retratadores*, p. 170. L. Gachard, *Don Carlos et Philipe II*, 2nd edn (Paris: Michele Lévy Frères, 1867) p. 135.
33. L. J. A. Villalon, 'Putting Don Carlos Together Again: Treatment of a Head Injury in Sixteenth-Century Spain', *Sixteenth Century Journal*, 26:2 (Summer 1995), pp. 347–65.
34. G. M. Espinosa, *Don Carlos: el príncipe de la leyenda negra* (Madrid: Marcial Pons, 2006), pp. 37–42.
35. L. Duerloo, *Dynasty and Piety: Archduke Albert (1598–1621) and Habsburg Political Culture in an Age of Religious Wars* (Burlington, VT: Ashgate, 2012), pp. 19–20; and G. Parker, *Felipe II: La biografía definitiva* (Barcelona: Planeta, 2010), pp. 406–16.
36. Kusche, *Retratos y retratadores*, p. 173.
37. J. Woodall, '"His Majesty's Most Majestic Room": The Division of Sovereign Identity in Philip II of Spain's Portrait Gallery at El Pardo', *Nederlands kunsthistorisch jaarboek*,

46:1 (1995), pp. 52–103.
38. Kusche, *Retratos y retratadores*, pp. 163–78.
39. Woodall, "His Majesty's Most Majestic Room", p. 71.
40. The two extant copies are privately owned in Madrid and Vienna. Kusche, *Retratos y retratadores*, pp. 151, 221–3.
41. Kusche, *Retratos y retratadores*, pp. 174–5.
42. Woodall, "His Majesty's Most Majestic Room", pp. 61–3.
43. J. M. Millàn, 'Archduque Alberto en la corte de Felipe II (1570–1580)', in W. Thomas and L. Duerloo (eds), *Albert & Isabella, 1598–1621, Essays* (Turnhout: Brepols, 1998), pp. 27–37.
44. Kusche, *Retratos y retratadores*, pp. 321–3.

9 Steele, 'Titian's *Clarissa Strozzi*: The Infant as Ideal Bride'

1. *Acknowledgements*: Aspects of this project were developed in presentations at the South Central Renaissance Conference and the Renaissance Society of America: for fruitful and encouraging discussions at these I thank, in particular, Liana de Girolami Cheney, Laurinda Dixon, Ellen Longsworth and the late Kate Frost. The intellectual stimulation they provided led me into avenues of exploration that always proved productive whether or not all results are incorporated directly herein. To Constance Cortez at my own institution I owe thanks for insistent encouragement; to Matthew Knox Averett, gratitude for organization, administration and perseverance in preparing and developing this volume; and to the readers at Pickering & Chatto, appreciation for their editorial expertise.
2. H. Wethey, *The Paintings of Titian, vol. II: The Portraits* (London: Phaidon, 1971), cat. 101, p. 142; and F. Pedrocco, *Titian* (New York: Rizzoli, 2001), cat. 123, p. 180.
3. L. Freedman, 'Titian's Portrait of Clarissa Strozzi: The State Portrait of a Child', *Jahrbuch der Berliner Museen*, 31 (1989), pp. 165–80; see also M. Jenkins, *The State Portrait: Its Origin and Evolution* (New York: College Art Association of America, 1947), pp. 1, 7, 11 and 31–3. On proportions, see J. B. Bedaux and R. Ekkart (eds), *Pride and Joy: Children's Portraits in the Netherlands 1500–1700* (Amsterdam: Ludion Press, 2001), p. 14, n. 12.
4. L. Freedman, *Titian's Portraits Through Aretino's Lens* (University Park, PA: Pennsylvania State University Press, 1995), p. 271. Pedrocco, *Titian*, p. 180, provides Aretino's text: '... it deserves to be ranked above all the paintings ever made ... , so natural is the image that she seems to be alive. I would praise the small dog that the girl is caressing if remarking on its qualities did it justice ... ' For the *topos*, see F. H. Jacobs, *The Living Image in Renaissance Art* (Cambridge: Cambridge University Press, 2005), pp. 1–30.
5. L. Reed, 'Art, Life, and Charm in Titian's Portrait of Clarissa Strozzi', in A. Classen (ed.), *Childhood in the Middle Ages and the Renaissance: The Results of a Paradigm Shift in the History of Mentality* (Berlin and New York: Walter de Gruyter, 2005), pp. 355–71.
6. See *inter alia* R. Brilliant, *Portraiture* (Cambridge: Harvard University Press, 1991), p. 58; J. Woods-Marsden, '"Ritratto al Naturale": Questions of Realism and Idealism in Early Renaissance Portraits', *Art Journal*, 46 (1987), pp. 209–16; P. Simons, 'Women in Frames: The Gaze, the Eye, the Profile in Renaissance Portraiture', *History Workshop*, 25 (1988), pp. 4–30; E. Cropper, 'The Beauty of Woman: Problems in the Rhetoric of Renaissance Portraiture', in M. W. Ferguson, M. Quilligan and N. J. Vickers (eds),

Rewriting the Renaissance: The Discourses of Sexual Difference in Early Modern Europe (Chicago, IL: University of Chicago Press, 1986), pp. 175–90; and B. Wilson, 'The Renaissance Portrait: From Resemblance to Representation', in J. J. Martin (ed.), *The Renaissance World* (New York: Routledge, 2007), pp. 452–80.

7. *De sculptura (1504), by Pomponio Gaurico,* eds and trans. A. Chastel and R. Klein (Geneva: Droz, 1969), pp. 128–9; and L. Campbell, *Renaissance Portraits* (New Haven, CT: Yale University Press, 1990), p. 27. See also Jenkins, *State Portrait,* pp. 43–5; and Brilliant, *Portraiture,* pp. 89–140. With regard to portraits of young women, see G. Langdon, *Medici Women: Portraits of Power, Love and Betrayal from the Court of Duke Cosimo I* (Toronto: University of Toronto Press, 2006), pp. 13–16 and 18–21; and, for children, see M. M. Methenitis, 'More Than Mirrors: Portraits of Children in Renaissance Italy' (PhD Dissertation, University of Texas at Dallas, 1995), p. vi.

8. S. Hickson,'"To See Ourselves as Others See us:" Giovanni Francesco Zaninello of Ferrara and the Portrait of Isabella d'Este by Francesco Francia', *Renaissance Studies,* 23 (2009), pp. 288–310, on p. 294, n.19; for an instance in which Pietro Bembo completed verbal depictions in discourse, see M. Rogers, 'The Decorum of Women's Beauty: Trissino, Firenzuola, Luigini and the Representation of Women in Sixteenth-Century Painting', *Renaissance Studies,* 2:1 (March 1988), pp. 47–88, on p. 49; and, for a portrait's character interpreted over time, see J. F. Bestor, 'Titian's Portrait of Laura Eustochia: The Decorum of Female Beauty and the Motif of the Black Page', *Renaissance Studies,* 17:1 (2003), pp. 628–73, on pp. 629–35. On portraiture's moral value, see Brilliant, *Portraiture,* pp. 128–9; and on Titian's multivalency and the dialogue form, see B. Aikema, 'Late Titian and the Others, Between Venice and Europe', in S. Ferino-Pagden (ed.), *Late Titian and the Sensuality of Painting* (Venice: Marsilio Editore, 2008), pp. 88–99, on p. 90. For similar interests at the Medici court, see Langdon, *Medici Women,* pp. 19–20.

9. Ferino-Pagden, *Late Titian,* cat. 1.1, pp. 146–8, with recent bibliography.

10. For review of literature, see M. King, 'Concepts of Childhood: What We Know and Where We Might Go', *Renaissance Quarterly,* 70 (2007), pp. 371–407. See also L. Demaitre, 'The Idea of Childhood and Child Care in Medical Writings of the Middle Ages', *Journal of Psychohistory,* 4 (1977), pp. 461–90, on pp. 463–7 and 473–81; M. King, *The Death of the Child Valerio Marcello* (Chicago, IL: University of Chicago Press, 1994); and R. C. Trexler, 'Ritual in Florence: Adolescence and Salvation in the Renaissance', in C. Trinkaus with H. A. Oberman (eds), *The Pursuit of Holiness in Late Medieval and Renaissance Religion* (Leiden: E.J. Brill, 1974), pp. 200–64. For *spiritelli* that intimate unbidden passions, see C. Dempsey, *Inventing the Renaissance Putto* (Chapel Hill, NC: University of North Carolina Press, 2001); and for pleasure in lively children, see Langdon, *Medici Women,* p. 99.

11. J. K. Sowards, 'Erasmus and the Education of Women', *Sixteenth Century Journal,* 13:4 (1982), pp. 77–89, on pp. 86–7. Although play activities characterize verbal representations of children until approximately age 10, the purpose of educating children lies in their future service to society; see E. Langmuir, *Imagining Childhood* (New Haven, CT: Yale University Press, 2006), pp. 138–9 and 142–8. For females' life cycle leading to marriage, see D. T. Kline, 'Female Childhoods', in C. Dinshaw and D. Wallace (eds), *The Cambridge Companion to Medieval Women's Writing* (Cambridge: Cambridge University Press, 2003), pp. 13–20, on p. 14; for females' roles in a patrilineal system, see A. Crabb, *The Strozzi of Florence: Widowhood and Family Solidarity in the Renaissance* (Ann Arbor, MI: University of Michigan Press, 2000), pp. 234–53; and for projection

of values on children, see C. England, '"The World Must Be Peopled": Children and their Context in Renaissance Florence', in J. F. Ruys (ed.), *What Nature Does Not Teach: Didactic Literature in the Medieval and Early-Modern Periods* (Tournhout, Belgium: Brepols, 2008), pp. 163–86. On developmental ages, see S. Shahar, *Childhood in the Middle Ages* (London: Routledge, 1990), pp. 23 and 92–3; and on shaping infants like wax, pp. 88–9; see also G. Dominici, *On the Education of Children* (*Regola del governo di cura familiar, parte quarta*), trans. A. B. Coté (Washington, DC: Catholic University of America, 1927), p. 37. For fragile innocence, see Bedaux and Ekkart, *Pride and Joy*, pp. 24–5; and for early education to preserve this 'bent' of character, see Shahar, *Childhood*, pp. 166–72; and G. Vigarello, 'The Upward Training of the Body from the Age of Chivalry to Courtly Civility', in M. Feher with R. Naddaff and N. Taze (eds), *Fragments for a History of the Human Body*, Part 2, Zone 4 (New York: Urzone, 1989), pp. 149–99, on pp. 168–76. Clarissa Strozzi's age, then, signaled the onset of simple educational practices designed to maintain her innocence and shape her malleable character toward virtue.

12. Cited by Sowards, 'Erasmus', p. 84, n. 29. On the goal of education, see Shahar, *Childhood*, pp. 166–72; and on females' education, see P. F. Grendler, *Schooling in Renaissance Italy: Literacy and Learning, 1300–1600* (Baltimore, MD: Johns Hopkins University Press, 1989), pp. 87–9; Sowards, 'Erasmus', pp. 79–84; England, '"The World Must Be Peopled"', 163–86; and Langdon, *Medici Women*, pp. 146–9. For wifely virtues, see P. Tinagli, *Women in Italian Renaissance Art: Gender, Representation, Identity* (Manchester: Manchester University Press, 1997), pp. 53–60.

13. On familial networks, see M. M. Bullard, 'Marsilio Ficino and the Medici: The Inner Dimensions of Patronage', in T. Verdon and J. Henderson (eds), *Christianity and the Renaissance: Image and Religious Imagination in the Quattrocento* (Syracuse: Syracuse University Press, 1990), pp. 467–92, on pp. 475–6. Clarissa Strozzi died 11 March 1581 aged approximately 41; see Wethey, *Portraits*, p. 142. For Filippo Strozzi, see M. M. Bullard, *Filippo Strozzi and the Medici: Favor and Finance in Sixteenth-Century Florence and Rome* (Cambridge: Cambridge University Press, 1980), pp. 8, 45–60, 79–85 and 173–8. For the Strozzi in Venice, see P. Simoncelli, 'The Turbulent Life of the Florentine Community in Venice', in R. K. Delph, M. Fontaine and J. J. Martin (eds), *Heresy, Culture, and Religion in Early Modern Italy: Contexts and Contestations* (Kirksville, MO: Truman State University Press, 2006), pp. 113–33; and R. J. Agee, 'Ruberto Strozzi and the Early Madrigal', *Journal of the American Musicological Society*, 36 (1983), pp. 1–17, on pp. 12–15.

14. Crabb, *Strozzi of Florence*, pp. 204–5; and N. R. Tomas, *The Medici Women: Gender and Power in Renaissance Florence* (Burlington, VT: Ashgate Publishing, 2003), pp. 14, 24–5, 51–3, 111–14, and 136–7.

15. M. Feldman, *City Culture and the Madrigal at Venice* (Berkeley, CA: University of California Press, 1995), p. 42, n. 62, at http://ark.cdlib.org/ark:/13030/ft238nb1nr/ [accessed 31 January 2013]. For Strozzi interests, see R. J. Agee, 'Filippo Strozzi and the Early Madrigal', *Journal of the American Musicological Society*, 38 (1985), pp. 227–37; and Agee, 'Ruberto Strozzi', pp. 1–17.

16. Wethey, *Portraits*, p. 142.

17. For an example suggesting physiognomic resemblance but lacking affective interaction, see Bronzino's *Portrait of a Lady*, in D. A. Brown (ed.), *Virtue and Beauty: Leonardo's 'Ginevra de' Benci' and Renaissance Portraits of Women* (Princeton, NJ: Princeton University Press, 2002), cat. 39, pp. 219–21; Langdon, *Medici Women*, pp. 24–32,

identifies the sitter as Maria Salviati. On physiognomic resemblance in Titian's oeuvre, discussed in text below, see L. Freedman, *Titian's Portraits*, p. 271; and M. Rogers, 'Man and Beast in Titian', in J. Woods-Marsden (ed.), *Titian: Materiality, Likeness, 'Istoria'* (Tourhout, Belgium: Brepols Publishers, 2007), pp. 125–38, on pp. 128 and 131–2.

18. M. Biondo, *De cognitione hominis per aspectum* [Rome, 1544], trans. as *Conoscenza dell'uomo dall'aspetto esteriore*, L. Rodler (Rome: Beniamino Vignola Editore, 1995), p. 83; on rosy lips: 'Quanto più le labbra sono rosse, tanto più risultano piacevoli, poiché piene di umore, proprietà che *indica pure buona costitutzione e sangue purissimo ...* ' While over frequent smiling can indicate lack of shame (manzanza di pudore), instability, emotional fragility, etc., nonetheless 'Il riso *rivela giocondità interior* ... Il riso è *qualità preziosa dell'animo* ... Chi ha trattato del riso, [presumably Galen], lo ha descritto moderato, poco frequente, tormentato, immotivato, eccessivo, alto, abituale; quello moderato *indica animo dolce e affabile ...*' (emphases indicate phrases translated literally by author for use in text). Biondo (1500–65) worked primarily in Roman and Venetian circles, was known to Pietro Aretino and wrote on diverse topics; for his biography, see *Dizionario degli Italiani* (Milan: Treccani, 1968), S. V. 'Biondo, Michelangelo'.

19. Biondo, *Conoscenza dell'uomo*, p. 75: 'Dalla forma: quella *conveniente, gradevole e amabile dimostra la bontà*, quella spiacevole e antipatica, l'opposto'; and p. 77: '*Gli occhi scintillanti manifestano forza d'animo*'.

20. Dominici, *On the Education of Children*, p. 39; for his biography, see the entry in *Dizionario Biografico degli Italiani*, V (1963), S.V. 'Banchini, Giovanni di Domenico', at http://www.treccani.it/enciclopedia/giovanni-di-domenico-banchini (Dizionario-Biografico)/ [accessed 22 August 2014]. For Plutarch's formulation, see his *Moralia*, trans. F. C. Babbitt (Cambridge, MA: Harvard University Press, 1931), pp. 353–5, LL 225F–226B; and, for evolution of the theme, see Bedaux and Ekkart, *Pride and Joy*, pp. 19–21, 102, 105, and 148.

21. P. Reuterswärd, 'The Dog in the Humanist's Study', *Konsthistorisk tidskrift*, 50:2 (1981), pp. 53–69. For Alciatus, see *Andreas Alciatus, vol. I: The Latin Emblems, Indexes and Lists*, ed. P. M. Daly (Toronto: University of Toronto Press, 1985), unpaginated 'Life of Andreas Alciatus and its Relation to his Emblems', pp. 228–9 and Emblem 41: '*Unum nihil, duos plurimum posse* (one man can do nothing, two a great deal)'.

22. M. Rogers, 'An Ideal Wife at the Villa Maser: Veronese, the Barbaros and Renaissance Theorists of Marriage', *Renaissance Studies*, 7 (1993), pp. 379–97, on pp. 387–90. See also A. R. Jones and P. Stallybrass, *Renaissance Clothing and the Materials of Memory* (Cambridge: Cambridge University Press, 2000), pp. 2, 6, 8, and 11; and M. F. Rosenthal and A. R. Jones, *The Clothing of the Renaissance World: Europe, Asia, Africa, the Americas. Cesare Vecellio's 'Habiti Antichi et Moderni'* (London: Thames & Hudson, 2008), pp. 15–20. For virtue, behavior and status inferred from appearances, see Rogers, 'Beauty of Women', p. 49.

23. For fabrics worn at Florentine festivities in 1550, see R. O. Landini and B. Niccoli, *Moda a Firenze 1540–1580: Lo stile di Eleonora di Toledo e la sua influenza* (Firenze: Ed. Polistampa, 2005), pp. 56–7, 68, n. 73, 82–5 (distinctions between gown and petticoat), and pp. 143–5 (slippers).

24. J. Arnold, *Patterns of Fashion 4: The Cut and Construction of linen Shirts, Smocks, Neckwear, Headwear and Accessories for Men and Women c.1540–1660* (London: Macmillan, 2008), p. 110, citing State Archives, Venice, *Terra*, R. 35, c. 24; she adds, 'further sumptuary legislation passed by the Senate in 1562 forbade the wearing of corsets on the grounds that they were harmful to women'. Giulia da Varano delle

Rovere (d.1547) wears an early version of the bodice condemned by the Venetian senate in her portrait, painted by Titian *c*.1540; later versions extended the bodice's point further below the waist: see Wethey, *Portraits*, cat. 90, p. 136; and P. Dal Poggetto (ed.), *I della Rovere: Piero della Francesca, Raffaello, Tiziano* (Milano: Mondadori Electa, 2004), p. 321. With regard to dress of infants, see Langmuir, *Imagining Childhood*, p. 105; for fifteenth-century practice, see C. C. Frick, *Dressing Renaissance Florence: Families, Fortunes, & Fine Clothing* (Baltimore, MD: The Johns Hopkins University Press, 2002), pp. 164–7; for dress and carriage to display status and beauty, see J. Bridgeman, "*Condecenti et netti*": Beauty, Dress, and Gender in Italian Renaissance Art', in F. Ames-Lewis and M. Rogers (eds), *Concepts of Beauty in Renaissance Art* (Aldershot: Ashgate, 1998), pp. 44–51. As for corseting and vasquine, see V. Steele, *The Corset: A Cultural History* (New Haven, CT: Yale University Press, 2001), pp. 6–7; and Vigarello, 'Upward Training of the Body', pp. 154–5. According to M. W. Bulgarella, 'The Burial Attire of Eleonora di Toledo', in K. Eisenbichler (ed.), *The Cultural World of Eleonora di Toledo: Duchess of Florence and Siena* (Burlington, VT: Ashgate Publishing, 2004), pp. 207–24, on p. 215, stays [vasquine] consisted of three parts, one back and two fronts secured with a row of paired hooks and eyes. Although inventories omit reference to skirts to be sewn to vasquine, Eleonora's funeral stays have stitches on the lower hem that suggest this possibility: see Landini and Niccoli, *Moda a Firenze*, pp. 131–2 and fig. 64. Prior to the mid-sixteenth century, metal corsets evidently functioned only as a corrective orthopedic devices; see Vigarello, 'Upward Training of the Body', pp. 175–6; and Steele, *The Corset*, pp. 4–5, citing the French surgeon Ambroise Paré (*c*.1510–90). With regard to practices after 1550, see Landini and Niccoli, *Moda a Firenze*, p. 131. For late-century trends, see Cesare Vecellio's *Spose Sposate* (Bride after Marriage), in Rosenthal and Jones, *Clothing of the Renaissance World*, pp. 178–9.

25. V. Steele, *The Corset*, p. 12, n. 31, citing E. Roeslin, *Des divers travaux et enfantements des femmes* (Paris, 1536); Vigarello, 'Upward Training of the Body', p. 173; for Castiglione and courtly contexts, see Steele, p. 13; and Vigarello, pp. 155–9 and 176–84.

26. See, for example, E. Goodman-Soellner, 'Petrarchism in Titian's *Lady with the Musician*', *Storia dell'Arte*, 49 (1983), pp. 179–86; and B. D. Steele, 'In the Flower of Their Youth: 'Portraits' of Venetian Beauties ca.1500', *Sixteenth Century Journal*, 28 (1997), pp. 481–502, on pp. 493–9. With regard to issues of decorum that follow, see M. Rogers, 'Decorum of Women's Beauty', pp. 52–60, 62, and 69–70; for the averted gaze, see M. D. Garrard, 'Leonardo da Vinci: Female Portraits, Female Nature', in N. Broude and M. D. Garrard (eds), *The Expanding Discourse: Feminism and Art History* (New York: Icon Editions, 1992), pp. 59–85, on pp. 65–6.

27. See D. S. Chambers, J. Fletcher and B. Pullan (eds), *Venice: A Documentary History 1450–1630* (Toronto: University of Toronto Press, 2001), pp. 179–80, for 1562 regulations permitting a single strand of pearls to be worn during ten years following marriage. For the importance of appearances in assessing rank at the time of marriage, see A. Molho, *Marriage Alliance in Late Renaissance Florence* (Cambridge, MA: Harvard University Press, 1994), pp. 29 and 143. On forms and display, see D. O. Hughes, 'Sumptuary Law and Social Relations in Renaissance Italy', in J. Bossy (ed.), *Disputes and Settlements, Law and Human Relations in the West* (Cambridge: Cambridge University Press, 1983), pp. 69–99; L. Syson and D. Thornton, *Objects of Virtue: Art in Renaissance Italy* (Los Angeles, CA: J. Paul Getty Museum, 2001), pp. 37–77; A. W. B. Randolph, 'Performing the Bridal Body in Fifteenth-Century Florence', *Art History*, 21:2 (January 1998), pp. 182–200, on p. 187; *L'Oreficeria nella Firenze del Quattro-*

cento (Firenze: Studio Per Edizioni Scelte, 1977), cat. nos 186–92, pp. 295–8; Y. Hackenbroch, *Renaissance Jewellery* (London: Philip Wilson Publishers Ltd., 1979), pp. 5–8 and 24–36; and, for Florentine practices, see J. Woods-Marsden, 'Portrait of the Lady, 1430–1520', in D. A. Brown (ed.), *Virtue and Beauty: Leonardo's 'Ginevra de' Benci' and Renaissance Portraits of Women* (Princeton, NJ: Princeton University Press, 2002), pp. 63–87. For gems as dowry or counter dowry, see K. A. McIver, 'Daddy's Little Girl: Patrilineal Anxiety in Two Portraits of a Renaissance Daughter', in A. Pearson (ed.), *Women and Portraits in Early Modern Europe: Gender, Agency, Identity* (Burlington, VT: Ashgate Publishing, 2008), pp. 85–106, on pp. 91–5; and B. Witthoft, 'Marriage Rituals and Marriage Chests in Quattrocento Florence', *Artibus et Historiae*, 3 (1982), pp. 43–59, on pp. 44 and 50.

28. Rosenthal and Jones, *Clothing of the Renaissance World*, p. 178 (Vecellio indicates that married brides wear such girdles also); see also R. W. Lightbown, *Mediaeval European Jewellery with a Catalogue of the Collection in the Victoria & Albert Museum* (London: Victoria & Albert Museum, 1992), pp. 306 and 332–41; A. Bayer (ed.), *Art and Love in Renaissance Italy* (New Haven, CT: Yale University Press, 2008), pp. 128–9; and, for children's jewelry, J. Musacchio, *The Art and Ritual of Childbirth in Renaissance Italy* (New Haven, CT: Yale University Press, 1999), pp. 55–7. For Venetian legislation in 1505, 1541 and 1548 see Hackenbroch, *Renaissance Jewellry*, p. 24.

29. For pendants and pomanders, see Lightbown, *Medieval European Jewellry*, pp. 338–9, 355–8, and cat. 84, pp. 529–30. The pomander's design fitted four hollow segments to be filled with musk on hinges around a central core; by contrast, the top half of Clarissa's *Muskapfel* shows hinged segments evidently united to the bottom half with central screw. Confusion among pomander, *Muskapfel* and paternoster bead is exacerbated since the last sometimes were pierced to contain musk. Titian's *La Bella*, *c.*1536, wears an ornate chain with beads sufficiently ample to have functioned as *Muskäpfel*; see Wethey, *Portraits*, cat. 14, pp. 81–2.

30. On favoured gems for marital gifts, see Syson and Thornton, *Objects of Virtue*, pp. 41–3; and P. Castelli, 'Le Virtu delle gemme: Il loro significato simbolico e astrologico nella cultura umanistica e nelle credenze popolari del Quattrocento. Il recupero delle gemme antiche', in *L'Oreficeria nella Firenze*, pp. 309–92, on pp. 345–6. For pearls as purity, see Castelli, 'Le Virtu delle gemme', pp. 337–9; for *De lapidus* by Marbode Bishop of Rennes (1067–1108), see M. Belozerskaya, *Luxury Arts of the Renaissance* (Los Angeles, CA: J. Paul Getty Museum, 2005), pp. 56–7. For sixteenth-century reference to emeralds shattering when a virgin is violated, see L. Dolce, *Trattato delle gemme che produce la natura: nel quale si discorre della qualità, grandezza, bellezza et virtù loro ... Hora ... ristampato* (1561; Venice: G. Batt. and G. Bern. Sessa, 1617), p. 115: 'E'commoda questa pietra a coloro, che amano la castità: percioche non sostiene, che una vergine sia violata, ma si spezza. Frena il movimento della lascivia'.

31. *Andreas Alciatus, Latin Emblems*, Emblem 191 and p. 228; Cesare Vecellio, in Rosenthal and Jones, *Clothing of the Renaissance World*, p. 179; and, for lapdog as fidelity of *married* women, see Langdon, *Medici Women*, pp. 26 and 29.

32. Cited in G. Riley, *The Oxford Companion to Italian Food* (Oxford: Oxford University Press, 2007), p. 73; and see pp. 71–2. See also *The 'Opera' of Bartolomeo Scappi (1570): L'arte et prudenza d'un maestro Cuoco*, trans. and commentary Terence Scully (Toronto: University of Toronto Press, 2008): in addition to *ciambellette di monache* and *ciambelle*, Scappi also refers to *ciambellette di piu sorte* (p. 418), *ciambelle grosse, fatte con ova, zuccaro, & latte* (p. 409), *ciambellette* (p. 414), *ciambellotta, ciambelloni*, etc. (p.

729, S. V. '*ciambelle*'). For Scappi's boiled *ciambelle*, see recipe 148, p. 500. Also valuable is Platina, who incorporates earlier recipes of Maestro Martino; see Riley, *Companion to Italian Food*, pp. 411–13; and on Scappi, pp. 491–3. The object Clarissa holds has also been termed biscuit, bread round, or pretzel.

33. Beginning her notebook as early as 1580, the nun Maria Vittoria della Verde designed and produced '*staffette di pasta, ciambelle*', extremely elaborate stirrup shapes from yeasted dough that, together with her embroidery work, provided revenue for her convent in Perugia; see Riley, *Companion to Italian Food*, pp. 69–70. For *ciambelle di monache* and other types at banquets, see Scappi, *Opera*, e.g. pp. 392, 396, 399, 401 and 411.

34. Riley, *Companion to Italian Foods*, p. 73; Scappi, *Opera*, recipe 232, p. 531, for *crostoli* at Lent. Development of such delicacies stemmed from relaxation of Lenten restrictions on milk and eggs after the fourteenth century until usage during 'lean' periods became customary: see A. Capatti and M. Montanari, *Italian Cuisine: A Cultural History*, trans. A. O'Healy (New York: Columbia University Press, 2003), pp. 70–1.

35. Wethey, *The Paintings of Titian, vol. I: The Religious Paintings* (Oxford: Phaidon, 1969), cat. 87, pp. 123–4; and Pedrocco, cat. 105, p. 164. Although Freedman discusses the motif as childlike behavior, Titian took great care with dogs in narrative settings, for which see P. Artoni, 'I cani invisibili di Tiziano', in P. Artoni (ed.), *Il tempo e la rosa: scritti di storia del'arte in onore di Loredana Olivato* (Treviso: ZeL Ed., 2013), pp. 206–9, at http://www.univr.it/documenti/AllegatiOA/allegatooa_37833.pdf [accessed 30 August 2014]. In this case, reflectography reveals that Titian altered the dog's mouth from closed to open form, thereby enhancing vivacity and greedy desire.

36. For questions of genre vis-à-vis symbolic interpretation see G. G. Giusti, *Dolci a Corte* (Livorno: Sillabe, 2001), pp. 14-17, to whom the Dandini example is indebted (illustrated p. 16). For Dandini, see entry in *Grove Art Online, Oxford Art Online* (Oxford University Press), S.V. 'Dandini', at http://www.oxfordartonline.com/subscriber/article/grove/art/T021315pg1 [accessed 28 August 2014]. Already by 1610–12 Bernardino Pocetti had pictured a spaniel pursuing scraps of *ciambella* within the women's refectory of the *Ospedale degli Innocenti* in Florence, evidently an act of charity paralleling those represented above in Scenes from the Life of the Ospedale; see Langmuir, *Imagining Childhood*, pp. 50–4.

37. *The Florentine Fior di Virtu of 1491*, trans. N. Fersin (Washington, DC: Library of Congress, 1953), p. 37. See also Dominici, *On the Education of Children*, p. 58: 'If you see a needy pauper and can help him, be free to do so at once and do not stop to think, "I may be impoverished, therefore I should save". If you see the young oppressed, the widow or the helpless, you may wish to aid them as well as you are able'.

38. Freedman, 'State Portrait', pp. 170–3: only two others of Titian's portraits include fictive sculpture, and Freedman concludes that the putti allude to Clarissa's cultural heritage and nobility. On association of stone monuments with the patrician class, see D. Bohde, 'Titian's three-altar project in the Venetian church of San Salvador: Strategies of Self-representation by Members of the Scuola Grande di San Rocco', *Renaissance Studies*, 15 (2001), pp. 450–72, on p. 457.

39. Dempsey, *Inventing the Renaissance Putto*, p. 44; see also pp. 38–48 and 86–9. For reference to living children as *spiritelli vivi* (imps), see J. Bridgeman and A. Griffiths, *A Renaissance Wedding: The Celebrations at Pesaro for the Marriage of Costanzo Sforza and Camilla Marzano d'Aragona 26–30 May 1475* (London: Harvey Miller, 2013), pp. 86, n. 110, p. 48, n. 3 and p. 130, n. 219. For the *Offering to Venus*, see Wethey, *The Paint-*

ings of Titian, vol. III: *The Mythological Paintings* (London: Phaidon, 1975), cat. 13, pp. 146–8; and Pedrocco, cat. 45, p. 118.

40. This is made explicit in Filippo Baldinucci's *Vocabolario Toscano dell'arte del Disegno* of 1681, for which see S. Fermor, 'Poetry in Motion: Beauty in Movement and the Renaissance Conception of *Leggiadria*', in Ames-Lewis and Rogers, *Concepts of Beauty*, pp. 124–33, on p. 129.
41. Pietro Bembo, *Opere in Volgare*, ed. M. Marti (Florence: Sansoni, 1961), pp. 102–3; cited by Fernor, 'Poetry in Motion', p. 128, n. 13.
42. Matteo Bandello, *Il Canzoniere*, ed. F. Picco (Turin: Editrice Torinense, 1923), pp. 83–4; cited by Fermor, 'Poetry in Motion', p. 129, n. 15.
43. On Titian's use of beasts to evoke time's flux, see Rogers, 'Man and Beast', pp. 131–6; on painterly materiality as a process of becoming eliding with the Incarnation, see Bohde, 'Titian's Three-Altar Project', pp. 468–70.
44. Syson and Thornton, *Objects of Virtue*, pp. 47 and 57–8; J. Musacchio, *Art, Marriage, & Family in the Florentine Renaissance Palace* (New Haven, CT: Yale University Press, 2008), pp. 152–3, 233 and 251.
45. J. E. Cirlot, *A Dictionary of Symbols*, 2nd edn (Mineola, NY: Dover, 2002), p. 322; J. Hall, *Dictionary of Subjects and Symbols in Art*, rev. ed. (New York: Harper & Row, 1979), S.V. 'Swan', p. 294, and 'Muses', p. 217; G. De Tervarent, *Atttributs et Symboles dans l'Art Profane: Dictionnaire d'un Langage perdu (1450–1600)* (Geneva: Librairie Droz, 1997) S.V. 'Cygne', pp. 172–5; and *Andreas Alciatus, Latin Emblems*, Emblem 184 (insignia of poets). For the *Venus with Lute Player*, see Wethey, *Mythological Paintings*, cat. 45, pp. 195–6; and Pedrocco, *Titian*, cat. 215, p. 259.
46. Bridgeman and Griffiths, *Renaissance Wedding*, pp. 143 and 68.
47. The text is at http://www.allmusic.com/composition/il-bianco-e-dolce-cigno-madrigal-for-4-voices-s-2-18-mc0002441874 [accessed 5 January 2015]. Six Venetian publications of Arcadelt's books of madrigals circulated by 1542.

10 Averett, 'Uncle Urban Raises the Barberini Nephews: The Education and Expectations of Papal *Nipote*'

1. A short selection of important recent works on the Barberini includes F. Hammond, *Music and Spectacle in Baroque Rome: Barberini Patronage under Urban VIII* (New Haven, CT: Yale University Press, 1994), J. G. Harper *The Barberini Tapestries of the Life of Pope Urban VIII: Program, Politics and Perfect History for the Post-Exile Era* (PhD thesis, University of Pennsylvania, 1998), Kirwin (1997), Mochi Onori (2007), P. Rietbergen, *Power and Religion in Baroque Rome: Barberini Cultural Politics* (Leiden: Brill, 2006), and J. B. Scott *Images of Nepotism: The Painted Ceilings of Palazzo Barberini* (Princeton, NJ: Princeton University Press, 1991).
2. See Rietbergen, *Power and Religion in Baroque Rome*, pp. 139–40
3. G. Williams, *Papal Genealogy: The Families and Descendants of the Popes* (Jefferson, NC: McFarland, 1998), p. 165.
4. B. Hallman, *Italian Cardinals, Reform, and the Church as Property* (Berkeley, CA: University of California Press, 1985), p. 129.
5. G. Signorotto, 'The *Squadrone Volante*: "Independent" Cardinals and European Politics in the Second Half of the Seventeenth Century', in G. Signorotto and M.A. Visceglia (eds), *Court and Politics in Papal Rome, 1492–1700* (Cambridge: Cambridge Univer-

sity Press, 2002), pp. 177–211, on pp. 196–7.
6. Signorotto, 'The *Squadrone Volante*', p. 195.
7. Hallman, *Italian Cardinals, Reform, and the Church as Property*, pp. 129–70
8. L. Nussdorfer, *Civic Politics in the Rome of Urban VIII* (Princeton, NJ: Princeton University Press, 1992), p. 33.
9. W. Reinhard, 'Nepotismus: der Funktionswandel einer papstgeschichtlichen Konstanten,' *Zeitschrift für Kirchengeschichte*, 86 (1975), pp. 145–85.
10. G. Drei, *I Farnese: Grandezza e decadenza di una dinastia italiana* (Rome: La Libreria dello Stato, 1954), p. 18.
11. Williams, *Papal Genealogy*, pp. 170–1.
12. Some of these provisions were ignored by subsequent popes, but these measure were fully adopted through the course of the eighteenth century.
13. B. Emich, 'Kardinal Francesco Barberini. Ein Pastneffe zwischen Kunst un Politik', in L.M. Onori, S. Schütze and F. Solinas (eds), *I Barberini e la Cultura Europa del Seicento* (Rome: De Luca, 2004), pp. 111–16, on p. 112.
14. Rietbergen, *Power and Religion*, p. 143.
15. C. Pieyre, 'La légation du cardinal Francesco Barberini en France en 1625, insuccès de la diplomatie du pape Urbain VIII', in L. M. Onori, S. Schütze and F. Solinas (eds), *I Barberini e la Cultura Europa del Seicento* (Rome: De Luca, 2004), pp. 87–94, on pp. 87–94.
16. L. Pastor, *The History of the Popes from the Close of the Middle Ages*, 40 vols (St Louis, MO: Herder, 1952), vol. 28, p. 40.
17. Hammond, *Music and Spectacle*, p. 28.
18. Rietbergen, *Power and Religion*, pp. 158–9.
19. W. R. Shea and M. Artigas, *Galileo in Rome the Rise and Fall of a Troublesome Genius* (Oxford: Oxford University Press, 2003), p. 97. Though Urban was pope during Galileo's trial in 1633, Francesco was one of the ten cardinal judges. Francesco sought a compromise that would spare Galileo prison, but that deal was ultimately rejected by a majority of the judges. Still, Francesco was one of three judges who withheld his signature from the condemnation of Galileo; see S. Drake, *Galileo*, (Oxford: Oxford University Press, 1980), p. 93.
20. K. Wolfe, 'Ten Days in the Life of a Cardinal Nephew in the Court of Pope Urban VIII: Antonio Barberini's Diary of December 1630', in L. M. Onori, S. Schütze and F. Solinas (eds), *I Barberini e la Cultura Europa del Seicento* (Rome: De Luca, 2004), pp. 253–64, on p. 253.
21. Hammond, *Music and Spectacle*, p. 30.
22. P. Waddy, *Seventeenth-Century Roman Palaces: Use and the Art of the Plan* (New York: Architectural History Foundation, 1990), p. 335.
23. C. G. Nauert, *The Age of Renaissance and Reformation* (Washington, DC: University Press of America, 1981), p. 79–80.
24. Hammond, *Music and Spectacle*, p. 30.
25. N. Orme, *From Childhood to Chivalry: The Education of the English Kings and Aristocracy, 1066–1530* (London: Methuen, 1984), p. 237.
26. B. Castiglione and C. S. Singleton, *The Book of the Courtier* (Garden City, NY: Anchor Books, 1959), p. 38.
27. M. K. Averett, 'Becoming Giorgio Cornaro: Titian's Portrait of a Man with a Falcon', *Zeitschrift für Kunstgeschichte*, 74:4 (2011), pp. 559–68, on pp. 566–7.
28. J. W. O'Malley, *The First Jesuits* (Cambridge, MA: Harvard University Press, 1993), pp.

202–8.
29. Ignatius of Loyola, *The Constitutions of the Society of Jesus and Their Complementary Norms: A Complete English Translation of the Official Latin Texts* (Saint Louis, MO: Institute of Jesuit Sources, 1996), 4:14, p. 83.
30. L. Caruana, 'The Jesuits and the Scientific Revolution', in T. Worchester (ed.), *The Cambridge Companion to the Jesuits* (Cambridge: Cambridge University Press, 2008), pp. 243–60, on p. 245.
31. C. Carlsmith, 'Struggling Towards Success: Jesuit Education in Italy, 1540–1600', *History of Education Quarterly* 42:2 (Summer 2002), pp. 215–46, on pp. 220–5.
32. P. F. Grendler, 'Jesuit Schools in Europe. A Historical Essay', *Journal of Jesuit Studies*, 1 (2014), pp. 7–25, on p. 16.
33. F. Mormando, *Bernini: His Life and His Rome* (Chicago: Chicago University Press), pp. 35–40.
34. Disputes over protocol often erupted in the streets of Rome when something as simple as two carriages would meet. The noble of lesser rank was expected to stop and let the other noble pass first, but deciding exactly who was the lesser noble was often hotly contested. These impasses could lead to outright violence, as was the case in September 1634 when Carlo Colonna and Gregorio Caetani met in the streets of Rome. They and their entourages took to swords and the fight resulted in the death of Gregorio; see J. Hook, 'Urban VIII: The paradox of a spiritual monarchy', in A. G. Dickens (ed.), *The Courts of Europe: Politics, Patronage, and Royalty, 1400–1800* (London: Thames and Hudson, 1977), pp. 213–32, on p. 230.
35. Rietbergen, *Power and Religion*, pp. 189–94.
36. F. Hartt and D. Wilkins, *History of Italian Renaissance Art*, 7th edn (Upper Saddle River, NJ: Prentice Hall, 2010), p. 338.
37. A. Kosto, *Hostages in the Middle Ages* (Oxford: Oxford University Press, 2012), p. 68.
38. J. Benham, *Peacemaking in the Middle Ages: Principles and Practice* (Manchester: Manchester University Press, 2011), pp. 143–78.
39. M. Thiébaux, *Dhuoda, Handbook for Her Warrior Son: Liber Manualis, Cambridge Medieval Classics*, book 8 (Cambridge: Cambridge University Press, 1998), pp. 42–6.
40. Kosto, *Hostages in the Middle Ages*, pp. 72–7.
41. Williams, *Papal Genealogy*, p. 108.
42. Williams, *Papal Genealogy*, pp. 108–9.
43. Pastor, *History of the Popes Vol. 29*, p. 440
44. For a thorough account of the tapestries, see Harper, *The Barberini Tapestries*.
45. P. Waddy, 'Barberini Cardinals Need Places to Live', in L. M. Onori, S. Schütze and F. Solinas (eds), *I Barberini e la Cultura Europa del Seicento* (Rome: De Luca, 2004), pp. 487–500, on p. 487.
46. Hammond, *Music and Spectacle*, p. 18.
47. O. Pollak, *Die Kunsttätigkeit unter Urban VIII. Volume I* (Vienna: Filser, 1928), p. 305.
48. Pastor, *History of the Popes Vol. 29*, pp. 410–11. See also Rietbergen, *Power and Religion*, pp. 95–142.
49. Quoted from Pastor, *History of the Popes Vol. 29*, p. 411.
50. Scott, *Images of Nepotism*, p. 176. See also Rietbergen, *Power and Religion*, p. 137; and S. Schütze, *Kardinal Maffeo Barberini spatter Papst Urban VIII und die Entstehung des Römischen Hochbarock*, Römische Forschungen der Biblioteca Hertziana, Bd. 32 (Munich: Hirmer, 2007), pp. 27–30.
51. Rietbergen, *Power and Religion*, p. 137.

INDEX

abandonment, 6–7
Albert, archduke (Philip II's nephew), 150–1
Alberti, Leon Battista, 88, 92, 94–5, 98, 100, 105
Ana, Infanta of Spain (Ana, Queen of France), 37, 41
    portraits of, 41–3
Anguissola, Sofonisba, 133
Anne of France, Duchess of Bourbon (1461–1522), 30–1
Apollo, 12, 167, 181–3
Ara Pacis Augustae, 83–5, 90, 95–6, 98
Ariès, Philippe, 25, 110

Barberini, 19, 171–2, 174–9, 181, 183
Barberini, Maffeo *See* Urban VIII
Baronzio, Giovanni, 59, 62, 64
Basile, Giambattista, 71, 73–4, 79
Bedoli, Girolamo Mazzola, 137
Bellerophon, 180–1, 183
birth trays, 9, 100, 102, 104
Boccaccio, 73–4
bread, 75 *See also* ciambelle
broadsheet, 71, 78
Bronzino, 114
Buchan, William, *Domestic Medicine*, 118

Calabrese, Joan, 130–1
Carlos, Don (son of Philip II), 133–4, 138, 142, 145–7, 149–50
Carlos, María Cruz de, 42
carnival, 71–2, 76, 78
Caro, Annibale, 138
Charles V, Holy Roman Emperor (Philip's father), 108, 133–4, 137–8, 140, 147
Charlotte of Savoy (1445–83), 28
children, 9, 14, 72, 93

Christ Among the Doctors, 77–8
Christus patiens, 50
ciambelle, 162
civilizing process, 18, 29, 71, 80–1
classic clothing, special occasion clothing, 117, 129–30, 132
clothing, 4–5, 19, 29, 38, 40, 42, 79, 100, 111, 115, 117, 119–20, 125, 128–30, 132, 159
codpieces, 79, 115
Coello, Alonso Sánchez, 133
Collegio Romano, 16
commemoration, 32–3
Convent of the Descalzas Reales, 35, 39–40, 42–3, 45, 47, 133, 150
    relationship of royal family to, 35–8, 43–4, 47, 145, 150
    visual culture of, 37, 41–2, 45, 48, 145
coral, 2, 42, 45
corsets, corseted body, 119–20, 125, 159

Decameron, 73
Desco da Parto, 103–4
didactic literature, 176
dog, symbolism of, 93, 111, 114, 150, 153, 158–9, 162
dolls, 2, 8, 38, 42, 120
domestic abuse, 75
domestic life, 99
    ideal of domestic life, 118–19
dress, 2, 4, 19, 25, 44, 76, 79, 105, 120, 123, 125–8, 130–2, 146, 148, 159, 162, 169
Ducal Palace, Mantua, 83, 93–4, 96

education, 11–14, 16–17, 162, 171, 176–8
    of children, 7, 12, 99, 157
    of females, 15, 157

El Pardo, 133, 149–50
emeralds *See* jewels
Emperor Ferdinand IV, 45
Erasmus of Rotterdam, 14
Eucharist, 24, 90
exposure, 3, 5–6

fairy tales, 73 *See also* folk tales
family, 4, 7, 9–10, 14–15, 17–18, 21–9, 32–3, 35–6, 38–9, 41–2, 48, 59, 73, 75–6, 83–4, 86, 89–90, 92–3, 96, 98–102, 104–5, 108, 111, 115–16, 119–20, 123, 130, 133–4, 137–9, 141, 145, 157, 162, 165, 171, 173–6, 178–9, 183
Farnese, Alexander (Philip II's half-sister), 133, 181
Farnese, Ottavio, 137
Feast of Fools, 76–9
Feltre, Vittorino da, 94–6
Fernando, Cardinal-Infante, 47
    relationship with Sor Margarita de la Cruz, 38
Florence, 9–10, 31, 52, 64, 83, 86–7, 89–90, 92–3, 106, 108, 159
Florence Eiseman Company, 129
folk tales, 18, 71–2, 74–6, 78–81 *See also* fairy tales,
Fouquet, Jean (*c.*1420–80), 21, 24, 26, 28
Free Society of Artists, 122
furniture, 7–9, 42, 155

Gainsborough, Thomas, 117, 123–4, 127
Galileo, 171, 176
García Sanz, Ana, 36, 44
genre prints, 73
Gerson, Jean (1363–1429), 30
Ghirlandaio, Domenico, 83, 92–3
girdle, 161–2
    symbolism of, 161–2, 169
girlhood, 125–8, 131–2
godparents, 23, 30–1
Gonzaga, Ludovico, 83–4, 93–5, 98, 153–5
Goodman, Eleanor, 36

Habsburg family, 35–7, 41, 45, 48, 133–4, 137–9, 141, 146–7, 149
    affection among, 38, 145

    children of, 41, 44
    piety of, 38, 48
    portraits of, 41, 139
heaven, 27, 32, 42, 181
Hoffman, Martha, 36
Hogarth, William, The Graham Children, 122
Holy Roman Emperor (Philip II's nephew), 41
humanist, 26, 99, 140

illegitimacy, 6
Il Pentamerone, 74, 80
infant Jesus, 36–8, 40, 42, 44–5, 47, 86, 88
    images of, 36
infant mortality, 42
inversion, 72–3, 75–8, 80
Italy, 1, 6, 8, 10, 19, 50, 74, 80, 83, 86, 94, 99, 101, 108, 113, 115, 139, 141, 155, 159, 169, 171, 174, 178

Jason, 180–1, 183
Jean V de Bueil, Count of Sancerre (1406–77), 23
Jesuits, 13, 176–7
Jesús y Jodar, Francisco de, 36
    Exercicios of Sor Margarita de la Cruz, 36
jewels, 19, 42, 96, 159 *See also* Muskapfel, *See also* girdle
    symbolism of, 161
Joachim of France (d.1460), 28
John of Austria, Don (Philip II's half-brother), 133, 142, 145–6, 149–50
Juana of Portugal, Princess (Juana, sister of Philip II), 35, 133
    as founder of the Descalzas Reales, 35, 41, 145
    portrait of, 41

leggiadrìa, 165–6
Le piacevoli notti, 73
lineage, 23, 84, 90, 95–6, 98, 101, 105, 116, 165, 173
Locke, John, 8, 14
Longinus, 53, 55, 57, 59–60, 62, 65
Louis XI, King (1423–83), 28, 30
Luther, Martin, 72, 76

Madrid, 35, 39, 41, 43, 45, 134, 139, 145, 147, 149
Mantegna, Andrea, 83, 93–4
Margaret, duchess of Parma (Philip II's half-sister), 137
Margarita of Austria, Archduchess, 17, 36–42, 44–5, 47–8
   correspondence of, 38, 47
   devotion to infant Christ, 40–1
   Exorcicios of, 41
   poor children, 40–1
   proposed marriage of, 35
   royal children, 37–8, 40–2, 44
Margarita, queen of Spain (Margarita of Austria, Queen), 37–9, 41, 44, 48
   children of, 37, 43
   portraits of, 41
   relationship with Sor Margarita de la Cruz, 37–8
María Ana, Infanta (María Ana, Queen of Hungary, Holy Roman Empress), 38
   portrait of, 46
   pregnancy of, 39
   relationship with Sor Margarita, 38, 47
María, Holy Roman Empress (Maria, mother of Sor Margarita de la Cruz), 35
María, Infanta
   funeral portrait of, 39
Martini, Simone, 52, 54
masculinity, 18, 79, 100, 102–3, 108, 111, 115–16
mass liturgy *See* Eucharist
Master of the Urbino Coronation, 58–9
Master of the Yale Missal (MSS dated 1468–75), 21, 24–5
Maximilian II, Holy Roman Emperor (Philip II's brother-in-law), 17, 35, 41, 147
Medici, 12, 83–4, 89–90, 92, 98–9, 142, 157–8, 162, 169, 177–8
Modena, Barnaba de, 55–6, 64
Montefeltro, Federigo da, 83, 96, 99
Mor, Anthonis, 133, 135, 138–42, 145–6, 149
Muller, Ewout, 67, 69
Muskapfel, 161

Nelli, Nicolò, 67–8
nepotism, 19, 171, 173–5

Northcote, James, 117, 127

orphan, 86
Orsini polyptych, 53

Palma, Juan de, 36, 38–40, 42
Pantoja de la Cruz, Juan, 39, 41–3
Paris, Bibliothèque nationale de France, 22
Parmigianino, 137–8, 140
patron saints, 32
pearls, 131 *See also* jewels
Peasant's Revolt, 71
Philip III, king of Spain, 36–8, 43, 48
   children of, 44
   marriage of, 37
Philip II, king of Spain, 19, 35, 133, 137–8, 140, 145, 147, 149
Philip IV, king of Spain, 36–7, 47–8
   as prince, 35, 37–8, 42
   relationship with Sor Margarita de la Cruz, 47
Philip the Good, Duke of Burgundy (1396–1467), 28
physiognomy, interpretation of, 155, 158
Picta, Camera, 83, 93
Plato, 8
Poggini, Gianpaolo, 138
Poliziano, 92
portrait, portraits, 1, 9, 18–19, 21, 23–4, 27–8, 36, 38–9, 41–2, 44–5, 48, 83, 89–90, 92–4, 96–8, 108, 110, 115, 118–19, 125–7, 129–30, 133–4, 137, 139–42, 145–6, 149–50, 153, 155, 158, 161–2, 169, 172
   as representation, 19, 21, 25–7, 72, 84, 93, 104, 116, 123, 138, 142, 155, 158–9, 161, 169
   of females, 119, 125–7, 157–9
   of infant, 19, 28, 30, 36–7, 42–3, 72, 86, 88, 97, 118, 155, 157–8, 161, 163, 167
portraiture, 84, 93, 97, 117–19, 153, 155
Prestcsaille, Macé (fl. 1468–75), 17, 21, 23–33
Prince, Jehanne (d.1474), 17, 23, 25, 27–9
Protestant Reformation, 76, 81
puppy, 155, 158, 162, 169 *See also* dog, symbolism of

Renaissance, 3–4, 7–8, 10–11, 13, 18, 71, 73, 80–1, 83–4, 86, 98–101, 116, 173, 176–8
Reynolds, Sir Joshua, 18, 117–18, 122–7, 130, 132
Rimini, Giovanni da, 59
Rimini, Giulianda da, 59, 62–3
Rimini, Pietro da, 59–61
Robbia, Luca della, 11, 20, 89
Rousseau, Jean-Jacques, 8, 14, 118
Rúa, Jorge de la, 133, 145–6, 148
Rubens, Peter Paul, 12–13, 172
ruby *See* jewels

Sánchez, Magdalena, 36, 143, 151
Santa Trinità, 83
sapphires *See* jewels
Sassetti Chapel, 83, 92–3, 98
School of Rimini, 49, 57
senses, five, 31, 110
S. Maria Donnaregina, convent, Naples, 52
Society of Artists, 122
Son, 77, 110
spiritelli, spiritella, 165–7
stays, 159 *See also* corsets, corseted body, 124
St Bernard of Clairvaux (1090–1153), 30–2
Stephaton, 49, 55, 57, 59–60, 62, 64–5
stepmothers, 75

St Michael the Archangel, 21, 25
Straparola, Giovanni Francesco, 71, 73–4, 79
Strozzi, Clarissa, 19, 153, 155, 157–9, 162, 165, 167, 169
St Saturnin, Tours, France, 23, 27, 32
Supplicationes variae, 49–52, 55, 57, 65
swaddling, 23, 25, 28, 38, 118, 120
swans, symbolism of, 153, 167

Teti, Girolamo, 179
The Royal Academy, exhibitions of, 18, 117, 119, 122–3, 127
Theseus, 180–1, 183
Titian, 108–11, 139–40, 154–5, 158, 164, 168

Ulysses, 180–1, 183
Urban VIII, 19, 171–2, 174, 180
Urbino, 58–62, 64–5, 83–4, 96–7, 99

vasquine, 159 *See also* corsets, corseted body
Venice, 73, 114, 157
Veronese, 105–6, 111–12, 114, 160
Vienna, 39, 41, 46–7, 79, 89, 134, 146–7, 150
violence, 1, 18, 71, 75, 80, 92, 115

Wenceslas (Philip II's nephew), 150
World Upside Down, print, 67, 71–81